MW00809681

# THE FOREVER GIRL

# The
# FOREVER
# GIRL

## By David Pagel
## & Harold I. Stevens

**MEGALITH**
PRESS

Copyright © 2017 by David Pagel

All rights reserved.

Published by David Pagel, Megalith Press, Duluth, MN

ISBN-13: 978-0692806722

**Acknowledgements:**
The author owes a great debt to the following individuals for generously contributing their time and talents: editors Amy Glomski and Dina Post, and graphic designer Rick Kollath (kollathdesign.com), who illustrated the book covers and maps, and designed the interior.

All photographs culled from the many albums of Harold Stevens.

For Mike

# CONTENTS

## PART TWO: DEBT OWED

# THE FAR EAST

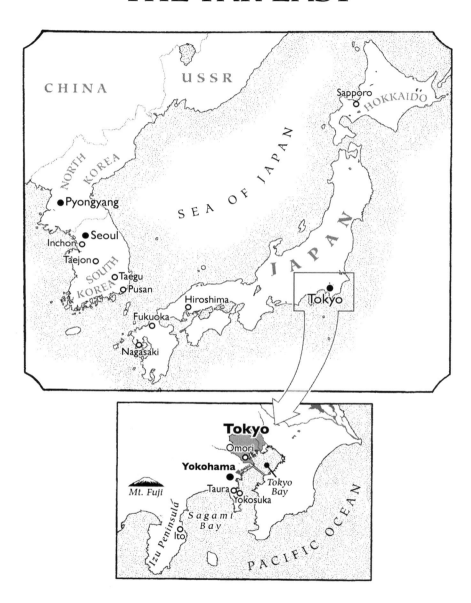

# THE FOUR PHASES
# OF THE KOREAN WAR

June 25, 1950

Sept. 14, 1950

Nov. 25, 1950

July 27, 1953

# THE FOREVER GIRL

# PROLOGUE

THE OLD MAN is a study in determination. Each step in the snow is a triumph, the unlikely result of intense focus and sudden, lurching movement. Hot pain flares in his knees and back. He leads with the entire upper half of his body—like the bowsprit of a ship cutting a gale—his spine angled acutely, the combined result of old battlefield injuries, infirmities of age, and the weight of devastating loss. It is his bereavement that drives him and defines his ambition. His motivation is so great that despite his age and disability, despite the glazed terrain beneath his feet and his jerky, precarious carriage, he moves steadily, resolutely, against all odds. Grace takes a backseat to forward progress when you are chasing a dream.

It is said that every person's life contains one good story. His life is a string of narrative pearls. Tales spanning nine decades—linked episodes ranging from the wildly romantic to boldly criminal. There are continuous threads: love, war, a career of patriotic service bookended by shadows of the mushroom cloud—a uniquely personal journey with highs and lows paralleling his own strengths and shortcomings. There are parts that make him immensely proud, and others he wishes could be undone, ignored, rewritten. But with his years comes the understanding that life is a sum, and to be considered fairly it cannot be measured selectively. Everything adds up.

More than considered, he wants his life written down. It is not vanity that compels him, at least, not a sense of *self*-importance. Rather, he desires a full and tangible accounting because it is the only way he can ensure the memory of another is secure and celebrated. His story is the mirror. Like clear water in a basin, it is real but defined by the reflections it echoes. To him, it is her story that must be preserved, because reflections and echoes are all that remain.

For two years he has struggled with how to proceed. As a schoolboy, he never applied much thought or energy to the intricacies of the written word—to education at all. Filled with the impatience and shortsighted independence of youth, he left school after the ninth grade. Years later, wiser but still fiercely self-reliant, he applied his drive and intelligence to furthering his education, but writing was never the focus. Now, near the end of his life, he must find the words. This urgency has propelled him down sundry and unfamiliar paths, even to a workshop for aspirant writers.

There, he listened intently as the instructor lectured about the craft of storytelling. Her counsel to *write what you know* thrilled him because it was a strategy in lockstep with his desire to breathe life into chapters living solely in his heart. But it soon became clear that this class was a forum for developing broad skills, and his need was immediate and intensely focused. At the end of the period, after the teacher had assigned homework—short stories written about random topics—he approached her with his personal agenda.

"I'm only interested in writing one story," he told the instructor, "and it's not a short one." He hesitated, having come to the meat of it, confessing his ambition out loud for the first time. "I want to write the story of two lives that became one. The story of my wife and me: how we came together, and how we stayed together…" and although he did not say it, he thought, *despite a woman's perfection, and a man's failings.*

"I don't have a short story," he continued, "but I have this." He handed her several pages covered in precise, almost mechanical handwriting, the paper stained and smudged as if blotted by a weary wrist or heavy shirtsleeve. "This is a letter I wrote to my wife two days before she died…" He gathered himself, considering carefully the words to advance his inquiry into uncharted territory. "I don't know if my writing says what it is that I feel, or if it's something anyone would ever want to read. But this is the beginning—or maybe the ending, of what I want to say."

She read his letter, her concentration broken only by an occasional hard swallow. Afterward, she said to him, "Not only do you have the ability to communicate your feelings…" Now it was her turn to pause, to clear spontaneous emotion from her throat. "Not only should you tell this story, you *must* tell it."

As he pushes onward through the cold and snow, he thinks back to that moment. The teacher's advice was like the pistol shot beginning a race, and yet with the infusion of energy he gathered from her encouragement, more weight was added. He'd cleared a hurdle, but now he faces an even more daunting obstacle. Although he has always had confidence in his ability to express himself in conversation—and also, apparently, in the form of a letter—an undertaking of the breadth and scope he envisions may be too much. Physically, the task is almost certainly beyond him. The failing mechanics of his body are more than a hindrance. The nerves and muscles in his extremities have been crushed and torn, his bones grate in their joints, worn beyond limits or repair. His fingers are locked into stiff mitts that can barely grip a pen, never mind peck a typewriter, the only kind of keyboard he has ever known.

It hasn't stopped him from trying. Despite all this, he has managed to laboriously scratch out over a hundred biographical pages. And yet when he reads them, he finds his life has no life at all. Translating his ideas into writing confounds him. Words that captivate when spoken aloud fall flat as the paper they are written on. Organizing and composing a biography is so much more complex than penning a heartfelt letter. He has come full circle to face an inevitable, undeniable truth: he is not a writer of books, and he has no time to become one.

But he is a storyteller. With a mind as clear and nimble as a mountain spring he regularly gives voice to a bubbling cascade of memories chronicling epic journeys and tantalizing discoveries, warring between nations and within a man's own nature, life-changing debts paid and life-saving debts owed. In this way he can do justice to the wheeling cavalcade of places, people, and events that make up the varied spokes of his life, and to the exotic and exceptional woman at the center, who connects them all and around whom everything revolves.

So he walks. A frail old man buffeted by a raw wind, but with the will and purposefulness of a legion. The ground may be obscured by snow, but his path forward is clear. He will tell his story and engage someone else to write the words. Throughout his life, whenever he has faced a personal or professional challenge, he has met it with unflappable self-control and a stoic determination to do his best. But if he did not possess the ability or means to achieve what he desired, he applied his intellect and resourcefulness to exploring options, considering alternatives, and, if necessary, seeking help.

And this is how I came to find him after his journey through the clawing weather, bent, but far from broken, upon my doorstep.

# Part One
# Debt Paid

# Chapter 1
# AGREEMENT
# 契約

"THERE'S ONE THING you have to know from the beginning—this is a love story."

The old soldier pauses as emotion wells in his eyes and hitches his lungs throughout a deep breath. "I'm sorry, but this is difficult for me to talk about, even years later..." his voice trails off as he stares out through frosted panes at barren trees and icy drifts, a bleak winter landscape that mirrors his soul. "She turned my whole life around. I became what we were together. When she went, it all went with her."

Harold Stevens has not lost everything, just the things that matter most. At the age of eighty-seven, his youth is long departed, along with his immediate family; he has outlived all fourteen of his siblings. Good health is also a memory. Four tours in Korea, two during wartime, have exacted a heavy toll on his legs and back. In the years since, his battered musculature has continued to deteriorate so that his days are largely defined by short moves from chair to chair with the aid of a sturdy cane. His nights are a litany of endless pains.

But for one who has lived and endured so much, Harold's face, starkly lit by the white world beyond the glass, is remarkably un-lined; some heaviness around the neck and jowls marks the only places where his skin has lost elasticity. Despite his involuntary lack of exercise, he still cuts a trim figure, with none of the pudgy thickening around the belly that is the usual, inevitable result of a metabolism winding down. But neither is he wasting away. His pallor is healthy, his voice robust, and the only sign that the thick shock of hair crowning his head belongs to an elderly man is the lack of color, although there are still traces of black mingled among the neatly parted thatches of gray. In fact, when he's sitting as he is now, backboarded in a living room chair, rather than stooped over his cane—his spine straight and true as one of the vertical stripes on his red plaid shirt—Harold could easily pass for a man fifteen years younger.

On the inside, however, time has piled over him like glacial ice, grinding away, piece by piece, the things that once made him whole. Two years ago came the crowning blow, as he sat at the bedside of his beloved wife of fifty-seven years, gripping her hand as the pulse faltered, then fell silent. From that moment he has been a man lost in grief, wracked with survivor's guilt, genuinely perplexed by the fact that he's still here while everything familiar and cherished has turned to dust. In his despair and self-reflection, he has seized upon a way to justify his longevity and breathe life back into the shades of the past. Memories are ephemeral, he has decided, but a memoir—his thoughts transferred to ink on paper—is a mechanism for turning back the clock. A book has the power to resurrect and the permanence of stone. It can also be a ledger for balancing the scales. For these reasons, he deems it a worthy forum for a testimonial, and a reckoning. Written words will record his triumphs, his struggles, and carry his adoration for his vanished wife forward so that after he has followed her into memory, an account—and an accounting—will endure.

"This is not just my story," he emphasizes. "This is a love story about the two of us. There's only me to tell it, and it's not easy for me, a lot of it, because I didn't really understand anything about love. For a number of reasons—youth, fear of rejection, denial…things that were part of my upbringing and my nature—I didn't realize how much I was in love with this girl. I want people to understand how I went through life, for some years, not realizing how deeply my feelings went, and how I came to the realization that I'd loved her from the day we met." He draws another long breath, but steadier now, his sorrow giving way to determination. "Now, I understand that from start to finish, this is a story about love."

Harold has come to me through a mutual acquaintance, a doctor, one of the multitude he has seen over the years for his myriad aches and pains. This physician also happens to be a woman whose parents were first-generation Japanese immigrants. Since his earliest days as a soldier stationed in the Orient, Harold has dabbled in the languages of that region. "I thought I would try speaking a little Japanese to her, just to test the waters," he told me later. To his surprise, the doctor not only understood him, she was fluent. "What she came back at me with was way beyond my pay grade," he had smiled. "I barely understood a word—I had to tell her to slow down!" His eyes twinkled, "When I was a young man, that's not something I could have imagined me ever saying to a woman." Despite the weighty physical and emotional burdens he carries and all that he has lost, Harold still possesses a trait that has defined him since adolescence: he is a bit of a rascal. In particular, his conversation trends toward waggish or self-effacing humor accompanied by a sly grin or a wry chuckle. When it comes to a seasoned wit, the man has salt.

While the doctor checked him over, he had chatted with her about his late wife, his desire to write a book, and his need for assistance. She told him she knew a writer who did that sort of thing for a living. Harold called me that very day. We agreed to meet at my house the following afternoon at one o' clock. Harold turned up at eleven in the morning. At the time, I attributed his early arrival to age—muddled memory, regarding the details of our appointment. Later I came to understand it was simply his enthusiasm to get the project underway that caused him to jump the gun. Harold is nearly ninety years old. He does not have a minute to waste.

During our phone conversation, he had briefed me on his history. Despite the thirty-two year difference in our ages, Harold and I have some things in common. For one, we share a strong connection to Duluth, Minnesota. I came to this bustling Great Lakes port city to attend college. Captivated by the scenic expanse of Lake Superior and enamored by the town's blend of big-city amenities and folksy charm, I never left. Harold, on the other hand, was born and raised here, but shipped out to the Pacific while still in his teens. Other than family visits and several brief periods between overseas postings, he did not move back to Duluth until he was an old man. In between, however, his journey has veered down avenues of experience utterly foreign to me, ranging from forbidden Far Eastern romance to routinely holding the means to destroy entire cities in the palms of his hands.

Today, it is as though Minnesota is determined to make up for all the winters Harold has missed. In my defense, I had fully intended to clear the snow from my sidewalk and salt the icy patches on the two series of concrete steps before his arrival. Instead, he surprised me, not only by turning up hours earlier than expected, but also by neatly negotiating terrain that would give a musk ox pause.

Yet, despite his iron-willed tenacity, Harold is no bull. One thing that was not apparent over the phone is the degree of his frailty. In terms of his health, he is not one to complain or wallow in self-pity, and he's not looking for sympathy. Still, when I opened the door to find an alarmingly bowed octogenarian, braced like a windblown mountaineer upon my stoop, his first words had been to let me know that according to the Americans with Disabilities Act, my steps do not pass muster. "What this place needs," Harold advised sternly, "is a damn railing!"

After rescuing him from the elements, I took his coat. Despite the clinging snow, I did not ask him to remove his shoes. The man had just scaled Everest; he deserved a parade, not the indignity and new challenge of skating across my wood floors in stocking feet. Harold took a moment to size me up. I'm taller than he is, but most men are. As the self-proclaimed runt in his family, he has been accustomed since childhood to looking up in order to meet another's gaze. Old age and a bent back have been no help on that score. But he has also spent a good portion of his life as an imposing army sergeant who once called cadence for an entire battalion, and even now, nearly folded in half, his bearing and voice carry the air of authority. "I'm Harold Stevens," he announced with polite assertiveness and a surprisingly firm handshake, "and I'm very pleased to meet you." Still a bit flustered at his premature and seemingly miraculous appearance upon my ice-slick threshold, I greeted him in kind, but spoke with genuine concern when I asked, "How are you?" In response, Harold offered up what I have come to know as his pat answer to any inquiry regarding his wellbeing: "I'm still above ground," he shrugged. Then, with surprising dexterity—spryness, even—he'd shot past me, out of the entry, beelining for the living room, some place where we could get down to business.

"Tell me," I asked, catching up, as he finally unburdened himself from his cane and settled into an armchair, "why do you want to write a book about your life?"

It had taken some time for Harold to reply, not because the answer is hard, but because his wounds are still raw, the sense of loss so keenly felt, and speaking from the heart is at odds with the impassive, battle-hardened disposition of a soldier.

"I want it more than anything—" voice cracking, he quickly shifted his gaze beyond the window, but the facade had fractured and emotion bubbled out, "for my wife."

And that is when Harold tells me that theirs is a love story, and how—as is the cruel and inevitable fate of soul mates—when one half is irrevocably lost, the other is left incomplete and bereft. In his case, the grief has manifested itself in a consuming desire to preserve his wife's memory by sharing their story of how he literally bought her freedom, and in turn, how her love rescued him.

It is a remarkable tale and one I truly want to help him write, but I need to make sure Harold understands that creating a book will demand a lot from him. He is going to have to submit to a lot of candid conversations, it will not be inexpensive, and it's going to take a while.

In terms of the work, Harold is willing and eager to do whatever is required. "I won't dodge anything that you ask me," he insists. "I'll be up-front with you. I want the good, the bad, and the ugly told, because I've done it all." He smiles pragmatically, "And I believe I'm safe. The statute of limitations has run out, so I'm sure I can feel free in disclosing my activities. Anyway," he reasons, "I don't think they'll send me to Leavenworth—I'm an old man!" He's kidding of course, but this gallows humor is a reminder that Harold has made decisions and done things in the past that may well have resulted in the authorities locking him up and throwing away the key.

He has brought with him a fat bundle of handwritten pages—his own failed attempt at putting his story down on paper. I tell him I'll gladly use his notes as a guide, but I am more interested in having him speak to me about his life in a series of interviews, beginning today, so I can glean the details from his own mouth. This delights Harold and he nods enthusiastically, "I want this story told using my language!" He doesn't mean word for word, but it is important to him that I am able to discern and communicate his point of view. This is something that, up to now, even he has not been able to pull off.

"When I was a kid," he tells me, glancing askew at the pages he's written, "English was not my favorite subject at school. Anything I could do to avoid an English class, I did. It wasn't because I was incapable of learning, I just didn't put forth the effort. And the teacher recognized that. She told me, 'Harold, you'd be a wonderful student if you came to class more often.' Skipping those English classes is something I've regretted my whole life." He exhales frustration at the apathy and lack of imagination of his younger self. "It's reflected in the way that I write, it's reflected in the way that I talk, and I know that. But I know one other thing: I can tell a story. And as long as you understand what it is I'm telling you, and you produce something that follows my line of thinking and expresses my feelings, then we're going to get along just fine."

With regard to the money it will take to create a book, Harold has done his homework; he doesn't blink when I shoot him an estimate. He is similarly unfazed when I explain that it is unlikely he will ever recoup much, if any, of his investment. "This isn't about money," he affirms. "It's about writing this book—telling the story that I need told."

But when I inform Harold that the project will likely take at least a year to complete, his face finally registers some anxiety. Time is a different kind of currency, and every passing day is another draw on his dwindling account. From his perspective, the goal is now tantalizingly close; he dreads the possibility of running out of road. Harold realizes he has little choice other than to let someone else do the driving, but he admonishes me to keep my foot on the gas, and if necessary, journey onward solo. He is so infused with purpose, so vigorously set upon this venture, that he catches me off guard when he adds one caveat to our contract. "I'm an old man. If I give up the ghost before this book is done, I need you to promise me something—you will finish it."

We have an agreement, and like this man's profound and affecting love, it transcends, "Till death do we part."

# Chapter 2
# ROOTS

# ルーツ

PERHAPS THE GREATEST testimony to the unassailable virtues of Harold's wife is that his family never said a bad word about her.

"My family could rip a person apart in about ten seconds if you gave them the chance," he rumbles. Harold is explaining to me how opinions grew like lemons on the Stevens' family tree, and they were constantly being squeezed for every drop. "There was always some kind of sour gossip or nitpicking going on about one person or another. Sisters talked about brothers, and brothers talked about sisters—and that included their husbands, wives, and children. But in all the years that my wife and I were married, and considering all the time my family spent around her, I was uncommonly proud of them," he remarks, genuinely astonished. "I never heard anyone say anything degrading about my wife. They all loved her."

Even so, Harold's regard for his family is complicated, and that's putting it kindly. He dearly loved his mother, yet he nearly wore her out with his insolent misbehavior. He was his little sister's guardian angel, though it cost him greatly. He got on well with his brothers, but it was decades before he could turn his back on any one of them without worry of catching a fist. As a kid, any associations with his siblings were purely Darwinian—survival of the fittest. It was the inevitable result of a large troop of kids growing up in adversity under a single roof, and in terms of sheer numbers and hard living, his family was a doozy.

"I am the sole survivor of a family of fifteen kids," he tells me, "and we never had anything in terms of money, so it wasn't an easy life. It was everyone for him or herself." It's understandable, however, if it often felt like they were all ganged up against him. His sisters bossed him like foremen being paid by the word and were free to cuff him at will, secure in the knowledge that Harold's mother would lash him with a suitcase strap if he even thought about striking back. His brothers were an equally rough and menacing crew, guided purely by their own self-interests. Indeed, the entire brood had moral compasses that spun like the tumblers of a picked lock—something that, according to Harold, they probably knew quite a bit about. "I couldn't walk up to a stranger and say I had an ideal family, because I think every damn one of them was crooked at one time or another." He smiles puckishly, "Of course, I can't point any fingers."

Harold Ira Stevens was born at the tail end of the Roaring Twenties: January 26, 1928, in Kelsey, Minnesota, an unincorporated smattering of homes scattered across boggy farmland, forty-five miles northwest of Duluth. Life there was a world apart from the pre-Crash *joie de vivre* holding sway in places like New York City, where young women flapped to jazz at the Cotton Club and men thrilled as Babe Ruth and Lou Gehrig led the Yankees to a decisive World Series victory. Meanwhile, in rural Kelsey, Harold's parents had their hands full trying to feed a family large enough to field nearly two baseball teams of their own.

Their patriarch, William Stevens, had fathered six children with a first wife. When she died, he remarried and sired another nine. Harold was sixth in line of this second batch. By all accounts, Harold's mother, Lottie May Preston, broke the mold in terms of maternal generosity; she mothered the whole lot as her own, treating Harold's half siblings no less attentively than her own children. "She raised them all," Harold tells me, with regard to the kids from his father's first family, "and they were always sisters and brothers to us. They were never half-anything."

Harold's father farmed and also worked for the forestry service where he was renowned for an uncanny ability to track peat fires—smoldering underground blazes that are difficult to detect and even harder to extinguish. But by the time Harold was born, his father was battling an even more insidious consumption. William had contracted tuberculosis, and would spend the next five years in and out of the Nopeming Sanatorium near Duluth. To be closer to this care facility, the family moved into an old farmhouse across the road from the fledgling Duluth airport. They spruced up a small outbuilding to quarantine Harold's father when he was at home. Although Harold was only five years old at the time, he has memories of huddling with the other kids on the grass beneath the sickroom window, listening to the radio programs—serials and big band broadcasts—that were his dad's favorite entertainment. Inevitably, William was transferred one last time to the sanatorium, and the music never played again.

"When my father died in 1933, he left eight children still at home with my mother," Harold tells me, "and the only thing that kept us alive was the fact that we went on relief."

This was during the meanest period of the Great Depression, and the relief he is referring to was a form of government assistance known as a "Mother's Pension." It was envisioned as a way to enable poor children to remain in the full-time care of a single parent—typically a mother. In reality, it was subsistence living. "We used to get a grocery credit," he explains. "It was just a piece of paper, but my mother could go to the market and purchase certain things. It wasn't much, and when it ran out, that was all for the month…but sometimes the grocer would give her bones so she could make soup. This was a hearty meal for us!" he says, with a hollow enthusiasm implying it was the exact opposite.

Social welfare also helped put a roof over the family; shortly after his father's death, Harold's mother moved them into public housing in Duluth's Riverside neighborhood. It was their first home with running water. Harold attended kindergarten there (he still has his report card that notes, ironically, his only mark with less than a perfect score was "storytelling"). Despite the bucolic name, Riverside was located amidst Duluth's outlying industrial sector. Harold roamed with the other kids exploring the grimy environs of the adjoining shipyards and steel mill. As soon as other lodging became available in town, his mother expediently transplanted her crew. They moved first into a third floor apartment in the Central Hillside district— a building that was less than ideal for a family teeming with small kids since the only access was via a rickety, seventy-five foot exterior staircase—before finally landing at a relative's house in an ethnic neighborhood known as "Little Italy."

For seven-year-old Harold, life as a Roman gladiator would have been easier.

"They hung me."

"What do you mean they hung you—by the neck?!"

Harold can't help but grin at my horrified incredulity. "Yeah, the neighborhood kids took a rope and strung me up! They hung me from a tree. My sister ran home screaming to my mother, who came and cut me down just as I was turning blue. Those Italians were mean!"

"They tried to kill you!" I reiterate, which in my book transcends meanness. "Why? Just because you weren't Italian?"

Harold chuckles, "Our family was a little bit of everything, and we didn't lay claim to anything." He shrugs, "My problem was that the Italian boys saw me as different, so they'd gang up on me. Whenever I got out of school, there would be three or four of them waiting to punch me around."

"You were just a little kid," I commiserate, "and small for your age…"

"I was the runt in my family," he nods, "but I could fight!" He squints like a rabid badger, a reminder that ferocity can reside in small packages. "That was something I'd had to learn early on because I had all those brothers. I'd been fighting them my whole life!"

In particular, Harold's older brother Lorin ensured he was well schooled in hard knocks. Lorin was five years his senior, blind in one eye (which may explain his cyclopean orneriness) and a Golden Gloves boxer who regularly amused himself by using Harold as his punching bag—or his blood sport rooster.

"Lorin used to make me fight other guys," Harold complains. "He'd corner some kid in the alley, and then he'd call me over. It might even be a friend of mine, but he'd tell me, 'Get over here and fight this kid!'" Harold shrugs, "And I'd fight him, because if I didn't, Lorin would beat the hell out of *me!*"

Once more, my face registers concern, and again Harold can only laugh, "I had weird siblings." He nods resignedly, "There were some sadistic individuals in my family."

But Harold occasionally managed to get in a lick or two, and with brother Lorin, he'd made at least one lasting impression.

"I'd cooked up some fudge," Harold recalls, "and Lorin had his eye on it. The last piece was on the platter, and I said to him, 'Don't take that!' So, of course, he picked it up and shoved it right into his mouth." Harold's retaliation was so instinctive and disproportionate Lorin never saw it coming. "I grabbed that heavy crockery platter, and sent it to him airmail special delivery!" Harold cuts a horizontal stroke with his hand. "Lorin already had a scar above his eye, one flat scar..." His hand slices upward to complete a right angle. "I added the other half of his initial to that! *L*," he stresses, "for Lorin! Oh god," he chuckles, "how he bled!" Of course, any immediate sensation of victory was tempered by the realization that unlike the biblical David, Harold's missile had only managed to enrage Goliath. "I went out of that room like a bullet and he was right behind me; if he'd caught me I know he would have strangled me on the spot!" Once again, his mother's timely intervention saved his bacon. Harold describes how, as the brothers chased through the kitchen where she was laboring, "She grabbed the poker out of the woodstove, stepped between us, and waved that thing like a glowing club in Lorin's face. Mother snarled at him, 'Back off, or you'll get the beating of a lifetime!' Lorin was chafing and pawing with fury," Harold stresses, "but she stopped him dead in his tracks! He went out of there cowed and bleeding like a stuck hog," he snorts, before adding solemnly, and I suspect without exaggeration, "but if my mother hadn't been there to threaten him with that poker, I'm sure he would have killed me!"

To dispel any notion that his mother is also coming off as a bit of a sadist, Harold assures me otherwise. "My mother never abused us," he insists, "but she didn't spare the rod either. If you got a whipping, you'd earned it. And I deserved every one," he notes, "and probably a couple extra that I dodged—although I didn't get away with much; she saw to that."

In truth, Harold's mother waded a daily path so inundated by parental duties she could barely keep her head above water. By all accounts, she was a well-intentioned, deeply Christian woman, who regarded the perpetual trial of ensuring her mob was adequately fed, housed, and disciplined as her cross to bear. She may have found comfort in her belief that God rewards those who endure such testing, but it was still a thankless and exhausting challenge. "I do believe that sometimes she was just running out of energy," Harold reflects. "I could measure it by the heat of that suitcase strap." He shifts a little at the memory. "My mother used to say that those whippings hurt her more than it hurt me." He rolls his eyes, "Of course, every parent tells their kid that right before the lashing starts. In Mom's case, though, I think saying it was her way of sending a message to the Almighty that she was trying to do the right thing."

Thanks to his mother's religious embrace of corporal punishment, and regular drubbings courtesy of his brothers and sisters, Harold had learned at a young age how to take a beating—and how to dole one out. These skills would prove invaluable for survival in Little Italy, especially after his near lynching by the playground Mafia.

"I had my eye on one of those guys," Harold squints. "He was the instigator of the bunch. His name was Harry Richardson."

Not a very Italian sounding name, I remark.

"He had Italian blood in him—enough to lead the gang. He was the one who'd put that noose around my neck, and he always had a few guys with him to back him up. Well, one day old Harry made the mistake of wandering down the street all alone…" Harold's mouth curves wickedly and he smacks his fist so forcefully I jump like there's a bee in the chair. "I caught up with him and I beat that kid to a pulp!" he leers gleefully. "I knocked his ass down and I made sure he *stayed* down."

I ask him whether this was because he wanted revenge, or because he thought that if he took down the leader, the others would leave him alone.

"That too," he exclaims, neatly scooping up both rationales, "and you know what? After that, there wasn't another Italian kid that ever tried to take me on!"

Of course, all this talk about his rough and impoverished childhood is merely a prelude to the real story—the one Harold is itching to tell—but he wants the circumstances of his growing up in the hopper, and so for the next few weeks this will be our focus. "These are things you'll need to know about," he explains, "because I think they're important for understanding what comes later. I think it will help to explain..." he blows a heavy sigh, "why I sometimes acted the way I did."

Though Harold may have regrets regarding certain past events and behaviors, he is not ashamed of his hardscrabble upbringing. Indeed, he remains in awe of his mother's wearying efforts to keep her family afloat despite their desperate circumstances. He also understands that his checkered past was a crucible that gave him the tools to seize on future opportunities—including one that would ultimately free him from the family spiral.

That's especially clear to him now that he is rudderless. For the first time since he was a teenager, Harold is without the steering influence of the other woman who still awes him, the one who helped him chart a new course, put wind in his sails, and did her best to guide him away from the rocks and shoals that sank his siblings and are littered with their wreckage.

He has too much humility to say it, but I think the reason Harold wants me to know his background—how both nature and nurture predisposed his family toward poverty, pregnancy, and prison—is to fully appreciate, thanks to his wife, how far he would go, and how different his life would become.

# Chapter 3
# FIGHTER

ファイター

HAROLD'S APARTMENT is a mess. Or at least, that's what he would have me believe.

"My wife was such a neat person. There was never a speck of dust in any of the places where we lived together. She was well known for her cleanliness and the beautiful homes we had. Since she passed away," he sighs, "I haven't kept this place up." Harold shakes his head gloomily. "I should probably get a cleaner in here before something takes root in this carpet."

In fact, the place is neat as a pin. Sure, there are probably more photo albums piled around than at the National Archives, and biographical notes and other documents are spread out across what appears to be a desk but is actually the dining room table. Even so, there are no dirty dishes in the sink or piles of mail building up, no clothes on the doorknobs or any of the other things that one might associate with being untidy—like at my house. Frankly, I am amazed and a little embarrassed by Harold's definition of what constitutes sloppy housekeeping. If this is his idea of unclean, doctors probably could have performed surgery in here when his wife was in charge.

We are talking today at his home, partly because I feel meeting here is easier and safer than having him risk the icy gauntlet to my front door, but also so I can get a better sense of the man. One way to glean insight into a person's nature is by observing how he feathers his nest.

My first impression, despite Harold's claims to the contrary, is that he runs a tight ship. For example, a glance into his bedroom reveals that his bunk is pulled together tidily. This is something that would be easy for any person living alone to neglect, especially someone hobbled with Harold's disabilities, but his bed is neatly made with tight, crisp folds that would pass an army inspection. Of course, I expect nothing less from a career military man with a dutiful and distinguished record of service—of which the framed rows of medals and other decorations on his wall speak volumes. Other than this, however, the apartment's decor is primarily an expression of the tastes and talents of his wife, with silk embroideries, porcelain vases, and other Asian influences throughout. The albums and framed photographs stacked on every level surface are testimony to Harold's perpetually reflective mood, now that he is alone.

"Have a seat over here," he tells me, as he lines up for a landing and then thumps backward into a recliner. "Sit right there on the couch. Help yourself to that candy in the dish. Feel free to get rid of any of those throw pillows. I don't know why we have to have all these pillows! I keep telling her—"

He catches himself. It is hard to let go of the old routines. For fifty-seven years he and his wife playfully bickered about the little things married couples pick about, like sofa pillows. But it's been over two years now since he has told her anything face-to-face.

"I'll be just fine," I assure him, perusing his candy. "Pillows and all. In fact, I think by the time we're done with the book, this couch and I are going to be old friends!"

"Not too old, I hope," Harold says, tapping his watch. Ticktock.

As during our first meeting, Harold is outfitted in a natty plaid, although today's shirt is checkered blue and white and highlighted with zippy stripes of teal. Other than the changes of wardrobe and venue, it is as though our previous meeting never ended—before I have time to consult my notes or even frame a question, Harold's razor-sharp memory and keenness to get the ball rolling take over and he dives in, picking up precisely where we left off. "I was telling you how I survived Little Italy."

"You said you fought back," I confirm, rifling through my transcripts. "You beat the tar out of…"

"Harry Richardson," Harold confirms. "Yeah, I became a pretty notorious fighter in that part of town."

To be clear, Harold insists that his banner was more white than black. Other than in self-defense, his proclivity for raising his fists was rooted in ethical principles, not rancor. "I wasn't a mean or bad natured kid," he asserts. In fact, it was the opposite. "I never liked a bully. Size didn't matter to me. If I saw a big guy throwing his weight around and if he persisted in being that way, I took it upon myself to teach him a lesson. And that got me into quite a bit of trouble."

A facet of Harold's personality that has plagued him since childhood—vividly demonstrated when he flung a stoneware plate, discus-style, into brother Lorin's skull—is an instinct to react without regard to consequences. By the time his mother finally moved the family away from Little Italy (where they'd managed to stick it out for over a year without Harold getting murdered) he had become a poster child for impulsive brawling. Now that he was living in a relatively placid neighborhood, Harold's dustups were no longer about survival. Instead, his troubles were rooted in a child's notion of justice born out of loyalty and in defense of his little sister.

"Starting with the third grade at Jackson School," he says scornfully, "that's when I really shined." Harold's grim smile confirms how much he did not. "I got into so many fights, and almost all of them were because kids were picking on my sister Floy." His face brightens at the memory of his little sister. Floy has always held a special place in Harold's heart. Of all the Stevens siblings, she was the good one. Floy harbored none of the others' burly aggression. "You only had to look at her to know she was different," he insists. "She was so small and so thin, she just didn't put the weight on like the rest of us." Of course, in the cruel marching band of childhood, this made her the kazoo—puny and different, a target for ridicule.

"In those days," he reflects, "they gave bottles of milk to all the kids at school. Everybody got one each morning. But because Floy was so skinny, the school nurse worried she was undernourished, so they made her drink two bottles of milk, one in the morning and another in the afternoon. Well, that made her stand out, and you know how kids are…"

"They teased her."

He bristles, "And if someone bullied my kid sister, I felt like they probably needed to get smacked good and hard to wise up! And that's exactly what I'd do. I'd beat the living daylights out of them!"

"That can't have gone over well at school."

"Oh, that principal, she *loved* me," he drips. "I sat on the bench outside her office so many days that she got tired of looking at me. She didn't want me there and the teacher didn't want me in class, so things were pretty tough for me at school."

But it was nothing compared to when he got home.

"My older sister Dorothy was an insufferable tattletale," Harold mutters bitterly. "Every time I did something wrong at school—and I managed to do something wrong nearly every day—she'd race home to crow to mother, *'Harold's in trouble again!'* So when I got home, my mom would be standing in the doorway, ready with either the strap or a whip-thin piece of wood from an orange crate." He winces, "She was a real artist with one of those!"

Time and again, the district's truant officer had to be dispatched to Harold's home to advocate for his readmission to school. As Harold tells it, the man was practically his personal lawyer. "He would come up to the porch and sit down alongside me and he'd say, 'Harold, what kind of trouble did you get into this time?' It was the same old story: 'Someone picked on my kid sister, and I had to smack 'em.' He'd shake his head, 'Why do you always have to smack 'em?' And I'd tell him, 'I guess it's just built into me.' He'd sigh and say, 'Okay, let's take a walk over to the school.'

"So we'd go see the principal and the teacher, and the truant officer would work to convince them to take me back. He'd have me apologize. I'd tell them I was sorry, and that I'd try to do better and try harder not to disrupt the class—I had those words memorized because I had to say them so often. The teacher had a soft heart, so I'd go back to class and get through maybe a week, until something new would erupt, and then," Harold points toward the door, *"Out!"*

It all came to a head when he was in the fifth grade. His penmanship instructor was painstakingly drawing out examples on the chalkboard, but the teacher insisted that his pupils also take out their flipbooks and follow along as he worked. That didn't make any sense to Harold.

"Why did he think I needed to look at my penmanship book if he was doing it all on the board?" Harold steams, even after nearly eighty years of venting. "Well, of course, I was the only student who didn't have the book on my desk. The teacher said, 'Where's your book?'

"'It's in my desk.'

"'Get it out.'"

Harold grits his teeth, "I didn't set out to be obstinate. Even then, all I would have had to do was take out that book and I'd have been fine. But that would have been too easy. I don't know why I was always challenging things," he sighs, "but I told him, 'I don't need the book. I can see it all right there on the board!' The teacher said, 'I want you to take out that book and put it on the desk right now.' I said, 'I don't think I will!'

"As usual," Harold acknowledges, "I was being stubborn, but it was one time too many. He showed me the exit, and it was the last time I was ever in the Jackson School. After that, no matter how hard my mother or the truant officer pleaded, they wouldn't take me back."

For Harold's mother, his getting kicked out of school was the last straw. As he'd arced toward delinquency, she had tried putting the fear of God in him, both with the strap and by dragging him to church. At best, the former delivered only a momentary respite from his wayward antics, and religion just fanned the flames of insubordination—it took him less than five minutes to escape Sunday school by climbing out through the bathroom window. At night he would pull the same stunt from his upstairs bedroom, sneaking out onto the roof, jumping to a nearby tree, and shinnying down to join with the other urchins ratting around downtown Duluth. Once, his mother caught Harold red-handed—and black-kneed—climbing in through the basement coal chute after a night of mischief. He had become a taxing drain on her time and energy, resources that were already spread thin attending to a houseful of other difficult children. At her wits' end after his expulsion, Harold's mother asked one of her older daughters to take him in. His mother could only hope that a change of household and a fresh start in a new school might straighten him out.

"She sent me off to live in Duluth Heights with my sister Gladys and her husband, Max," Harold tells me. "I may have been stupid in a lot of ways," he reflects, "but not dumb enough to challenge my older sister."

"Why was that?"

A sharp puff of breath betrays the dread instilled by the sheer physical presence of Gladys, "She was a big, *big* woman…she could back me into a chair with just her voice!"

"You make her sound like some kind of bear," I laugh.

"That would be a fair description," he nods. "She was mean as a grizzly too. All she had to do was level a milk bottle or a fist in my direction and I'd tow the line."

"She would hit you?!"

"Never," Harold insists. "She didn't have to. She just had to look like she was thinking about it."

Remarkably, this arrangement worked well for three years. Harold made it relatively without incident through the sixth grade and two years of junior high school. Of course there were still occasional altercations and episodes of misbehavior. Once, after the teacher caught him dropping pencils to ogle a girl's legs, he was told he would have to pass the next test or she would flunk him for the whole semester; purely out of defiance, he scored nearly one hundred percent. But under the watchful eye of the formidable Gladys, and with the compulsion to champion his little sister far removed, the fights were less frequent. If he did get held after school, Harold would race the bus home on foot to arrive at the usual time, lest Gladys even consider that he had stepped out of line.

But if outwardly he was a model inmate in his sister's home, on the inside Harold was a kettle ready to boil. The heat was supplied by Gladys' strict edict that he must complete his household chores before being allowed outside in the evening.

"That sounds…reasonable," I suggest.

Harold sets me straight. "That's the time all the young people used to gather," he grouses, "to shoot marbles and bat around before dark—this was how you mixed with the other neighborhood kids."

Meanwhile, he was stuck indoors mixing dish soap and water. "One of the rules my sister laid down was that it was my job to do all the washing up after dinner before I could go out. Now, if that only happened once in a while," he allows, "I probably wouldn't have thought anything of it. But it was *every* damn night. Sometimes Max worked overtime and the family would eat late, and I wouldn't get to go out at all!"

I remain unconvinced. "It still sounds to me like a run-of-the-mill responsibility for a kid," I persist. "I mean, how many people did you have to do the washing up for?"

"Well," he frowns, "there was me, the two adults, and it seemed like they were adding more kids every year. I can't tell you the exact number at that time, but my sister had nine children!"

I'm warming to his predicament.

Harold was desperate. He viewed pulling perpetual KP duty for Gladys' entire platoon as slave labor, pure and simple. He didn't dare defy his sister outright, but life under her authoritarian rule had become unlivable. Harold practically wails, "I felt like I was being robbed of my youth! I knew I had to get out of that house, once and for all. That's when I finally said to myself, there's only one way I'm ever going to be free of the goddamn dishes…and that's if I do something drastic."

# Chapter 4
# EXILE
# 島流し

THE NEIGHBORS must have thought the Germans had invaded. In living rooms and on front porches up and down the block there could be heard a din of breaking glass that shattered the tranquility of evening crickets and muffled radio music like a Panzer tank rolling through a greenhouse, determinedly grinding every shard to sand beneath its treads. One after another, whole panes erupted with explosive crashes, followed by staggered reports as any remaining fragments hinged back and forth from caulking before dropping from the emptied frames. Throughout the neighborhood, dogs barked with nervous excitement, house lights flicked on, and people peered out anxiously from behind curtains and blinds, their mouths agape at a scene of wanton destruction that went on and on and on. All who witnessed it were likely thinking two things: thank goodness that house is empty, and Harold has finally gone mad.

"Honest to god, I stood in the street and threw stones through every window in the front of that house! I broke every one! And then I started working my way around the building, and before I was done, I had destroyed over twenty windows. By the time I finally ran out of glass to smash, my arm was so sore I couldn't have thrown another rock!" Harold cups one elbow tenderly, "I sometimes wonder if the arthritis in my arm and shoulder is because of that day," he chuckles, only half-kidding.

He can laugh about it now, but Harold is the first to admit "that day" wasn't his proudest moment. In his defense, he tells me, he was just a kid—barely a teenager, and his rampage wasn't an act of senseless or impulsive vandalism. In fact he had thought it out quite rationally, plotting every detail to ensure no one would get hurt. He had targeted that particular house because it was a county foreclosure, sitting empty; to his mind, it didn't even belong to anyone. And he did not try to run away or deny his actions, though he knew there would be serious consequences. Getting caught was key to his plan.

"My thinking was this: I'm going to do something that will land me in Red Wing—that was the state reformatory school at the time. They called it a school," he explains, "but it was a prison for juvenile delinquents."

Harold felt sure there was already a bunk at Red Wing with his name on it (most of his brothers and sisters were alumni of this and similar institutions, so as a candidate for admission he practically had legacy status) but he did not relish the idea of incarceration. "Nevertheless, I decided I'd rather be in jail," he reasons, "than locked up where I was, getting belittled by my peers for having to do the dishes night after night. I'd welcome reform school if it got me the hell away from Gladys and her damn chores!"

I ask him whether the cops showed up while he was still breaking windows, or did they come fetch him at his sister's house?

"They never did come," he says, amazed. "Gladys and Max took me down to the police station in the morning. I'm sure they got a phone call: *Bring that animal down here!* I had to face a judge, and I knew he was going to throw the book at me and ship me off to someplace—most likely Red Wing."

The proceedings were indeed focused upon who would take custody of Harold, but reform school was not even mentioned. Astonishingly, the discussion centered on remanding him to the care of one of his siblings. To Harold's great relief, it wasn't Gladys.

"My brother Harvey was there in the courtroom! I suspect my mother may have had something to do with that," he smiles broadly.

"Harvey was her oldest son, and she leaned on him whenever she needed help. I can only surmise that my mother asked him to intercede on my behalf. Harvey told the judge, 'I live across the bay on the outskirts of Superior, Wisconsin. I'm married and I have plenty of room in my house. If you'll allow it, he can come live with me.'"

This sounded pretty good to a court that was weary of weeding the Stevens' garden; every time a judge sent one off to the reformatory, two more popped up to take his or her place. If the Minnesota taxpayers could rid themselves of one of these hooligans by shipping him off to another state, why not? With the rap of a gavel, Harold was sentenced to exile.

To say where Harvey lived was Superior was a stretch on several counts. In fact, his home was located well outside the town, in an isolated, rural district; *Godforsaken!!* is the term and punctuation Harold volunteers. Making matters even more unsatisfactory for a born troublemaker like Harold: "The only other children for miles around were a few farm kids," he laments, "and most of them were goody-goodies that weren't interested in having any *real* fun."

In terms of amusement, Harold had to be content with sneaking sloe gin at barn dances or getting behind the wheel of his brother's old Chevrolet and ripping up and down the gravel roads. Harvey not only taught and permitted Harold to drive, he schooled him in the mechanical workings of the Chevy and other machinery, so Harold regarded his brother as a tolerant and tolerable guardian. Harvey's wife was another matter.

"I didn't always get along with her," Harold acknowledges flatly. "One time she and I got into a big row and I stomped out of that house ready to blow! Harvey and I had sawed up a whole bunch of wood for the stove and left it in a big pile. I grabbed an ax and took my frustrations out on that firewood. I hacked the whole damn pile! When Harvey came home, he saw all that split wood and said, 'What the hell happened here?!' His wife said, 'Harold got mad at me.' He told her, 'For chrissake, get him mad at you more often!'"

To Harold's chagrin, living far from civilization was not a reprieve from having to attend school, and not even an excuse for showing up late. By a cruel twist of fate the school building, seemingly one of the only other structures in the entire district, was located directly across the road from Harvey's home. But Harold quickly came to regard the teacher there as kindly and patient, so he made a conscious effort to apply himself to his studies and not do anything to cause her trouble. Ironically, in terms of his public education, this school year would be his undoing, but at the time, he was moving forward by leaps and bounds.

"It was just a little two-room country schoolhouse," Harold explains, "where the teacher alternated teaching the different grades. One year she'd teach the ninth grade, the next year the tenth, then back to the ninth again, and so on, back and forth. Well, I was supposed to have the ninth grade, but that year she was doing the tenth. So I had to skip a grade; I went straight from the eighth grade to the tenth."

I ask him if that was hard. Wasn't he lost compared to the other students?

"Not at all," Harold glares, straddling a line between feigning umbrage and real annoyance. "I wasn't a dummy! I had a brain—when I chose to use it! No, I just took it in stride and jumped ahead a grade. It didn't cause me any trouble at all—" he frowns, "well, not for another year or two anyway."

Despite his remarkable academic progress and Harvey's benevolence, country living did not agree with Harold. Put simply, he was bored to tears. From where he was living in Wisconsin, he could glimpse Duluth's bustling hills and crowded skyline in the distance, a constant reminder of the big city with all its alluring temptations and depravities. After a year of penance in the wilderness, Harold felt he had done his time, so he appealed to the highest arbiter of justice he knew.

"I asked my mother to let me come home," he says. "I still had a bedroom in her house, and I begged her to let me live there again."

"What made you think she would take you back?" I wonder, admiring his cheek. It was a bold proposition, considering how much trouble he had given her in the past.

"Well," he explains, "I had to commit to promises about my behavior at home and at school…plus, by this time, I was old enough to work odd jobs and bring a little money into the family. I thought that seemed like a fair trade," he beams, adding, "and she agreed!"

In fact, sorting out his schooling would be the greater challenge. In Wisconsin, Harold had successfully graduated the tenth grade. He assumed he would start the next year as a junior at Duluth's Central High School. Noting he'd skipped a grade, however, the state of Minnesota insisted he fill in the blank. It was a step backwards, but his pledge to his landlady to walk the straight and narrow meant Harold had little choice other than to about-face and take the ninth grade.

Also true to his word, Harold did his best to secure part-time work after school and on weekends. He shined shoes and worked in a market, anything to turn a quick buck. One of these jobs was helping to unload produce deliveries for a trucking company. Even though he had previously raced Harvey's Chevy all over rural Wisconsin, Harold likes to joke that this delivery job is where the husband of one of his sisters first taught him how to drive—although "abandoned him to it" would be more accurate.

"That brother-in-law," Harold notes with genuine disgust, "he'd spent more time in jail than out! But somehow he got a job driving a delivery truck and he asked me to help him load and unload potatoes. He backed the truck down a steep hill, and we'd just started unloading when he saw a policeman that he recognized coming around the corner. 'Harold, you've got it!' my brother-in-law said, and he took off running down the alley and was gone! He just left me there with that truck full of potatoes! Well, I didn't have any choice. I had to get that truck moved—"

"Wait," I interrupt, "why was that?"

"Well, I couldn't just leave it there!"

"*He* did!"

Harold grunts, "Boy, did he ever! This was a five-ton truck stacked full of hundred-pound bags of potatoes, and we'd only taken about two of those bags off before that no-good brother-in-law decided to bolt!" Harold reaches one hand forward and begins energetically working an imaginary shift lever. "But I was confident I could drive it—" He grits his teeth and mutters, "Well, I'd seen him work the gears anyway…the real tricky part was starting out with a

**35**

fully loaded truck going uphill." His feet lever in opposition, "You had to ease off the clutch and come out smooth." He sags. "Except I didn't come out smooth!" Alarmingly, Harold starts jolting in his chair as if he's being electrocuted; considering his brittle bones, it's like watching china dishes clatter in an earthquake, but he's trying to make a point. "The whole rig was jerking and jumping," he quavers. "I bounced that truck for blocks, all the way up the hill!"

Now that Harold was a teenager, the city presented a whole new array of enticing and illicit ways for him to court trouble: pool halls, backroom gambling, alcohol—sometimes, the forbidden fruit practically put itself in his mouth.

"I could buy liquor anytime I wanted," he declares. "Evidently, the clerk thought I was old enough because he never asked me to show a draft card or other proof of age."

I reflect that this must have made him quite popular with the other teenagers.

"Oh yeah," he affirms. "The drinking age was twenty-one, so I used to buy booze for my friends all the time." He leans toward me confidentially, "When I was young, I always looked older. Now that I'm old," he twinkles, "I look like a kid!"

He's having a little fun, but it's no joke. Harold has indeed been blessed with a hard-to-pin-a-number-on appearance from an early age—the pictures in his albums are proof of this. For one thing, he has always had that hair. Photos of him as a teenager depict dark eyes and darker eyebrows set beneath a rakish pompadour of sable hair nearly a decade before anyone ever uttered the name Elvis. I think it's a safe bet young Harold was a bit of a ladies' man. According to him, it is a bet I would lose.

"I didn't have a lot of romantic experience with girls," he admits frankly. His mind drifts back to torrid summer nights and cars with steamed windows and seats the size of couches parked beside the moonlit expanse of Lake Superior. Unhappily, Harold reveals, the only backseat encounters he ever saw were in a rearview mirror. "I was the designated chauffeur," he says, dejectedly. "I drove the car while my friends fogged up the glass." He frowns, "No, I was dumb about girls."

"What do you mean *dumb?*" I ask him. "You were certainly familiar with girls; you had all those sisters…"

Harold grinds his lower lip. "I was shy," he mumbles.

Gun-shy is more like it.

"I had sisters alright," he squints, "a whole houseful of sisters who smacked me around any time I stepped out of line! Trust me," he practically trembles, "that's enough to make any boy anxious around women. If I had ever accidentally walked in on any one of them while she was dressing, she'd have thrown me out the upstairs window—through the glass! I think that same fear carried over in my…education, if you will, with girls." Harold offers up this example: "There was a girl I liked, and so I took her out. I finally got up the nerve to park the car and we shared a few kisses. Somehow I got the signals mixed—I thought I'd gotten the okay to get a little fresh, nothing too serious—and I got slapped!" Harold fixes me earnestly. "It may or may not have just been her way of telling me to slow down, but that rejection scared the hell out of me. I took her straight home! No," he breathes, "it was safer for me driving the cars for the other guys. I just didn't have the guts to experiment with girls. To be very honest with you, I was afraid of women."

He may have been an underachiever with the fair sex, but by the fall of 1943, Harold had accomplished something no one else in his family had ever done. He'd completed every grade from kindergarten all the way up through the tenth—albeit with the last two in reverse order. The previous year had been utter torture, as he suffered through curriculum meant to prepare him for material he had already learned, but he'd stuck it out. He was looking forward to finally moving on to Central High School—and was therefore dumbfounded when he was informed he would have to remain in progression in the Duluth school system. By decree of the district administration, he would be attending high school all right, but as a tenth grader, studying the same courses he had covered two years earlier in Wisconsin. To Harold's mind, the only thing worse after being made to step down a grade when he had already proven himself capable of moving ahead a year, was being forced to repeat a grade he had already completed. Such rigid, nonsensical thinking (particularly from an institution tasked with cultivating the opposite), coupled with the prospect of facing yet another term without learning anything new, were too much. Harold describes to me his first day at Central High School. "I went in the front door and right out the back." It was also his last day. Harold Stevens washed his hands of public school.

"What then?" I wonder. "Did you even have a plan?"

His eyes brighten and he nods enthusiastically. "There was a world war going on! The biggest fight ever, and if there was one thing I loved," he grins, "it was a good fight! I just had to kill some time and hope it would last long enough for me to get into it because I wasn't yet old enough to join up."

Until then, Harold would literally drift, but not in the nautical sense. Like a vagrant.

"I went on the bum."

# Chapter 5
# HOBO
# 漂泊者

A NEW DAY, a new plaid shirt—alternating shades of navy and robin's-egg blue. Just as we're settling in, once more in Harold's living room, his cell phone rings. I'm frankly surprised he owns such a thing. Harold wants nothing to do with touchscreens, email, or the World Wide Web. No thank you; he'll get his correspondence and information the old-fashioned way, on tangible paper instead of conjured from the digital ether. For a man with his health issues, however, a mobile phone is a vexing but prudent concession.

"Hello…" he says, "*hello?!*" Either there's nobody on the line or Harold hasn't got the patience to engage. He hangs up. Moments later it rings again. "Yes?!" he barks into the glassy brick, then immediately pulls it from his ear to inspect the gadget. "It says *listen*," he growls, "but to what?!"—even though from the tiny speaker I can hear a voice clamoring on about a limited, once-in-a-lifetime offer. But these entreaties are falling on deaf ears, or at least those of a man who sorely misses the kind of phone you can slam into a cradle to make your point. Harold does the next best thing. He punches a button and blocks the number—now there's an app he can appreciate. Somewhere on the globe, a telemarketer has met his match.

Harold knows all about distant lands. He has traveled the world and lived for extended periods in countries where the customs are as confounding to a Minnesotan as bonsai to a timber baron. But by the age of sixteen, other than his yearlong banishment to Wisconsin, Harold had never ventured beyond the confines of his hometown. With school in the rearview mirror and a war somewhere over the horizon, he felt it was high time to hit the road and explore.

"In terms of my education about the world," he tells me, "I decided to start providing that for myself." He pursued this by the only practical method of travel available to a teenager of little means. "I hopped freight out to the West Coast," he smiles. "We saved train fare that way."

When he says "we," Harold isn't referring to the other bums, just one in particular. Surprisingly, it was brother Lorin who had hatched the plan for the two of them to ride the rails, looking for work along the way. Surprising, because, until now, any stories involving Lorin have typically ended with somebody having one foot in the grave— usually Harold. But after a few years of living apart (including a stretch or two at Red Wing for Lorin) his older brother's aggressive tendencies, at least toward Harold, had mellowed. Indeed, during their western sojourn, Lorin seems to have kept his eye (and he only had one) dutifully trained on his younger sibling.

"My brother looked out for me," Harold acknowledges. When I ask what he means by that, he tells me, "Lorin stayed close to me in those boxcars. He was worried about the other tramps getting hold of me. He taught me how to hide my money from them. Hell, I never had much, maybe five or ten dollars, but that was a lot to men who had nothing."

"It sounds dangerous," I remark, envisioning a long list of perils two boys might have faced traveling in the company of rough men— not to mention jumping on and off moving trains. Harold nods, and then surprises me with one I have not considered.

"We almost died of thirst!" he exclaims. "We didn't have any water, and the train just kept rolling across the plains. I remember when it finally stopped, we went running down to the river—the *Missouri River*," he emphasizes, "The 'Big Muddy.' That's what they call it," Harold laughs, "and boy, what an understatement!" He jams his tongue between his teeth and spits a mouthful of imaginary grit. "But we didn't have any choice. It was the only water for miles around and we had to drink it to survive. So we strained it through our teeth. That was the first of many lessons on that trip: if I was going to hitch a ride on a freight train, always carry a jug of water!"

I ask him about the other part of the plan. "Were you able to find work?"

"Sure," he says, telling me how, ironically, their first job was for the railroad. "We got hired as laborers icing refrigerator boxcars, muscling three-hundred-pound blocks of ice. I worked in the icehouse, right in the rail yard. The building had ramps running down to the platform..." Harold's cheeks flush with amusement. "Let me tell you how dumb I was. I had a two-wheeled cart and I took five bags of rock salt and stacked them on that thing—only I didn't appreciate how heavy the load would be. I finally got the cart tipped back, but on the way down the ramp I lost the balance point, the handle went up, and I held on—" he exhales a merry snort, "and it flipped me right over the top! The guys were all standing around roaring with laughter. 'Looks like Harold got an education!' they shouted. And I did. I learned my lesson." He sighs, "It seems like I was learning something new nearly every day."

Despite all the hard work and Harold's acrobatics, the boys were earning little more than a bunk in a boarding car and three squares a day. When they heard the railroad was hiring track workers for better pay, the Stevens brothers jumped at the opportunity.

"We did that awhile somewhere out West on the side of a mountain," Harold recounts, adding that this was where he fell victim to one of the more traditional hazards of tramping: "I nearly got myself disemboweled there in a knife fight with a Mexican fellow."

"A knife fight..." I repeat.

He nods, "With a Mexican." Harold draws a line from his navel to his hip. "He cut me from here to here. I have an obvious scar."

I have an obvious question. "Why did he do that to you?"

"Because he was a goddamn thief!" Harold spits. "He'd stolen something—I can't even remember what it was, and I challenged him on it!" It quickly becomes clear, however, that what Harold terms a fight was an attempted murder. "Before I knew it," he grunts, "he'd pulled a blade and made a swipe across my belly..." Again, he uses his hand to indicate a slice that nearly cut him in half.

"But just then my brother showed up, and that was the end of it. Lorin beat that guy to within an inch of his life," Harold says evenly, "and left him lying in a heap alongside the tracks."

"What about you?! You must have been hurt badly!"

He shrugs, "I was bleeding pretty good, but we taped it up and I survived." He taps his temple, "Again, an education."

A stabbing is certainly one way to gain wisdom about picking a fight with a shady drifter, and, in this case, Harold took both points. "To my credit," he says, with all the hard-earned conviction of someone who decides to quit smoking after burning down the house, "I learned from that. And I never went toe to toe with a guy like him again, on that trip or the others."

In fact, Harold made three different journeys west by freight train during this period. After his outing with Lorin, he traveled a few times with a foster brother (yet another wayward bird his mother had added to her nest) and on these trips it was Harold who was in charge. He volunteers an example of his seasoned leadership. "By now," he explains, "I knew where the hobos had their camps along the way." I'm thinking this was important information for avoiding these vagrants and minimizing unpleasant encounters. In fact, he tells me, it was an opportunity to scrounge a meal—as the beggars' beggar. "These men would scavenge a town searching for scraps and then they'd gather on the outskirts and throw it all in a pot to make stew. In those camps, we could always bum a little to eat!"

Along the way, he worked a diversity of jobs, including a stint in an aluminum smelting plant north of Spokane where he'd had to lie about his age to get hired. To be fair, Harold had good reason to consider his years on earth as just a number. By vagabonding across the country and working shoulder to shoulder with adult men, he had proven—to himself, anyway—that youth was not an impediment to doing these things, or anything else he set his mind to. Of course, what he wanted most of all was to get into the war. Despite being just sixteen, Harold now felt the equal of any of the young men who were streaming overseas to fight in Europe and the Pacific, but two formidable obstacles stood in his way: the United States government and his mother—and in that order of ascending difficulty.

"When I got back to Duluth, I learned that a couple of my friends were heading off to join the navy, and I wanted to go too," he explains, "but if I was going to join up, I'd have to exaggerate my age. You could enlist at seventeen, with a parent's permission. So I went down to the recruiting station and filled out all the papers. Then I took my birth certificate and doctored it up to make me a year older—and I did a damn good job of it!" he says, with the buoyant self-assurance of a master forger.

So much for Uncle Sam. Maneuvering around his blood relative would not be as easy, and he knew it. Harold decided the best tack was to tell, rather than ask.

"I had the forms spread out on the table and I said to my mother, 'Mom, I've decided to join the navy. There are some papers here all ready for you to sign.'" To Harold's way of thinking, he was not soliciting dishonesty; all he needed was her unwitting consent. But if she discovered his alterations to the document, signing it would make her complicit—it literally defined bearing false witness—and breaking a commandment was a thing Harold's mother would never knowingly abet. Everything depended upon her not detecting his handiwork.

It only took her about three seconds.

"She said to me, 'Son, there's a little discrepancy in these papers.'" Harold blows a heavy sigh of resignation, "Of course, I'm still playing dumb. 'Oh? What's that, Mom?' She said, 'You were born in 1928, not 1927.' The jig was up."

In desperation, Harold pulled out all the stops. "I begged her to let me go. I even tried to convince her that the navy was my only hope for staying out of jail! I said, 'Mom, you know better than anyone that I can get into more trouble in one day than most people will in a lifetime! If I stay here, it's only a matter of time before they lock me up!' But she was smarter than me—and infinitely more honest. She said, 'No, son, what becomes of you will be determined by God's will and your own choices. I won't lie for you.' She wouldn't sign those papers."

"You must have been angry with her."

"No…" he pauses, searching for the proper sentiment, "I was… discouraged. Disappointed. But I respected her, and I couldn't blame her. She was a devout Christian woman. She studied the Bible every night and filled the margins with everything she thought it left out. She'd given her life over to raising her children, but asking her to sin for one of them—that wasn't fair."

Harold also wonders whether his mother's religious principles were the sole reason she steadfastly refused to send him to war. "I believe she also had a soft spot in her heart for me," he reflects. "I think maybe she felt she had one son that might someday make something of himself—if I didn't get killed along the way." Harold looks me in the eye. "You know, she'd talk to me. If I'd sit down and want to ask her advice, my mother would always talk to me, and that wasn't true with my older brothers, Harvey and Lorin, or even with my younger brother, Howard."

"What would you and your mother talk about?"

"Oh," he muses cagily, "like whether I'd gotten somebody pregnant."

He gives me a sly wink. At least one time anyway, Harold did more than just drive the car.

"This was a few years later," he explains, "when I went to her and told her, 'Mom, I think I may have put a girl in the family way.' And she had an answer for me. She said, 'Son, you made your bed, now go sleep in it!' In other words, you did this, now take charge." Harold cocks one eyebrow thoughtfully. "It didn't seem like particularly useful advice, but she used that expression a lot with me. Whenever I made a stupid mistake, that's what she'd say. She never sympathized with me when I got myself in a jam, but she listened to me, and I think she thought more of me because I had the guts to come talk to her about it. Still," he chuckles, *It's your bed, now sleep in it!*—that was always her answer."

"She taught you to take responsibility."

"She sure as hell did." As if reading my mind, Harold adds firmly, "And, by the way, the girl wasn't!"

# Chapter 6
# SEABEE
# シービー船

H AROLD'S ADOLESCENT yearning for combat is a hard thing for me to wrap my head around. When I was sixteen years old, the Vietnam War had recently ended, the draft was also history, and among boys of my generation there was palpable relief that we would not be called up to fight communist expansion in remote Asian jungles. Sentiments ran much differently during World War II.

In December, 1941, when the Japanese launched their devastating surprise attack on Pearl Harbor, it fueled a roaring furnace of American resolve to strike back at the ruthless aggressors. In beleaguered Britain, Winston Churchill later admitted going to bed that night and sleeping "the sleep of the saved and thankful," with the certainty that the United States would now apply its considerable will and resources toward defeating Japan, and by extension, its ally Nazi Germany.

Harold was just thirteen years old, still chained to the sink in his sister Gladys' home, when word came of the attack in Hawaii. Like most Americans alive on that day he remembers the family huddling around the radio listening to bulletins detailing the destruction. The next day Congress declared war, and soon leering, bucktoothed and bespectacled caricatures—exaggerated and ugly representations of the enemy—were commonplace propaganda in newspapers and other publications. Whole families of Japanese Americans, now considered untrustworthy at best, were rounded up and interned in detention camps. The potent blend of anger, paranoia, and patriotism was galvanizing, particularly for young men.

"After Pearl Harbor, all I had in my heart was hate," Harold chews hotly. "So many Americans had been killed. Just the words, 'sneak attack' boiled my blood! Not long after that, I had a good friend who was one of the first young guys I knew to enlist in the army. He volunteered, was sent over to Europe, and in no time at all he was killed. I thought about these things a lot and I built up feelings of rage. I wanted to join the fight and..." his fists close reflexively, "I wanted to hurt those who were hurting us."

"And you weren't worried about being killed yourself?"

According to Harold, the prospect of being wounded, maimed, or worse on the battlefield did register upon his youthful sensibilities, but barely, and was overshadowed by an infectious determination to defend home and country. "I was a very patriotic kid," he tells me, "and I wanted to do my part. I wasn't out to be a hero, I just wanted to be one of the men who went there and did the job."

"One of the *men*..." I emphasize, but Harold only noses the bait.

"There were a lot of sixteen-year-olds who lied about their age and went into service during the war," he shrugs, "including many guys I knew personally—friends of mine."

When I speculate about the extent to which a boyish sense of immortality might have fanned his enthusiasm and fueled a false sense of security, Harold tells me that in his case it was indeed significant. "At age sixteen I was invincible," he nods. "I had no fear!" After a moment of thought, he qualifies, "Hell, I was more scared of putting my hand on a woman's breast than I was of going to war," he frowns, "and that's a fact!"

Though deeply frustrated at his mother's refusal to back his underage attempt to join up, Harold was not willing to forge his parent's signature, as some of his friends had done—not yet anyway. He accepted that her convictions precluded her from perpetrating a lie, but he had his limits. Harold anticipated his mother's support once he came of age or he would not hesitate to dust off his counterfeiting skills. "I told her, 'Alright Mom, I'll be seventeen next year, and then

I'm going into service. With your consent, everything will be on the up and up. But if I have to lie to get in, I will!'"

In the meantime, he found work driving anything on wheels, including construction, garbage, and delivery trucks (despite the baptism-by-fire driving lesson courtesy of his jailbird in-law, Harold was by now an accomplished truck driver—even going uphill). In January, 1945, when he finally celebrated his seventeenth birthday, in accordance with his wishes, though doubtlessly with a heavy heart, his mother signed off on his enlistment papers. The path was clear for Harold to join the U.S. Navy.

"Why the navy?" I ask.

He's not entirely sure. "I couldn't swim worth a damn," he admits. Harold speculates, "Maybe because so many guys I knew were going into the navy."

I wonder whether the rage he'd felt at the outbreak of the war had anything to do with it. "By choosing the navy you must have realized there was a high probability you would end up fighting the Japanese. Was your decision, even in part, fueled by a specific hatred?"

Harold is not entirely comfortable with this word—in fact, he abruptly softens on the primacy of revenge as his motivation for military service. "By the time I joined up I don't know that I *hated* the Japanese…" He thinks for a moment, then rephrases, "I had a strong dislike." Although this seems the definition of hate to me, in Harold's mind, particularly in light of subsequent events, the two are very different. "Right after Pearl Harbor," he explains, "there was a period of time when I think everybody despised the Japanese, myself included. But I didn't understand the complexities of war. I didn't realize there were good Japanese and bad Japanese…not yet."

There may be another influence at work here. "Hate was a word my mother never used," Harold tells me, "but I had anger, that's for sure. The Japanese had hit us when we weren't looking—it was like punching someone from behind. The way I saw it, the war was about fighting a bully, and I never shied from that. I just didn't have the brains to realize how tough this bully was!"

First stop: Chippewa Falls, Wisconsin, where Harold swore his oath and was formally inducted. (In fact, he had first attempted to sign up at Fort Snelling in Minnesota, where a military psychiatrist rejected his application due to Harold's predisposition for—of all things—fighting. Undeterred, he simply reapplied in the next state over.) Then it was off to basic training at Great Lakes Naval Base in Illinois. There, he had his first run-in with military discipline and was made to run seemingly endless laps around the facility's expansive training field. His infraction—fighting.

"We had to stand inspection every morning," Harold explains, "and having a neatly made bunk was a big part of that. One morning, after I had made up my bunk nice and tight—sleek as can be—I went off to breakfast. While I was gone, one of the other recruits rumpled up my bed!"

"Was it an accident or did he mess with it on purpose?"

"Just out of meanness," Harold says, irritated. "I wanted to kill the guy…"

"Did you hit him?"

"Did I *hit* him?!" Harold does a double take. "He was on the ground and I was pounding the daylights out of him! But in a situation like that you don't have time to get in more than a few licks because there are so many people around, including a few tattletales who'll run to get the chief petty officer, and that's what happened. As punishment, they made me do a hundred laps around the grinder holding a rifle over my head. But," he gives me a satisfied smirk, "so did the other guy."

Normally, boot camp lasted six weeks, but after less than a month Harold was abruptly assigned to an outgoing unit and shipped off to Camp Endicott Naval Construction Training Center in Davisville, Rhode Island. Probably because of his truck driving experience, he had been selected for one of the navy's celebrated Construction Battalions, C-B for short (traditionally spelled out as "Seabee"). This meant Harold's itch for duty in a hot zone would likely be satisfied; after the Marines, Seabees were often next ashore. In the South Pacific, the construction battalions were tasked with quickly building airstrips, bridges, and other supporting infrastructure, often while the battle to secure an island was still raging around them. Their mission called for them to defend themselves and whatever they were building, and this required Seabees to be as adept at combat as they were at engineering. That's what Camp Endicott was all about.

"Davisville was primarily an assault training area," Harold tells me. "All the preparations we got there were headed up by Marines, battle-hardened veterans who'd already served in the Pacific, and those trainers didn't take pity on us! In fact, they tried to drown me—twice!"

I settle in.

"One of the training exercises was a mock landing on the beach," he enthuses, "where they had the ground all doctored up with fake explosives. The landing craft we were using had a wooden hull and they didn't want to venture in too close to shore because a rock might knock the bottom out. When we got the order to storm the beach, we were still a long way out. Well," he mutters sheepishly, "I was a sailor who couldn't swim. So I asked one of the Marines, 'How deep is the water out here anyway?' He drew a line across his chest, 'About up to here. Now *go!*'

"*Christ!*" Harold sputters, "I stepped off that ramp and it was about two feet over my head! The last thing I heard before I went under was him barking at me, '*And don't get that weapon wet!*' I'm gurgling toward shore, trying to hold my rifle over my head with both hands…"

"But you made it!"

"Barely. And once I'd dragged myself onto the beach, they'd laid a trap for me there too! The instructors told us, 'When we blow the whistle, you drop to the ground. It doesn't matter where you are, you hit the deck!' I came running up out of the surf, explosions going off all around me, charging up that sand when suddenly I heard the damn whistle and I went flat—right into a hole full of mud! I'm sure the Marine with the whistle planned it that way," he grumbles, "because he timed it just right! And when I started to pick my head up, he put his foot on my helmet and sank my face right into that muddy puddle. 'Keep your head down!' he growled."

"It does sound like they tried to drown you twice," I agree.

"They sure did," he nods, "but I count all that as one! Another morning they had us put on our navy whites, and they marched us over to this huge Quonset building with a square structure on top.

I thought, *I wonder what the hell this is?* We walked into the building and it's a swimming pool! Huge!" Just contemplating what was in store for him (or perhaps ahead of the game) Harold's heart sank. "But swimming was only the half of it," he exclaims. "On one end of the building there was a high platform with a big cargo net hanging down into the pool. At the other end I saw steps that went right to the ceiling and beyond, up into that square tower on top. The Marine instructors told us, 'You men are going up those steps and when you get to the platform on top you'll walk out to the edge and you'll stop there. When you feel a tap on the shoulder, you will step off.'"

"How far down was it?"

"At least sixty feet!" he estimates. "But the truly artful part was that when we hit the water they expected us to strip off the blouse—remember, we were in whites, which are tight-fitting to begin with—and then knot the sleeves to trap air and make a floatation device! With a shirt!" he stresses. "If you managed to live through all that, you had to swim the length of this Olympic-sized pool and climb the giant net hanging on the other side. They told us, 'When you get to that platform at the top of the net, you will have accomplished your day.'"

None of this was optional, Harold reminds me, and no lifeguards were on duty. "You either did it or drowned," he says. "So up the stairs I go, all the way into that tower on top of the building, where I cautiously stepped out onto the platform, got right up to the edge and glanced down—that water looked like it was about a mile and a half away! I was about to step back to see if it was too late to switch to the army," Harold laughs, "when the instructor *tapped* my shoulder," he says, miming a sturdy shove, "and over I went! I swear, on the way down, I inhaled all the oxygen in that building!" Harold fills his lungs with a gasp so huge his eyeballs practically press the lenses of his glasses. "When I punched that water…" his hand missiles downward as his chest deflates, "I went straight to the bottom! And I'll tell you what, I think I drank half the damn pool trying to get my white jumper over my head and tying up the sleeves. That's a pretty hard thing to do! Then came the swim, and again…" he pokes his chest with a thumb, "not a strong swimmer—I must have used fifteen different strokes trying to reach that net! I was out of wind and full of water, but I finally made it over there. And then it was a damn job climbing up that! But I did it, and I was never so happy to get out of a building in my life."

It occurs to me that there was a method to all this madness. "I suppose it was training to simulate jumping off a sinking ship," I speculate, "in case your boat got torpedoed and you needed to swim to the next one over?"

Harold points a finger at me and nods firmly. "That's exactly what it was for. Yeah, Davisville, Rhode Island," he reflects, "that place was a challenge, but it was probably some of the best training I ever had. Those Marines had no mercy on us, but they were just doing their jobs. They'd been through hell in the war and that's where we were headed. They knew they wouldn't be doing us any favors by going easy on us. The fitness training was also good," he muses, "hours of it, in and out of the gymnasium. I enjoyed that... I never turned down a chance to get tougher," he explains. "I even tried boxing there!"

"Hold on," I remark, "you were a fighter from way back!"

"A street fighter, yes. But I'd never boxed before. When they asked for volunteers, I thought, well, why not? They told us to pick a partner, and there was a taller guy, standing quietly in back. I went over to him and asked, 'Have you ever boxed before?' He said, 'No, I never have.'" Harold rolls his eyes. "Well, he had! Once we got going he was picking me off left and right, dancing around just like a practiced gentleman fighter, popping me pretty good." His eyes narrow, "When I realized he'd lied to me, the brawler in me came out! I closed in on him, threw a punch and came right around with my elbow and nearly took his jaw off the front of his head! The instructor shouted, 'Hold it right there! That'll be enough of that!' He pointed at me, 'You're out!' But I figured the guy had tried to sucker me, so I didn't feel too badly about ringing his bell."

"Well," I calculate, "if that's the only trouble you got into in Rhode Island, with all the mud and water and barking Marines, I guess that's not too bad."

Harold nods agreement. "But only because I didn't get caught."
Of course.

"I did go over the fence on an 'unofficial' liberty," he acknowl-edges, "with a friend of mine who knew a girl in Providence. We used a ladder to get out, but we had to climb the fence when we got back because while we were gone somebody moved the damn ladder! It was a high fence, middle of the night, pouring rain; I was cursing at him and he was cursing me—it was a miracle we didn't get ar-rested by the MPs—or shot."

"What were you *thinking?*"

Harold blinks, "He had a date...with a girl!"

"But why did *you* go?" I laugh, "To drive?!"

"Hell, no. We took a bus."

"Well, what did you do while he was on his date?"

He stares at me as if I've asked the stupidest question on earth. "I watched! The last girl I'd gone out with had slapped me." He taps his temple, "Always learning..."

# Chapter 7
# TINIAN

テニアン島

TALK ABOUT a slap in the face—Harold has cancer.

My heart sinks when he tells me this, but he is taking it in stride. At this point in his life, Harold is used to his body's varied protestations, breakdowns, and outright rebellions. The fact that some of his bladder cells have risen up in insurrection doesn't surprise him—hell, he tells me, he and his bladder have been at odds with one another for years. This latest diagnosis genuinely does not seem to concern him, other than the fact that it means he will be spending more time with doctors and in hospitals, people and places he has had his fair share of and then some—that thought fills him with a dread darker than any cancer.

Of course, this development is the catalyst for another lengthy discourse upon the fact that he is the sole remaining survivor of fifteen siblings—not to mention having outlived his wife and all his closest friends—and his perpetual bewilderment about why this is so. Then he settles upon the only reason that makes any sense to him.

"We've got a book to write," he says, determinedly.

Time to get cracking.

Today's shirt is red. A tartan red, naturally. Red like the rising sun at Harold's back as he journeyed westward as a seventeen-year-old naval recruit fresh out of assault training—west toward the Pacific and another rising sun, the one emblazoning the banner of the enemy.

"Let's talk about being in the military," I suggest.

"That'll be a long and ugly conversation," he grumps.

I press on, stressing that up till this time he had operated pretty independently, more or less at odds with being told what to do by anybody. But in the navy he was expected to follow orders 'round the clock. Was that a tough adjustment for him?

"Not really," Harold says. "I was assigned to the Seabees. I was part of a group now. That's all I ever wanted; make me a part of a unit that did this or that, and I would do my best."

Even so, I insist, he was no stranger to bucking authority. In that sense, the navy must have been his worst nightmare. "What kept you from squaring off the first time a sergeant barked at you to take a lap? I mean, you'd given your mother such a hard time…"

As I've been prattling on, Harold has gradually leaned closer to me until we lock eyes.

"I was proud!" he says quietly, and then he spells it out for me with a laundry list that is quite literally that. "When I joined the navy, I was given two dress uniforms: white and blue. I had dungarees. Five sets of underwear and socks. *Three* pairs of shoes! Can you imagine? Me, a kid who came from nothing, suddenly having all these things?" He eases into his chair again and shakes his head in wonder. "I'd never had more than one pair of shoes at a time in my whole damn life! And these were nice clothes, crisp and clean. When I put on that uniform, I looked good! Pride," he reiterates. "I felt it, maybe for the first time ever." He shakes his head definitively, "I wasn't going to risk losing that."

Of course, the military did have its ups and downs. One unfortunate drawback that held true throughout his entire career was exemplified during the train ride from Rhode Island to Harold's port of embarkation in California. For the long trip across the country, each sailor was assigned a sleeping berth and served daily meals in a mess car. When I suggest that it must have felt a relative luxury to be traveling west by train and, for once, not riding in a boxcar, he muses, "I dunno, being a hobo beat the navy in some respects."

"How's that?"

"The food was better."

Almost as soon as he arrived at Camp Parks near Oakland, California, Harold got a lesson in the foibles inherent in military bureaucracy. "This was the staging area," he tells me, "where thousands of men from all over were streaming in, and the navy organized us into smaller groups for shipping out. The trouble was the way they arranged us..." he rolls his eyes. "It was alphabetical!"

When I look at him questioningly, Harold explains why this was a problem: "We had twenty-six guys in our group named Stevens! Whenever they'd have us fall in to call the roll, they'd shout, *Stevens!* And we'd all just look at each other until someone yelled back, *Which one?!*"

Aboard the troopship, Harold stood apart from the other Stevens by not getting seasick. "I had enough brains to spend most of my time outside, breathing that good fresh air, rather than down in the hold where guys were constantly getting sick!" When he did venture below deck, he certainly was not suffering. Harold had pulled duty organizing the ship's stores, and took the opportunity to clandestinely feast on canned peaches and other delicacies that ordinarily would be few and far between.

After a week at sea, the ship docked at Pearl Harbor, where he saw firsthand the devastation wrought during the Japanese attack three and a half years prior. "They had cleaned up a lot of it by then," he tells me, "but there were still wrecked ships sticking out of the water—the *Arizona* and a few of the others."

While in Hawaii, he was witness to another display of ugly aggression, and for once, Harold had the good sense to stay out of a fight. "We were housed in barracks," he recounts, "a long building with double-decker bunks. I had an upper bunk, and I was just sitting there one evening when a riot broke out!"

Harold is not exaggerating. This was not just a few guys blowing off steam; it was an ugly, no holds barred, free-for-all. "They were out to kill one another!" he stresses. "Everybody was getting smacked around pretty good until the military police arrived!"

I ask him what set it off.

"It was a racial deal. This was during the time when they were integrating the navy. Up till then, blacks could only serve as cooks or stewards, but now they were being put in as equal sailors, and that didn't sit well with some of the other recruits. That's what had happened; a race riot had broken out in the dormitory! I didn't want any part of that," his eyes widen, "and then the Shore Patrol showed up with automatic weapons—Tommy guns!" Harold gulps, "That was my introduction to armed combat!"

"How did you manage to stay out of the fray while all this was going on?"

He points downward, "I was underneath that bottom bunk!"

After surviving what must have felt like the second battle of Pearl Harbor, Harold bid farewell to the Stevens brigade as the men were dispatched to their assigned units. He was attached to the 38th Seabee Battalion, currently at work carving out a grid of airstrips on Tinian Island in the Marianas. Everything about this assignment was a mystery to Harold. "I didn't know the first thing about building a runway, and I didn't know what or where Tinian was until I got there."

In fact, Tinian was a dot of land with tremendous strategic importance. In the final year of the war, as Allied forces in the Pacific pushed farther and farther west, cities on the main Japanese islands had become principal objectives for long-range bombing. Comprising thirty-nine square miles of relatively flat terrain and located 1,500 miles from Japan (just within the range of B-29 Superfortress bombers), Tinian was an ideal location to base aircraft for sorties over Tokyo and other targets in the enemy's homeland. The hard-fought battle to wrest Tinian from Japanese control had taken place during the previous summer. By the time Harold arrived—with the exception of a few, elusive, holdout fighters—the island was secure and airfield construction was in full swing. Despite misgivings about his lack of construction experience, Harold was delighted to find he was able to make a valuable contribution to the work detail.

"They made me a dump truck driver," he says brightly, "which was something I actually knew how to do! When I got to Tinian, they had the four huge runways on the North Field pretty much complete, but there was still a lot of finishing work to be done, attaching aprons and pads for the bombers. The Seabees were dynamiting the island's coral outcrops, crushing it, and mixing the aggregate into asphalt. My job was hauling crushed coral to the work sites."

"I'll bet it was a relief to know the enemy wasn't going to be taking shots at you while you were doing it!" I remark.

Harold nods, "The Marines had the island pretty well mopped up." He adds, "Oh, there were still a few snipers hiding out in the sugarcane fields…and one night someone blew our dynamite dump. It shook the entire Marianas' chain when that went up!"

I wonder if he ever encountered any of the Japanese while he was there.

"Not directly," he tells me, his voice tensing, "but when I pulled guard duty at night, sometimes I'd hear a shot or two. I knew they were out there!"

Snipers and saboteurs aside, Harold seems to have enjoyed his time on Tinian. In particular, he liked working alongside the older Seabees, whom he greatly admired and respected. "Most of them were talented construction professionals: engineers, carpenters, plumbers—gentlemen in service. Great guys," he extols. "A dumb boot like me had no special skills. I was just there as a laborer, but they took me in, treated me well, and I learned a lot from them. They looked out for us younger guys. They warned us, don't do this and don't do that," he stabs a finger emphatically, "and stay away from the Pink Lady!"

"Wait…who?—there were women on Tinian?"

Harold snorts. "I wish! I hadn't seen a female since Hawaii when I'd had my picture taken with a hula girl!" No, he explains, the Pink Lady was moonshine—derived from colorful torpedo fuel that was 180 proof alcohol. To discourage any temptation to imbibe, the navy inventively blended it with diarrhea-inducing Croton oil and a distinctive rose-colored dye. But as Harold soon discovered, sailors applied equal determination and ingenuity to removing the toxins. "Some of the mechanics had gotten their hands on a drum of this stuff," he tells me, "and they'd cobbled together a still to filter out the poison and peddle it as booze they called the Pink Lady."

"Did you ever try it?"

"Only once," he stresses, followed by a mock fit of choking. "My throat was so burnt up from that torpedo juice," he gasps hoarsely, "I couldn't talk for days!"

Throughout Harold's time on Tinian, long-range bombers departing on missions to the Philippines, Okinawa, and Japan were commonplace—and so were crashes. The ponderous weight of the fully fueled, ordnance-laden Superfortresses shook the ground as they rumbled down airstrips nearly two miles long, struggling to get airborne. The ends of the runways were littered with the wreckage of planes that had not quite made the leap.

Then, in early August, Harold noticed some unusual activity. Two B-29s were sequestered at one end of the field, surrounded day and night by a detail of Marine guards. No one was allowed to approach the security perimeter without special clearance. The bombers were parked over concrete pits designed for loading some kind of special payload. Harold couldn't get near enough to discern any markings, but if he had, he would have seen enigmatic words painted on the fuselage of one plane that were, in fact, the name of the pilot's mother—*Enola Gay*. Today, that fuselage is hangared in the collection of the Smithsonian's National Air and Space Museum in Washington, D.C., along with the *Wright Flyer* and Lindbergh's *Spirit of St. Louis*, for having made one of the most significant— and notorious—flights in history. On August 6, 1945, *Enola Gay* dropped an atomic bomb on the Japanese city of Hiroshima. Harold was there when the plane departed Tinian on that fateful mission.

"It took off at night," he says.

"Did you see it leave?"

"No, but I heard it roaring as it warmed up to go. Hell, I wasn't going to run out in the middle of the night just to watch an airplane take off. I could see that all day long! But in the morning, it was gone."

"Were there any rumors," I ask him, "about what that plane was carrying or where it was going?"

He shakes his head. "We didn't know anything about it."

"Had you or anyone else in your group ever heard of an atomic bomb or some secret weapon that was being developed?"

"Only what was in the newspapers," Harold replies. "We didn't know any more or less than the average guy on the street. Oh, there was speculation about secret experiments and rumors the government had tested some sort of new weapon in Nevada, but we didn't know any specifics—except, supposedly, it made one hell of a bang!" Harold narrows his gaze, considering, "We knew there was something different about those two planes on Tinian because they were both so heavily guarded, but we had no idea what it was."

"So, when that first plane left," I venture, "never in your wildest dreams were you thinking that the war could be over in just three or four days..."

"No," he replies firmly. "In fact, our battalion was preparing for the invasion of Japan. Before the atomic bombings, we were busy loading all of our equipment onto landing crafts—LSTs. My LST was one of countless ships in the Mariana Islands staging for the invasion. I was on that boat, at Tinian, when the atom bombs dropped. We didn't know it at the time, but there was a good chance the Japanese would surrender, and we would be occupying Japan instead of invading. All we knew was that we had to be ready to go when the order came to move out."

"When did you hear about Hiroshima?"

"It was strange," he reflects, "because after the first plane left, we didn't hear anything right away. A day or so later we heard the news about an atom bomb. Then the second plane took off and we heard Nagasaki was bombed. We could put two and two together."

Unbeknownst to Harold, just being there when that second B-29 departed may have been the most dangerous moment of the war for him and the other sailors on Tinian. The plane was indeed carrying another atom bomb, a roly-poly wrecking ball with fins, aptly nicknamed "Fat Man." It was a completely different configuration from the elongated, enriched-uranium "Little Boy" weapon dropped by *Enola Gay*. The Fat Man bomb was a plutonium device packing even more of a wallop, but the designers also worried it might accidentally detonate if exposed to fire. On the previous day, they had watched in horror as four B-29s—fueled to the wingtips—had crashed in succession on Tinian's runways. Among the scientists, there was a huge sigh of relief when the plane lugging the five-and-a-half-ton Fat Man finally cleared the trees.

"When the second plane took off," I ask Harold, "where was your LST anchored?"

"Practically underneath it."

In other words, ground zero.

"Later," he continues, "after the second bomb dropped and the Japanese gave up, we weighed anchor. The mission was occupation, not invasion. We were on our way!"

# Chapter 8
# YOKOSUKA
# 横須賀

WE'RE GETTING CLOSER, nearer to the heart of things. Closer to *her*. I know this because the emotions Harold displayed during our first meeting—long reflective pauses and sudden upwellings of grief—are beginning to reassert themselves. Up till now it has been relatively easy for him to talk dispassionately, even humorously, about the early part of his life. His wife had no role in his growing up. While he was slugging it out at school and tramping the West, she was a world away, a literal prisoner of her own upbringing. But now the two paths are converging. At this point in his narrative, it is getting harder for Harold to reflect upon his trajectory without being continually reminded of her, and these thoughts can give rise to halting and deeply emotive moments of nostalgia.

"As I sailed toward Japan," he tells me, "I knew very little about that country…" Harold pauses, searching for the proper thread that will unravel the fabric of the Japanese mind-set. After a few moments of expressionless concentration, he frees a stitch. "But if you can wipe the war from your mind, including the warmongers who convinced the people they would be disrespecting their Emperor by not fighting, then I think what they've achieved as a culture is amazing. My wife, she was very proud of her country…"

And just like that, Harold falls to pieces.

"Tell me about the boat ride," I ask cheerily, hoping this might help him regain his composure by focusing on something new. It works, as his attention is now drawn to the prize idiot who has described crossing fifteen hundred miles of open ocean in a landing craft as a "boat ride."

"You've obviously never been on an LST," he sniffs, frowning.

The initials are a scrambled abbreviation for "Tank Landing Ship," but a World War II-era LST wasn't so much a ship as a self-propelled barge with a nose that opened like a set of French doors extending well below the waterline. To Harold's mind, this was not a confidence-inspiring design for a boat. Furthermore, LSTs were used to haul much more than tanks. In this case, the Seabees had packed it with trucks, bulldozers, cranes, and other construction paraphernalia. There was ample room to store equipment, but other than berths for the ship's small crew, there were no accommodations for people.

"The LST was basically an empty hull," Harold informs me. "It didn't have troop quarters. You picked out a corner where you weren't likely to get run over by a shifting truck, and that's where you slept. The lucky ones were those quick enough to stake a claim *in* the trucks."

"How long were you at sea?"

"More than a week," he says, and then it is Harold who is guilty of understatement: "We were delayed by the weather."

The "weather" was Typhoon Jean, a nasty whirl of low pressure that raked the Philippine Sea with sustained winds of one hundred miles per hour. In fact, in the months surrounding the end of the Second World War, the Pacific was that ocean in name only. Extreme weather events were so destructive that the War Department had little choice but to consider them a threat on par with the enemy. Indeed, in June, a typhoon east of Okinawa had pounded the Third Fleet, damaging dozens of ships and destroying scores of airplanes. In October, a category-3 storm in the same region would wash hundreds of ships and boats ashore, sink another dozen, and kill or injure nearly two hundred American servicemen. Like those storms, Typhoon Jean also spawned tornadic winds and mountainous waves capable of flipping a destroyer, but it thankfully tracked due west of

U.S. bases in the Marianas. For Harold and the other Seabees riding its tail in the hollow shell of an LST, there was no escape.

"We were only a few days out of Tinian when the storm hit us, and I can tell you this," Harold says solemnly. "If I had my choice of ships to be on in a typhoon, the last one I would ever pick would be a *goddamn* LST!" He nods gravely, "I really thought I was going to drown! That thing was rolling and dipping, the waves would slam those clamshell doors up front and—" he smacks his hands in a concussive clap, "*Bang!!* I thought they were coming right off! With all the water washing over the top, and especially when we would begin to roll, I figured we were going down for sure!"

I wonder about the ship's cargo, finding it hard to imagine trucks and other vehicles remaining in place throughout the boat's frenzied pitching and keeling.

He nods, "Thankfully, none of it got loose. If we saw something start to go, we scrambled like hell to strap it down again!"

"Was this during the day or night?"

"Day *and* night! We were getting slammed for about twenty-four hours. I really thought I was a goner!" So much so, that during the darkest hours of raging wind and violent ocean, Harold made a life decision. "I was a sailor who couldn't swim," he confesses solemnly, "and so I vowed to myself that if I somehow managed to live through this, I would not stay in this navy!"

Harold's first view of Japan was in some ways strikingly reminiscent of what he had seen at Pearl Harbor—a sprawling naval base scarred by the ravages of war. His unit, the 38th Construction Battalion, had been assigned to Yokosuka, one of the principal shipyards of the Japanese Imperial Navy, located at the mouth of Tokyo Bay. The previous July, planes from the carrier *Yorktown* had attacked Yokosuka's vast boatyard and military arsenal. As Harold's LST entered the harbor, he sailed past the shattered hulks of ships sunk in the raid.

"You can see a big hole in the side of one," he says, pointing to a photograph of a capsized hull, like a bathtub toy turning turtle. It's part of a photo album, culled from his encyclopedic collection, splayed open across his lap. Harold is a biographer's dream, having obsessively documented and captioned seemingly every important moment throughout his life. This particular album is chock-full of images from his early days in Japan, including wrecked ships in the neck of Tokyo Bay.

"That was where we landed," he tells me, "in Yokosuka, a huge navy yard where the Japanese had been producing one- and two-man submarines and battleship gun tubes. The Allies had already set up a headquarters there, and then we arrived with the main wave of the occupation."

As they had throughout the war, the Seabees waded ashore in the company of Marines, but this time they met no resistance. According to Harold, the only rumbles of protest that occurred during the handover of this former Japanese stronghold came from deep inside the island itself.

"My first night in Japan was very memorable," he tells me, "I was sleeping in an upper wooden bunk when, suddenly, everything started moving! I didn't know what was going on—stuff was falling off the walls and things people had set at the heads of their beds went crashing!" What Harold experienced is a relatively common occurrence in that seismically active archipelago—a mild earthquake. But to a kid solidly grounded in the Midwest, for whom one of the few solid things in life had been the Midwest ground, the temblor felt as though the earth itself was running riot. Like the barracks melee he had witnessed in Pearl Harbor, it promptly sent Harold scurrying to his safe place. "In no time at all I was on the floor, under that bunk!"

One of the first priorities of the occupation was to transform Yokosuka into a working hub for American and Allied naval operations. That meant quickly getting the base repaired, adapted, and up and running at full capacity. The Seabee battalions were tasked with public works, including small construction, the maintenance of buildings and other structures, and the operation of utilities. Specifically, Harold can sum up his unit's responsibilities with just five words: "We maintained a coal pile."

To me, this sounds about as thrilling as a lump of the stuff, but he informs me that it was actually a plum assignment. That's because, for stocking the coal, Harold lived out every boy's idea of heaven. He got to play with trains.

"One of the basic things we did was operate this little railroad inside the base…" He points to a photograph of a pair of smallish, stout-looking steam locomotives. "The primary purpose of these trains was to pick up gondola cars loaded with coal from the main station, move them into the base through the gate, then down to an area near the pier that was reserved for unloading." His finger slides across the page to a picture of Japanese workers armed with shovels. "Day laborers would knock down the sides of the railcars to get as much coal out as possible and then shovel out the rest. We also had a little dozer down there to push the coal around so they wouldn't have to do as much by hand."

Although Harold would eventually learn to operate the locomotives, his initial duty assignment was not as enviable. "My job, when I first got there, was standing guard on the labor crew working the coal pile."

I ask him if these men were prisoners.

Harold shakes his head. "They weren't being forced to work," he explains. "These were Japanese men hired to do manual labor; they were paid to do it."

I wonder why they needed to be guarded.

"Security. This was a military base," he reminds me, "and up until a few weeks prior, these people had been the enemy. But the fact is," he insists, "they weren't looking to cause problems, and I never had trouble with any of them. They just wanted to work. Hell, some of them even became my friends."

He shows me another photo. It is of him, a grinning seventeen-year-old, standing next to a diminutive Japanese. "See this little guy here? His name was Imai. I swear he couldn't have been more than fifteen or sixteen years old, but he was part of the work gang."

In the picture, the runt of the Stevens' litter towers over the boy. "How tall were you?" I ask.

"Oh, five foot seven, give or take."

"He can't even be five feet tall!"

"That's what I'm saying! He looked like a little kid. But he was one of the laborers on this pile, and if he wanted to be there, I didn't question his age. We got along fine. In fact, he used to throw me down that coal pile!"

Harold doesn't even give me a chance to ask the question.

"There was a Japanese school nearby where I had seen children assembling outdoors in the morning for calisthenics, and one of the things they were doing was throwing each other—you know, judo." He grins, "I didn't know anything about that, but it looked to me like something that might come in damn handy! So I asked Imai to teach me a couple of hip throws. He was reluctant at first—probably thinking I was an American guard, and if he started tossing me around someone might pick up a rifle and shoot him! But I kept pestering him, and he finally agreed. Well, by the time he got through with me," Harold laughs, whisking at his arms and chest, "I was as black as the coal! But I kept saying, '*Do it again! Do it again!*'" He leans in earnestly. "I was bound and determined to learn that damn judo."

This surprises me, partly because I cannot imagine the little boy in the picture tossing more than a salad, but mostly because a defensive and disciplined form of martial arts doesn't seem like Harold's style. It turns out he was looking to supplement, not supplant, his street fighting skills.

"I figured if I knew enough to get a guy off his feet, then I could kick him into oblivion—something I was already an expert at doing! So this kid taught me two or three different approaches, and boy..." Harold chuckles, "he wiped that coal pile clean with me! But, like I said, we got along fine. He even asked me to take his sister to a movie—and I did! How's that for fraternizing with the enemy?!"

He is being facetious, of course, but Harold has opened the door to something I have often wondered about the American occupation of Japan. After four and a half years of fighting one another, tooth and nail, across the Pacific—from the treachery at Pearl Harbor to the radiated rubble of the atomic bombings—there were simmering resentments aplenty, on both sides. So, when American military forces and the Japanese people suddenly found themselves living side by side, what kept these feelings from flaring into brutal subjugation or angry defiance?

"There was some of that…" Harold says, and after a pensive silence he softly repeats, "there was some of that. But I'll tell you something you may find hard to believe. The men who fight the wars usually aren't the ones filled with hatred once it's over. The soldiers are the ones who say, 'Enough is enough. Enough fighting, enough killing, enough hate.' They understand that the enemy soldiers—mind you, not their politicians or leaders—are just people like themselves who fought for their country and did what they were told to do."

"Is that how you felt about the Japanese?"

Harold thinks long and hard. "I watched their soldiers coming back," he says, at last. "As they were being repatriated from the various islands in the Pacific, they would arrive at the train station in Yokosuka—a hundred, maybe two hundred at a time. And they would stand around there in large groups, waiting for other transportation to the four winds." He thumbs through his book until he locates a photo (of course) depicting just this: a crowd of men milling about the railway station. "I never tried to mix with them," he explains, "but if I happened to be passing by while they were there, I would acknowledge them, and often they would greet me in return. But I'll admit," he says soberly, "I would have felt uncomfortable walking among that group—worried about what might happen to me. That fear was there."

It is important to Harold that I understand he was never outwardly threatened. Rather, his unease was an empathetic reaction to the plight of these weary, beaten men. "It must have been hell to be one of those defeated soldiers," he muses grimly. "They went away very proud people, and came back humbled. I can't imagine…" He reflects, "Well, maybe I *can* imagine, because I certainly wondered how I might feel in their situation, and what I might be tempted to do to a lone American who wandered into the group. I thought about that a lot. Those men, their families, their entire country suffered greatly in the war, and in the end, all they achieved was epic loss and humiliation. They'd been willing to die for their Emperor. He was a god—when he passed through the streets, people couldn't even look at him! And now, even he had to bow to us, the Americans." Harold shakes his head stoically.

"What thoughts and feelings run through another person's mind? I can only guess." He taps the photo of the crowded platforms, "But when I saw those groups of soldiers heading back to their homes, I never felt hatred. I had sympathy."

In Yokosuka, as on Tinian, Harold enjoyed the camaraderie of the senior Seabees in his unit, particularly when they invited him to live with them in the rail yard where they were billeted in relative luxury aboard a converted train carriage. Despite his bunk's utility as a makeshift earthquake shelter, Harold jumped at the opportunity to trade the wooden pallet for something akin to how he had bedded down during his hobo days. Once again, he was sleeping on rails, although this was definitely a step up.

"There were thirteen of the older guys living down there when I moved in," he tells me. "They were in a coach they had turned into living space with running water and burners for heating and cooking. They'd made it into pretty nice quarters," he enthuses.

Soon after he moved out of the barracks, two things occurred that would redefine the course of Harold's tenure in Japan, and in fact, his entire life. First, one by one, the old-timers living with him accrued enough service points to be discharged and were rotated back to the States. Thus, only a few months after arriving in Japan, Harold found himself virtually alone, running a railroad that connected the base's waterfront with the outside world, supervising a crew of grateful-to-be-employed, willing-to-turn-a-blind-eye workers, and bunking in solitary comfort far from prying eyes.

The second thing that changed Harold's life forever was making a new friend, one who would introduce him to a number of intriguing foreign experiences and opportunities.

First up, the black market.

# Chapter 9
# RACKETEER

# 密輸業者

I T WAS A well-oiled operation. Each newly arrived vessel was
brimming with sailors eager to peddle a variety of in demand
commodities hoarded from the ship's Exchange—whiskey, cigarettes,
sugar—at exorbitant profits. As the men came ashore, however,
Marine guards at the landing meticulously searched their boats for
these contraband items. But rather than arrest any would-be smug-
glers or seize their merchandise, the guards waved them (with greased
palms) down the pier, toward a place where transactions could be
made—albeit for wholesale prices. With no other choice, the sailors
grumbled off along the waterfront in search of a name. It was the
only other information the Marines would give them: "Ask for a guy
named Stevens."

"You were a bit of a gangster!"
I'm registering my astonishment at the scale of Harold's rack-
eteering operation during his navy stint in Japan. He laughs and
waves a hand dismissively, but there's no denying his scheme was
built upon the same illicit opportunities that gave rise to the boot-
legging empire of Al Capone: when sought-after goods are deemed
illegal or highly regulated, demand soars, and a lucrative black market develops. The only question is who will emerge as the criminal

mastermind to exploit the situation. In postwar Yokosuka, he was a seventeen-year-old kid from Duluth.

"I didn't know anything about smuggling before I landed in Japan," Harold insists. "But I saw things, and I got educated."

"Such as…?"

"Well, seeing what Barney was doing with his little car was the beginning." Harold's face softens. "I'll tell you a simple truth. It was Barney who opened my eyes to a lot of things." His tone conveys such affection that I can only assume he's talking about a good friend, in all likelihood another navy man. I'm right, except for one unexpected detail. Barney had fought for the other side.

"Michio Barney Nozaki." Harold shows me a picture of an Asian man in his early to mid-twenties, whose face conveys an intelligence and maturity beyond his years. In the photo, he is dressed in a crisp shirt and slacks because, by the time Harold met him, Barney's days in uniform were behind him. "He was ex-navy," Harold says, emphasizing, "the *Japanese* navy!"

"And his name was Barney?"

"I thought for years it was a nickname," Harold squints, "but that was his real name."

I'm thinking there is a lot more to Barney than meets the eye. Of course, Harold is already out in front of me. "When I was first introduced to Barney, he amazed me by speaking perfect English. I was naturally quite curious about that, but I didn't want to pester him with too many questions—hell, his country had just lost the war! Barney had been a naval officer at Yokosuka. Now he was working as an interpreter and overseeing the labor crews I was using to operate the locomotives and unload coal. It was his job to hire, fire, and keep time on these workers. It was my job to make sure he did it right."

I ask if that means he was Barney's supervisor.

Harold informs me that, although this was technically true, it was a collaborative partnership. "Barney and I worked together; in fact, our desks faced one another in the roundhouse. Each day that I took the crews out to the coal piles I had a conversation with him, and I always let him know that when it came to the laborers, it was his show to run. Over time, we befriended each other, and eventually

I felt I knew him well enough to ask him where he'd learned English. Barney told me he'd been born in Chicago! He was from a wealthy, educated Japanese family living in the United States. His father and his uncle were both graduates of the University of Iowa."

"So how did he come to fight on the side of Japan?"

"The family had significant business concerns there, and when Barney was still a child, they had to go back to survey and rebuild their properties after a big earthquake. By the time they were ready to return to the States, the Japanese government had been taken over by the military, and their permission to leave was denied. So Barney got an engineering degree at Keio University in Tokyo—a really top-notch school—and was drafted into the navy. He'd been stationed at Yokosuka, as a lieutenant in charge of building these little submarines."

I shake my head. "Where he ended up employed as an office accountant working under a seventeen-year-old American…"

Harold fixes me sternly, "Well, I'd turned eighteen in January! You know," he notes pensively, "working for me never seemed to bother Barney."

"And the two of you became close friends?"

"We did. The more I got to know Barney, the better I liked him."

I can't help but note the differences dividing these men, not least of which is the ocean (both literal and figuratively) between their formative underpinnings. Everything about Barney's privileged upbringing was a far cry from Harold's rough-hewn childhood. I feel I must ask, "What was it that Barney saw in you? What was the connection between the two of you that led to this important friendship?"

Harold considers. "I think it was respect for one another. I was good to Barney. I let him do his job. And he never treated me like a stupid kid. We both knew I didn't have the book knowledge he had. When we talked, we talked at my level, but he never made me look bad. In fact, Barney made me look good. And he was determined to teach me things about his country and his culture."

"Including introducing you to the black market?"

Harold's brow furrows, as if underlining again and again a point he wants to make perfectly clear: "I never involved Barney in any of my black market activities! He was strictly small time. However," Harold admits, "he did set things in motion…"

Harold's friend may have tossed him the ball, but there is no way Barney or anybody else could have anticipated how far Harold would run with it—over the goal line, out the stadium, through the streets, and beyond the city limits. Harold describes the handoff:

"Barney had this little car that was so small it didn't have a trunk, so he'd mounted a wooden box on the back—it was about the size of a small suitcase. One day I saw him monkeying with that box, and I walked over to see what he was up to. I was amazed when he showed me that the box had a false bottom! It was for smuggling cigarettes—Barney would occasionally buy a carton or two from arriving sailors, and then he used this box to smuggle them off the base!"

"He trusted you enough to show you that?"

"By that time, we were good friends. He knew I could also get cartons of cigarettes from the base Exchange, that's like a retail store for military people, and he offered to transport a few out the gates for me in this false bottom. That was the key; once they were off the base, I could sell them for good money—people couldn't get enough of them! But the Marines controlled the gate, and they had strict orders not to let these things pass. Barney used the hidden compartment in his car to get stuff out. It was something he would do every now and then—but not often. He didn't really need the money, and he was smart enough to know that the more items you moved, the bigger the risk of getting caught."

"When you saw that little box Barney used for smuggling a few cigarettes, what did you think?"

Harold taps his temple, "I thought, *I have a railroad!*"

To his credit, Harold started out small, just a few cartons of cigarettes secreted away in Barney's car. As a budding entrepreneur, however (not to mention a lifelong opportunist), he soon upped his volume by buying cigarettes off other sailors and liquor from junior officers—which meant he had to seek out smuggling avenues with greater capacity than a wooden box. By loitering near the gates, watching as the Marine guards conducted their searches, Harold learned what *not* to do. For example, he quickly rejected military jeeps as too risky since they invited a shakedown, and the bare-bones design offered few nooks and crannies for stashing goods. "I could hide more in my pants than in one of those vehicles," he claims.

I laugh, but he is not kidding.

"It was true!" he insists. "The uniforms Seabees wore for going off base included combat boots with trousers that bloused over the tops. I could fit a lot of cigarettes inside those pants."

Eventually, however, he settled upon a less covert alternative that offered almost zero risk of being caught. He simply bribed the guards.

"Unlike regular navy sailors," Harold informs me, "the Seabees got along well with the Marines." This mutual goodwill, the legacy of storming beaches in support of one another, was the lubricant he used to slide past the Marine checkpoint. "At first, all I had to do was befriend them, and they would pretty much turn a blind eye. Later on, when I needed their direct involvement, I brought them beer from the local brewery."

I ask if he offered the guards money.

"Hell, no!" He frowns amusedly, "*I* wanted the money, and they were perfectly happy with that Japanese beer! In fact, for a few quart bottles, they would do pretty much anything I asked."

What Harold asked was that the Marines continue to do their job ferreting out and blocking illegal imports, but with one addendum—he wanted the guards to funnel any incoming contraband straight to him.

"When ships docked at Yokosuka," he explains, "the naval and merchant sailors would get into small boats and come to the fleet landing gate. Anyone who wanted to go into town had to go through that gate, and they'd all try to bring in stuff to sell in order to have a little Japanese money to spend. But the Marines would tell 'em, 'Nope! You can't bring any of that through here.' The sailors were stuck. They sure as hell didn't want to haul it back to their ships— that was just asking to be caught. So, we gave them another option. I had the guards detour them—" Harold pauses, then measures his words in a manner befitting a kingpin, "I had the guards *suggest* that if the sailors went down the slip a little further, at the roundhouse, there might be somebody there who could help them out."

"Were you geared up for that kind of volume?" I wonder.

He snorts. "By this time, I had graduated to using the trains! Every day after unloading coal and other supplies, my workers pushed the empty gondolas and boxcars back through a gate leading to the outside station. Guess what?" he chuckles. "I had the key to that gate, and those cars weren't empty! I also had a couple of guys on the outside waiting to receive the goods and sell them for me. I started out moving just a few cartons of cigarettes, but one thing led to another, and business just took off—especially when I saw all the things sailors would try to bring in off those ships!" Harold says with amazement, "They'd load fifty-pound bags of sugar into those boats! The guards told them, 'Sorry, you can't bring that in, but—'" He smiles, "They'd have no choice other than to come see me, and I'd make them an offer." He laughs merrily, "All I ever touched was money! I'd pay them a fair price—but a lot less than what I would sell it for. Then I'd call a couple of my Japanese workers and say, 'Put this in the railcar.' I always had a car waiting on the siding—hell, if anyone in charge had ever looked inside one of those, I'd probably still be in jail!"

Of course, this raises the question: Who was minding the store at the Yokosuka Naval Base? Surely there must have been a chain of command, superior officers to whom Harold was accountable. When he talks about his luck avoiding the attentions of "anyone in charge," to whom is he referring? And where were they while he was assembling and overseeing a smuggling operation worthy of a pirate king?

"My area was just one little part of a huge facility," Harold explains, "and it was a working rail yard. There was no reason for officers to come wandering down there."

"You must have had a supervisor…"

"I had someone who was in charge of me," he acknowledges. "A lieutenant in charge of public works."

"How often would he check on you?"

"Never."

"Really. Why not?"

"There was no reason! I had that yard and that coal pile running like a Swiss watch," he grins. "As far as that lieutenant or any of the higher-ups were concerned, I was doing a fine job."

"What about Barney and the other Japanese who were working with you on a daily basis? Surely they must have known what you were up to."

Again, Harold stresses, "I didn't involve Barney in *anything* crooked. Barney wasn't stupid; you can bet he knew what I was doing, but I made sure his hands were clean. And in terms of the workers, all I had to do was give them a little extra pay, or toss them a few packs of cigarettes, and they'd help me out any way they could. I thought nothing of jumping up in an engine with them when they were moving a trainload, to observe how they operated those small steam locomotives—I figured in case I ever had to get rid of a carload of something fast, I better know how to do that." Then he adds, with no pun intended, "I didn't want to be left hanging!"

Remarkably, Harold's lucrative, underground railroad—a black market conduit that was, in fact, an actual train—still had a lot of untapped moneymaking potential. Every car he moved netted him hundreds of dollars in yen, but he was dealing strictly in conventional goods and only filling a tiny portion of the available space in each railcar. Diversifying or upping his capacity could have pushed his profits into the thousands, but the simple truth is that the impetus for Harold's criminal enterprise wasn't greed. At his core, he has always been a man grounded in practicality, with ambitions that mirror basic market forces—supply and demand. When he needed a few extra dollars, he mustered the resources to get them. That is what his smuggling activity offered him, and that is what he took from it. Even as his earnings wildly outpaced his desires, he was not tempted to excess or moved to squirrel away a treasure trove. The fact is, Harold had no need for mountains of cash.

Those days were coming to an end.

# Chapter 10
# MARIKO
# 真理子

A GOLDEN YELLOW SHIRT.

It is the sunniest variant so far to emerge from Harold's signature collection of checkered flannel. As such, it's an apt choice for what promises to be an illuminating conversation. Today, Harold will be shining light on events that occurred over the course of a single remarkable evening. It began as an overture of friendship, progressed from an awkward misunderstanding to a banquet of sensory delight, and by the time it was over, his world had been flipped upside down. As we settle into our now familiar places—Harold in his well-worn recliner, me on the couch—it is nothing less than the turning point in the life of this man we will be mining today.

Gold indeed.

Six weeks after befriending Barney, Harold was invited out for a night on the town.

"Barney wanted me to experience the culture of Japan," Harold explains, "so he asked me whether I might like to accompany him for the evening." Barney promised Harold a meal, plus entertainment he would never forget, and he said he would cover all the costs. Even for a prospering racketeer, the generosity of the offer was too compelling to pass up.

Six decades after the fact, the launching of this expedition still works Harold into an excited state that has him speaking in brisk, buoyant sentences toward an exuberant crescendo: "Barney made all the arrangements. I didn't know where we were going. I didn't know *what* we were doing. He wouldn't say anything specific! It wasn't until we got there that he told me *we were visiting a geisha house!!*"

I ask him if he even knew what a geisha was.

"No, I didn't," he blinks. "Not really. I had no real knowledge of Japan or its traditions. But when Barney told me 'This is an *okiya*—a geisha house,' I had a notion...I had been to a place once before that someone, not Barney, had told me was a geisha house. That time, I opened the door to find half-a-dozen women—all naked!—who talked me into taking a bath!

Harold throws up his arms to signal anticipation of impending bliss. "I thought, *Oh glory! I'm in heaven!*" But his hands, like his hopes at the time that this outing with Barney would be another prurient experience, are soon brought back down to earth. "I learned very quickly how different a legitimate geisha house and real geishas are from all that."

"Were you thinking this night might include..." I'm searching for a polite euphemism, completely ignoring the fact that Harold was a sailor.

"Sex!" he enthuses. "I didn't know what was going to happen. But when I saw that classy building, I was pretty sure I wouldn't be taking another group bath!"

In fact, the geisha house in the Omori suburb of Tokyo was miles away and a world apart from the city's red-light district bathhouses and seamy dens of prostitution. "A grand, traditional, wooden building," is how Harold describes it. He elaborates, "If you wanted to take a photograph of a uniquely Japanese structure, that geisha house would have been a fine choice. It was decoratively painted and had all the classic Oriental trappings. But the purpose wasn't for tourist appeal," he explains. "This was an authentic Japanese building."

Harold continues, "We entered by crossing a little walkway over ornamental landscaping—like a dry stream feature. As Barney and I approached, the doors slid open, and we were ushered into an entryway. It was a sort of patio with an elevated platform, where we sat on cushions while we took off our shoes. That gave me a few tense moments," he admits, "as I did a once-over to make sure I didn't have holes in my socks! Thankfully, there were also slippers there for us to put on."

"Who was it that let you in?" I ask.

"A young girl opened the door—probably a maid. Behind her was the woman who owned the house. She was there to greet us. The girl made sure our shoes were placed neatly under the edge of the patio. I remember thinking, *I wonder if my shoes will be here when I come back?*"

A geisha house hosts singular and unexpected surprises, but one look at the proprietress should have been enough to convince Harold this was not a place where people steal shoes.

"The owner of the okiya was a very elegant lady," he tells me, "probably in her late forties or early fifties, dressed impeccably in a fine silk kimono. She didn't speak much English, so Barney introduced us to one another. I learned later that her name was Mrs. Fusa Suda, but I never called her that; I referred to her by her title, which was 'Mama-san.' That's how Barney introduced her, and that's how everybody addressed her, so I followed suit.

"From the entry, we stepped onto a walkway between two paneled walls. That honeyed wooden floor shone like polished glass," he marvels, telling me this was not uncommon in finer Japanese establishments. "To achieve it," Harold explains, "a cleaning woman gets down on her knees with a cloth under both hands, then raises her rump and walks the rags all the way down to one end of the hall and all the way back again a number of times each day. I've seen it being done," he remarks, "and it's grueling work, but you can't believe the depth of the finish. The passage in that geisha house was like a mirror." In fact, the whole building had a richly appointed and sophisticated air—which only added to Harold's growing sense of discomfort. Having grown up in desperate poverty, as he was led up the lavishly maintained, gleaming hallway, he thought anxiously, *I'm in over my head!*

"We followed that lacquered walkway," he continues, "into the interior of the house where Mama-san slid open a panel door to a room. Following Barney's lead, I took my slippers off—the flooring inside was tatami matting, and you don't walk on those straw mats wearing any kind of footwear, even slippers. The walls were colorful sliding panels—some kind of thin board with a paper finish that could be reconfigured to expand the room for hosting larger parties. The space was set up for us with a traditional low table, maybe four-feet square, and padded cushions on each side."

Harold was already feeling like a fish out of water; this room didn't afford him so much as a puddle. "As soon as I stepped in and saw that short table I realized, oh my god, they expect me to sit on the floor with my legs folded up! Never in all my life was I able to cross my legs and sit down on them," he moans. "Never! After making humble apologies for my lack of etiquette, I plunked down with my legs sticking straight out. Barney sat across from me, and when Mama-san exited, I whispered to him, 'What the *hell* am I doing here?!' Barney smiled and said, 'You're going to have company shortly—' He hardly got those words out of his mouth when the door slid open again, and a young woman stepped inside and knelt down on a cushion, and when I looked across at that girl I thought, *that's the most beautiful woman I've ever seen in my life!* She had on a silk kimono of the richest colors; she was clearly a geisha. And she just took my breath away. I had never imagined a girl could be that beautiful."

"Can you describe her to me?"

Can he ever. In Harold's memory this geisha's countenance still carries more depth and clarity than any photograph in his vast portfolio. Using his mind's brush, he paints a luminous portrait of a face round as a midsummer moon with delicately proportioned features. The arching, almost circular eyebrows framing her perpetually smiling eyes contributed to the doll-like impression, but her mouth was broad rather than heart-shaped, with a sensuously full lower lip that instinctively caused Harold to bite his own. "She had very clear skin," he gushes, "and she wore natural makeup, not the traditional white face of the geisha and no elaborate wig—just her own hair made up beautifully."

It seems unusual to me that the girl's face wasn't decorated with the heavy cosmetics that are the hallmark of a geisha. When I ask him about it, Harold shrugs, "Maybe because I was an American. Barney had arranged everything, and perhaps he thought a more natural look would be appealing to a Westerner…" As if in confirmation, Harold closes his eyes and starts rhythmically thumping his fist against his chest. It's not clear to me whether he is trying to convey a passionately inflamed heartbeat, or jump-starting an organ that has seized at the prospect of such singular beauty; either way, I take his point.

But it was not just the girl's extraordinary looks that had captivated him. Harold also found her poise and bearing mesmerizing. "It was so proper, so graceful—when she knelt down, it was like a ceremony! Then she got up and approached us, and the way she moved in her kimono was like flowing water, so deliberate, and so fluid." Although her figure was obscured beneath layers of silk and the large sash and bow of her obi, he could infer by her carriage that her body was lithe and practiced as a ballerina's. Indeed, she exuded such physical charisma that he imagined this must be what it feels like to meet a famous performer or actress—Harold knew instinctively he was in the presence of celebrity.

"Everything about her…" he sighs, practically melting into his recliner. "I was just agog at the way she conducted herself. And when she finally knelt down again, right beside me, I wondered whether I'd died and gone to heaven."

Incredibly, things only got better from there.

"Another geisha entered," he continues, "also a very beautiful lady, though she didn't bowl me over like the first girl had, and she too came around the table and sat down with us. Barney made introductions, telling me, 'This lady'—indicating the first geisha—'is named Mariko. She will be your hostess for the evening, and this other lady will be my hostess.' And I was speechless. I really didn't know what to say. I was just…dumbfounded."

"Did you know what *hostess* meant?"

"I had hopes!" he says naughtily.

"Who made the decision about which of these women would host you?"

"Mama-san had assigned them, and Barney had a hand in it. But *I* made the decision," he declares.

"*You* did?" I remark with some amusement. "When she came in, you said, *Barney, I'll take the knockout!?*"

"Well, I didn't say it like that!" he scolds. "It was more of a reflexive *Wow!!* and my jaw practically fell off its hinges. Barney got the signal. He said, 'Okay, this woman will be with you!'"

Harold wasn't the only one at a loss for words.

"Mariko knew very little English," he tells me, pinching his finger and thumb nearly together. "She could recognize certain words and was quick on the uptake—she was obviously very intelligent. Barney was there to translate for us, so we were able to go back and forth making simple conversation. I told her that I came from the state of Minnesota, and I asked if she knew where that was. She told me basic things about herself: her family was in Tokyo, her father was still alive, she had a brother and a sister." Harold frowns, "I had a bunch of both," he grimaces, "but you can bet I didn't go into details about them!"

Despite understanding little of what Mariko was saying, as she spoke, her voice enthralled him. "Her Japanese," Harold notes, "it was different than any I'd ever heard before. Her voice was clear, but subdued and musical. And her smile…" He sighs wistfully. "She was a *very* entertaining young lady."

Deliberately or not, Harold has used the perfect word. "Geisha" translated into English means "person of the arts," specifically an entertainer. Although this highly specialized tradition of women, skilled in artistic and social talents, is rooted in the courtesans of medieval Japan, by the mid-twentieth century a purely nonsexual form of the profession had become ingrained in Japanese culture. Select girls were rigorously schooled from young ages in skills (ranging from playing music and dancing, to politics and other topics of cultured discourse) required to achieve the status of *geisha*: an elaborately made-up and costumed woman, employed for her consummate abilities to provide attractive, entertaining, and hospitable companionship.

But no sexual services. A geisha's principal clientele were wealthy men, her place of business was typically a brothel-like pleasure house—like the one Harold is describing—owned and administered by a Madam-like overseer, so it is understandable how distinctions between geishas and prostitutes could become muddied, particularly

in the minds of culturally ignorant American servicemen. (There was,
however, a darker side to a geisha's life and profession, but we will get
to that soon enough.) On this night, Harold was learning more with
every passing minute about the geisha's impressive talents, and the
social graces she employed to entrance her client and make him feel
as though the sun revolved around him. Not that Mariko needed to
dangle much of her cultured bait—from the moment she first smiled
at Harold, the fish was in the boat.

"Throughout the evening, it was a joyous sort of thing, full of
sake, food, and music," Harold says, sounding like he might still
be a bit drunk from the experience. "They danced for us, and they
sang…both geishas were skilled players on the shamisen (a three-
stringed Japanese instrument). We laughed and we talked. Because of
the language barrier, we stuck with general conversation. I found out
Mariko was four years older than I was. She could hardly believe I
had only just turned eighteen; she told me she thought I was older. I
told her I thought she was beautiful…"

"You just dropped that into the conversation?" I grin.

"Sure!" he asserts, earnestly. "Oh, yes. I couldn't help but tell her
that, because she'd knocked me out from the moment she walked in
the room."

"What exactly did you say?"

"I said it outright, 'I think you're the most beautiful lady I've ever
seen!' And I meant it. The other lady was also quite lovely, but in a
beauty contest, Mariko would have won, hands down—no question!
She was just the most gorgeous and fascinating person I could ever
imagine."

"And did you imagine that this evening still might include some
hanky-panky?"

Harold snorts and deflates a bit. "As soon as I saw those women,
I knew by the class they embodied that this wouldn't be a night of
sex. Still, when you're a dumb eighteen-year-old with a brain drowning in sake, you can't help but test the boundaries—" His head
droops guiltily, like a dog that has eaten cake off the table.

"What did you do, Harold?"

"Well—let's just say I had…wandering hands!"

"You tried to touch her?"

"Mm-hmm."

"Inappropriately?!"

He winces.

"What did you do?" I repeat. "Pinch her? Reach inside her kimono?"

"Now you're just trying to learn my skills!" he frowns impishly. "Oh, I may have slid my hand under the table to get her by the leg—but I never made it there!" He complains, "It was another skill she had been taught, how to expertly thwart unwanted advances. She didn't slap my hand, but I'll tell you what, she politely deflected it and returned it to me with enough firmness that I got the message— *hands off!*"

The evening progressed happily, despite Harold's roving mitts (to his great relief, Mariko seemed cheerfully unaffected by the attempted groping). He describes to me how as each delicious chapter unfolded—conversation, music, food, and other delights—his appetite for new and exotic experiences was tested and expanded. I wonder if the same was true of his stomach. He was, after all, far removed from the meat and potatoes of the Midwest.

"Did you eat traditional Japanese foods?"

"Oh yes."

"What were they?"

"If I knew, I'd tell you!" he teases. His brow wrinkles, "In Japan, they feed you things that are very strange! But I didn't reject anything—I figured after pawing her, I better not do anything else to offend!" He considers, "It was probably dried squid, and maybe fish of some kind. These were served as snacks, and once we'd eaten that and imbibed even more sake, the women prepared a meal for us."

The main course was sukiyaki (which Harold pronounces "skay-yaki," in the Japanese vernacular). Although the dish is common— essentially a beef stir-fry—this meal, in keeping with the entire evening, was extraordinary. "In the geisha house," Harold explains, "they prepared sukiyaki using Kobe beef. It's very tender meat. In fact," he says, amazed, "the cow is hand massaged throughout its lifetime, to make it that way! This very expensive beef was sliced thinly, then stirred into a pan. Once it made a little grease, they started adding seasoned vegetables, including long onions sliced in sections, and bamboo shoots. They cooked it all right there on the table, in a flat pan over a charcoal brazier, and we were supposed to reach in with chopsticks and take a portion. Well," he slumps, "I wasn't adept enough to do that, so Mariko picked some up and put it in my rice bowl." Though initially embarrassed (Harold would have traded an entire boxcar of cigarettes for a proper fork) he soon came to regard his awkwardness with the twiggy cutlery as an advantage. "She had to help me a lot with the food…onions that would slide off…tomatoes—you can chase those around a plate all night long with chopsticks! Whenever I had trouble picking something up, she would do it for me. Eventually," he grins, "she just started feeding it to me…" If the enraptured look on his face at this moment is any indication of how he felt that night, I am guessing she could have put a beetle on his tongue and he would have gobbled it down. "I didn't know or care what I was eating," he confirms dreamily, "because my mind was definitely not on the food!"

"It sounds like you'd gotten past your fear of rejection!" I note.

To be clear (and putting his pert, investigative foray down to the booze), Harold tells me that his feelings toward this geisha were not rooted in lust. This was something more complicated and intense, unlike anything he had ever felt drawing him to a girl. In him, Mariko had stirred a heady blend of desire, intrigue, and respect born of this sensual and transformative evening. Her beauty and comportment were indeed intimidating, but he felt certain a prince would have melted in her presence. So skillful were her attentive ministrations as his hostess that Harold's social anxieties were similarly dissolved.

"This was a completely new and different experience for me," he concedes. "I was in the company of an astonishingly attractive and elegant companion, surrounded by luxury—it must have cost Barney a small fortune to arrange it all. I was clearly out of my depth, but I was being treated with the greatest respect I'd ever known." Harold returns to the meal as an example: "I grew up in a large family," he says, "and when it came time to eat, if you didn't get it quickly, you might not get it at all! Here, I had to fight my natural tendencies, and Mariko was dedicated to helping me slow down…relaxing me, and ensuring I didn't feel out of place. If I made a mistake, she worked to minimize whatever it was, or she demonstrated the correct way to do something without making me feel foolish. I paid very close attention to her, and she taught me so many things in such a short time that my mind couldn't take it all in. She was patient and kind and her expertise amazed me because everything, down to each little movement she made, was something she'd been trained to do, and it was all so beautifully artistic."

He reflects, "And I think that's what Barney had planned for me from the start, that I would see and appreciate another side of Japanese culture, outside the navy base, and expand my perspective as an American. His intention was to educate me about traditional Japan. And what better place to do that than an okiya, where tradition is brought to life…"

I ask him how the night ended.

"Too soon!" Harold moans. "I wondered where the hours went! But eventually," he sighs, "our time was up. The two ladies escorted us down to the entryway where we all said good night. My mind was spinning, and not just because Barney and I had drunk our weight in sake. As we wobbled out into the night, I had questions for him."

"Like…?"

"Like how do I see this girl again?! From the moment I'd laid eyes on her, I desperately wanted to spend more time with Mariko. I was hooked! But how did I stay hooked? This was no ordinary person. She was a geisha—and an elite geisha, at that. How could I be with a woman like her, other than by booking an evening at the okiya? Was there a way to get to know her outside the customs and boundaries of her profession? Never mind the hurdle of us not sharing a common language, was such a relationship even possible?"

"And what did Barney say?"

Trying to steer Harold clear of the military police while listening to him drunkenly babble this fantasy, Barney was muttering and swearing beneath his breath in Japanese, but the meaning was clear.

"He was telling me, *Good goddamn luck!*"

# Chapter 11
# OBSESSION
# 執着

ERHAPS BARNEY NEEDED a few days for the alcoholic fog to ebb—a clearer head to consider his chum's lovestruck entreaty. Indeed, to see if once Harold himself had dried out, whether he was actually serious about, or even remembered, his preposterous desire to romantically pursue a geisha. Perhaps Barney felt responsible. It was, after all, his idea to grow Harold's cultural awareness by immersing him in the beguiling charms of the okiya. Or perhaps he was just being a good friend. Whatever the reason—time, guilt, duty, or a combination—once he had sobered up and found Harold still besotted, Barney agreed to lend a hand.

But not before Harold tried to make a solo run at it.

"I was a young man with no brains," he admits, "pursuing a very beautiful lady, and I didn't know where it would end or how it would even begin. From the very start, I did some things I probably shouldn't have done..." he considers ruefully, "like returning to the geisha house alone."

I ask him if Barney had at least arranged the visit.

"No," he murmurs sheepishly, "I just showed up."

Although amenities procured at an okiya may be similar to a nightclub, cabaret, or fine restaurant, there are differences—the most obvious being that for an evening with a geisha, you do not just show up. Like any elite club or private party, it is just common sense that such an exclusive venue for entertainment is by appointment only. Harold had certainly gleaned this during his intoxicating night of indulgence there, but now that love was in the air, common sense was out the window.

"Did they even let you in?" I wonder.

Harold exhales another of his little snorts of embarrassment, "Being stupid and bold, I snuck in." He shakes his head, "I should not have done that. It was infringing on everything I had learned during my visit with Barney. But I did it anyway because I had a burning question I wanted answered: how do I arrange to see Mariko again—and more than once? I'd have swum a moat to find that out! So I went into the building alone and unannounced, and I didn't see Mariko, but I definitely had an encounter with the lady who ran the place." He shudders, "Needless to say, Mama-san was not happy to find me there. For one thing, she knew very little English…I don't think she even understood what I was asking."

"Were you able to get an answer to your question?"

"No," Harold says, underscoring, "and it was a *short* conversation. I knew then that I wasn't going to get anywhere without Barney's help."

First, however, Barney did his best to try to dissuade his friend, or at least help Harold confront the realities of the situation. "'If she was anyone else…' Barney told me, 'even a high-end street girl, maybe there would be a way to arrange social meetings, but you can't even be seen with a geisha!'" This was true enough. A geisha's livelihood was dependent upon her unsullied reputation, and there was no surer sign, in many cases quite accurately, by which a Japanese woman was judged to have "fallen" than by being seen publicly with an American soldier, or entertaining him regularly.

For the same reason, subsequent rendezvous at the geisha house were out of the question—not to mention the risk this would also pose for Harold. Despite the fact that these were not dens of prostitution, to discourage any suggestion of unbecoming behavior, the military had declared the okiyas off-limits to servicemen. This geisha house had made a calculated exception during Barney and Harold's big night out, but if a GI were to be caught frequenting such a place, it would land him in the brig and raise a cloud of suspicion over the business. Thanks to Barney's timing and a little luck, Harold had managed to dodge the MP patrols on his first visit; it was a miracle he was not picked up on the second. It is no wonder Mama-san had been alarmed to find a U.S. sailor wandering her halls in broad daylight.

Barney made one other thing very clear. Even if Harold could find a place to meet secretly with Mariko, and even if she agreed to see him, it would not be her decision alone to make. As a geisha, she did not hold the keys to her social freedom. Mariko was, in fact, an indentured employee, subject to constraints Harold would have to recognize and accept. First and foremost was the understanding that if he wanted to visit with her, even outside the confines of the geisha house, it could only be done with the consent and coopera-tion of Mama-san.

Despite all this, Harold was unwavering in his persistence to chase a wild goose (or, as he saw it, a bird-of-paradise), though admittedly dependent upon another's expertise to help him herd it toward the net. "I had no choice other than to rely on Barney," he tells me, "and his knowledge of the culture and language to help me achieve this."

For his part, Harold's friend could see the writing on the wall: *Shikata ga nai*. This oft-used Japanese expression of resignation sums up Barney's stoic surrender. The phrase approximately translates as, "nothing can be done about it," or "it cannot be helped," and embod-ies the Eastern philosophical concept of accepting one's fate by sim-ply giving in to situations beyond control. Clearly, nothing Barney could do or say was going to deter Harold from pursuing the geisha.

On the other hand, Barney reflected that if anyone could pull this off, it just might be this wide-eyed and handsome, rough around the edges, eminently resourceful American kid. Harold had a deep well of determination, but more than that, thanks to Barney's own tutelage, Harold had a wellspring of ready money—and he would need it. Barney came from a wealthy family, and even he shuddered at the prospect of what it might cost to essentially have a top dollar, much in demand geisha like Mariko on retainer. Now it was time to find out.

"With Barney's help," Harold recounts, "we contacted Mama-san and arranged an appointment. Together, Barney and I made another visit to the geisha house. This time, however, it was strictly business rather than pleasure."

That does not mean Harold didn't enjoy himself. To his utter delight, Mariko was also present at the meeting. "This time she was dressed in everyday clothing," he remembers. "She wasn't as dolled up as on the night we met, but she was still the most beautiful girl I'd ever seen…"

While Harold mooned from the sideline, Barney communicated to both women the young man's wish to see Mariko on a frequent and ongoing basis. He took it as an encouraging sign when they were not immediately laughed out of the room. However, Harold tells me, there were problems—the same problems Barney had previously spelled out. "Mama-san confirmed that Mariko could never be seen on the street with me," he notes, "or in any other public location, and having me make repeated trips to the geisha house would be too risky for all concerned."

It was Mariko, surprisingly, who offered a solution. "She had a friend," Harold says, "a woman whose husband had been killed in the war, who lived about twelve blocks up the hill from the okiya. Mariko said this lady had two children to support and would welcome the income from renting us a room where she and I could meet in private."

I need to back him up a bit. "Why," I ask, "would the woman who owned the geisha house even consider allowing one of her top geishas to entertain a suitor?"

The short answer is *money*.

"Geishas weren't allowed to have boyfriends," Harold acknowledges, "but I wasn't presenting myself as a prospective boyfriend. I was a paying customer. Barney had already made it clear to me that there was no way I could expect to see Mariko without compensation. So I asked Mama-san, straight out, 'I know it will cost money for me to spend time with Mariko, how much?'" He gulps, "Even Barney was a little shocked at the answer—two hundred dollars in yen per visit! *Plus* the room fee to the lady who owned the house."

"Holy smoke!" I exclaim, thinking, *that's a lot of cigarettes!*

As if reading my mind, Harold remarks, "I was definitely going to have to step up my black market activities!"

I also cannot help feeling that it all sounds a little salacious— renting a private room, two hundred dollars a visit... "Just what kind of get-togethers were you arranging to have with her?" I wonder. To me, it sounds like he was paying for a lot more than just sitting around and sipping tea. He wasn't.

"This did not include sex!" Harold emphasizes. "Mama-san was quite clear on that. A physical relationship was not an option. But at this point," he insists, "I wasn't thinking about that. I just wanted to spend time with her. To get to know her better."

"I have to ask, you were obviously head over heels for this woman—"

"I was *gaga!*" he affirms.

"Right," I nod, "but did you have any sense at all whether the attraction was mutual? Or, as far as Mariko was concerned, was this just another business arrangement?"

Harold weighs this. "She definitely knew how I felt about her— anyone could see I was hot on the trail. Why else would I be going through all this trouble to see her again? But I can't say it was the same for her...I think curiosity is what was going on in her mind."

There was one other condition that would have to be met in order for Harold to meet privately with Mariko at a secluded location. She would need a chaperon. But not in the traditional sense; not some dour matron to sit in a corner, clucking her disapproval and flashing eye-daggers each time Harold's roaming fingers began to twitch. In this case, the chaperon was necessary to protect the interests of Mama-san, to secure her investment against a geisha's own temptation to wander.

"A friendly and polite young gentleman, around twenty-two years old, dressed in a neat jacket and tie, topped with a wide hat," is how Harold describes the mandatory escort. "He was small—even shorter than I was, and I liked him immediately. He was introduced to me as 'Oki-boy.' It was a nickname he had because he'd grown up on Okinawa, and it's the only name I ever knew him by. Mama-san explained to us that whenever one of the geishas left the okiya to go shopping, walking, or anywhere else, Oki-boy had to accompany her.

But he wasn't there to protect her. It was his job to make sure the girl didn't try to run away."

In fact, despite his dapper charm and diminutive stature, Oki-boy was the shadowed face of the business made manifest. A geisha is not created overnight. By the time she has mastered the many talents required to earn her title, she will have spent years in preparation—in most cases, since childhood. And geisha training is not like ordinary schooling. It is a rigorous and immersive course of apprenticeship requiring the girl to live year-round at the okiya, separated from her family and the ordinary experiences of girlhood—although, by the standards of mid-twentieth century Japan, the lives of ordinary country girls were typically so bleak that being selected as a geisha novitiate might be considered lucky indeed.

"Girls were of no value," Harold frowns deeply. "In rural Japan, unless a girl could earn an income working in the fields or at some other form of labor, she was considered a drain on her family's resources. This was a hard thing for me to understand," he says darkly, "but it was not unusual for farmers to peddle their daughters off to factories, tea plantations, or linen mills, where they worked fourteen hours a day and where many of them got dust fever and died. And this wasn't criminal activity! It was done in the open and considered a normal way—an honorable way—for a girl to make a contribution to her family."

For a father, having a daughter who possessed enough promising beauty and intellect to be sold to a geisha house was hitting the jackpot, but it offered little escape for the child. Instead, this was the opening notation in a ledger of compounding debt that would carry forward throughout her life. Regardless of how high she rose in the geisha hierarchy, no matter how steep a price she might eventually command for her services, these numbers could never balance the years of investment owed to the business for her education, room and board, and expensive costuming. From day one, a geisha was doomed to a lifetime of servitude by her overwhelming and insurmountable debt. Thus, from Mama-san's perspective, a watchful eye was a necessary precaution to ensure her employees were not tempted to flee their obligations while they were out-of-doors. If Harold wanted to meet Mariko off the premises, Oki-boy was a nonnegotiable part of the deal.

"The fact that Mariko was basically a captive," Harold sighs, "was very difficult for me to accept. I didn't grasp the significance of it right away. This was Japan, and those were the traditions, but it took me a long time to comprehend that this is the way it was, and this is the way it had been for centuries, and there wasn't a damn thing I could do to change things."

*Shikata ga nai.*

# Chapter 12
# MEETINGS
# ランデブー

HAROLD CAN'T sit still and who could blame him? Two days ago he had surgery to remove the cancer from his bladder. The offending cells were scooped out via something called a "transurethral resection"—a procedure every bit as uncomfortably invasive as it sounds. The good news is the doctors seem confident that Harold's tumors are gone. But this happy prognosis is tempered by gutting pain throughout his urinary plumbing, the inevitable result of snaking a device the size of a pencil-thick knitting needle up the pipe to slice away at the insides of his bladder. Although this particular procedure was a novel ordeal, for Harold, hurting is nothing new. "I live on pain medicine," he mutters, shifting tenderly in his chair.

At least he's home again, glad to have traded a hospital gown for the familiar comfort of checkered flannel. And though he is still peeing out bits of bladder, his ribald humor is intact. When I press him on the upside of having had the surgery, he confides, "There was the thrill of being prepped for it by a nice young lady!" He chuckles wearily, "She did a lot of…inspecting. As far as I'm concerned, that nurse earned every penny."

"So money *can* buy happiness!" I remark, sensing a segue back into his narrative. "Even yen?"

"It certainly can," Harold nods, confirming that by the time the two would-be Cupids (he and Barney) had concluded their odds-on, fool's errand to the okiya, a plan that would allow Harold to meet regularly with Mariko had been worked out and agreed upon—albeit for an extortionate sum. "And that was the key," Harold stresses. "It was going to be risky for everyone; a geisha and an American were forbidden to mix, but it was going to happen because I was willing to pay top dollar."

All that remained was making the final arrangements for the meeting place with Mariko's lady friend, which Harold attended to in short order. The woman was indeed happy to provide them use of her sitting room. Since her husband's death, renting out space in her home was her only source of income, and she was fortunate to still have that. The Omori district was one of the city's few neighborhoods unmarked by the intense firebombing that incinerated much of central and western Tokyo. (One reason for this may have been the presence there of a POW camp—a notorious prison that had counted U.S. Olympian Louis Zamperini among its inmates.) But Tokyo was a metropolis of wooden buildings, so even areas not targeted by the bombings had been ravaged as the fires spread. Somehow, this woman's little house had escaped the flames. Now, things there were about to heat up.

"We met at this house up the hill," Harold smiles. "Mariko and I arrived separately and we took different routes to get there, but at last we were there together."

"This is just the third time you've ever seen her, correct?"

"Yes."

"What was the evening like?"

"Heaven…" he exhales, and I know by this reflexive, intoxicated sigh, he is not being flippant. "In some ways," he says, "it was similar to our first meeting. The room was set up with a low table, and we had food and something to drink."

I ask him whether she again performed any of the traditional geisha entertainment.

Harold shakes his head. "This was informal," he asserts. "*Very* informal. Like at our first meeting, she was made up naturally, but this time her clothing was also more casual." He reiterates, "No, this get-together wasn't about her entertaining me or playing instruments or anything like that. It was strictly socializing, getting to know one another. Questions and answers. They were curious about me—"

"They?"

"Mariko and Oki-boy."

"You mean to say he was right there in the room with you?"

"Of course."

"You were spending all this money for an evening with her—and him?"

"Yeah," Harold nods, "he was there too. But it was a good thing," he insists. "Oki-boy spoke pretty good English, so we had an interpreter!"

I see his point. Three is a crowd, but still less awkward than two mutely staring at one another across a table.

"So we talked," he says. "I had questions for her and she had questions for me. She was very inquisitive. She wanted to know all about my life and about me being in the navy. She was curious where I had been during the war, and I wondered the same about her. She told me that during the firebombings she'd been in the countryside. All the girls from the geisha house had been moved out of Tokyo until it was safe to return, so she'd avoided most of the bombing. But she had seen the aftermath: people burned, bodies floating in the rivers—she didn't blame me for that, and thankfully her family hadn't been hurt or killed."

Not exactly idle, first date chitchat, I reflect.

"We talked at length about the training she underwent to become a geisha," Harold continues. "Although," he notes grimly, "*endured* might be a better word. She explained to me that she was still in elementary school when she first came to the okiya, and hadn't known anything about what she would have to learn. And there was a lot to know! She had to be taught how to dress, how to speak, how to move—not to mention how to sit still, because talking with men is also an art."

Harold listened as Mariko explained to him how she had worked to acquire arcane talents, such as learning to sing traditional songs and perform dances that were centuries old—and how she had to hit every note perfectly and was expected to move with the grace of a swan, like a creature born to effortless beauty. Her studies had been rigorous and arduous; she'd learned three instruments simultaneously from an instructor who struck her knuckles with a cane whenever she made a mistake. But she hadn't complained. She had understood what she needed to do to succeed as a geisha and had applied her intellect and will to mastering all these skills.

Harold was in awe of her determination and fortitude. Everything Mariko related to him about her training only magnified how much she impressed him. He would not have thought it possible, but he felt even more attracted to her—and yet, thankfully, throughout this visit he managed to exercise self-restraint. "I behaved myself," he grins. "I had learned to keep my hands on top of the table." (I'm guessing the presence of Oki-boy also provided some incentive in this regard.)

And once again, the evening passed quickly and was over all too soon. At least this time Harold knew he could see Mariko again whenever he desired, provided he had the cash. "I gave Oki-boy the payment to take back to Mama-san," Harold says, "two hundred dollars in yen. *Ouch!*" he exclaims. "That was a lot! I was peeling it off, hoping I wouldn't run out! Then I paid the woman for the room, and it was time for me to go."

As it is for him now.

The urgency from Harold's bruised and swollen bladder cannot be denied a minute longer, and he excuses himself to find relief. While he's gone, I poke through his candy dish and fish out a toffee. Knowing these are my favorite, Harold has pilfered a hoard from the bowl at the reception desk of his retirement complex (a place he tellingly refers to as "the compound"). The housing plights of seniors are a frequent topic of Harold's impassioned grousing. Considering what it is costing him to live here, he thinks the desk probably ought to be handing out gold nuggets. He has no qualms about regifting their sweets.

While he's gone, I open one of his photo albums from Japan and contemplate the scene of his crimes: pictures of the rail yard at Yokosuka and the seemingly innocuous little trains that ferried coal by day, but were fueling his meetings with Mariko by night.

"I was making some pretty good hauls," Harold says, hobbling back into the room and finding me poring over his black market operation. "It was costing me a fortune to spend time with her, but I was making enough on the cartons of cigarettes and other things I was smuggling to carry on." He eases himself tenderly into the recliner, noting, "I continued to meet with her there in that little house at least a couple times each week for most of that year."

I am flabbergasted. *At two hundred dollars a pop?!* If my teeth weren't cemented together with candy, my jaw would be hanging slack with astonishment.

And yet, money aside, this arrangement was remarkably solid footing for fostering a relationship. It was essentially a parlor courtship—and what young couple would not benefit from ritual sessions of chaste conversation? Without the temptations and associated anxieties of physical intimacy, Harold could focus on listening to Mariko, and admire her many qualities beyond physical beauty. For her part, the geisha was free to indulge her curiosity and cultivate familiarity, perhaps, in time, even genuine affection, for this lovestruck teenager from halfway around the world. Plus, she got to learn English.

"In the beginning," Harold explains, "any direct communication between just the two of us was done by using facial expressions, hand gestures, and a lot of mumble-jumble to get our meanings across." Initially, he estimates that Mariko only knew about a dozen words in English. "But she was a very fast learner," he remarks. "She had to be. By nature, a geisha must have a magnificent mind and great aptitude for learning. Whenever I said something in English, a word or sentence she didn't understand, she'd ask me about the definition and pronunciation, and then simply add it to her vocabulary."

I wonder if he was learning any Japanese.

"She made it easy on me," he admits. "I was picking up a few words here and there, and eventually I learned to understand her language quite well, but in the beginning, she was doing the hard work by absorbing English so quickly."

Remarkably, as Mariko's language skills progressed, and with the rules of engagement firmly established, the couple began to enjoy greater privacy as Oki-boy gradually gave them space.

"He might be in another room or somewhere else close by," Harold informs me, "but by now he also wasn't afraid to leave the house for a while. He was a good kid. He was watching over her, but not in an overeager or threatening way. He had a simple job to do, and that was to ensure Mariko didn't fly the coop. He was there to keep her from being tempted down the wrong path."

I cannot resist teasing him, "And yet, he didn't have a problem with you spending time alone with her?"

"No," he scoffs, "he was very relaxed about it. He knew she could take care of herself and he knew I wasn't going to run away with her—where was an American sailor going to go in Japan?! Plus," he gives me a wink, "slipping him a few hundred dollars in yen now and then didn't hurt."

Astonishingly, over time, Mariko's inquisitiveness about Harold showed signs of developing into a real fondness. Perhaps it was his flattering fascination with her, or his boyish good looks and rough-hewn charm that were gradually winning her over. Maybe it was all the money he was spending—at the very least, it must have been a great compliment to be the object of such paying devotion. To this day, Harold is not sure.

"I don't know," he frowns, "because compared to her, I was a dopey, clumsy ox in every way. I was just a kid—she had those four years on me, but beyond that she was much more sophisticated and mature in every way…maybe it was pity!" he suggests, not entirely in jest. "Maybe she looked at me and thought, *boy, this guy could really use a little encouragement—what could it hurt?* I never asked her," he confides, "but there had to have been some kind of attraction because any time I asked to meet her, whenever I wanted to be with her, there was no question she would be there."

This was never made more clear than on a night when Harold phoned the okiya to inform Mariko he was deathly ill. He told her he felt like he was on his last lap, and all he wanted was to see her, implying his condition was so dire it might even be for the last time. He moaned to her that he couldn't even make it up the hill to their usual meeting place—he had barely managed to drag himself to a nearby pool hall before collapsing. Would she come to him even though it meant risking the strict rules prohibiting public contact between them? It seemed like he'd barely hung up the phone before she burst into the room and rushed to where he was splayed out, corpse-like, across one of the felt tables. Her brow knitted with concern as she considered his sickly pallor and sweaty delirium—then furrowed into anger as she deduced the cause of his suffering: Harold was raving drunk! And yet, even in his inebriated state, in the split second before Mariko's face transformed into the definition of fury, he noted her fleeting, but thankful sigh, signaling genuine relief.

But perhaps the surest signs that she was growing closer to him were the increasingly personal details she brought to their conversations. And nothing was a truer demonstration of this than when, after several months of meeting regularly with him, she suddenly confessed to Harold, "I want to tell you something important about myself...Mariko is not my real name."

# Chapter 13
# CHIYOKO
# 千代子

THE LITTLE GIRL loved her parents. Her father doted on her and made no secret of the fact that she was the favorite of his three children. His job sometimes kept him away from home for days or weeks at a time, but whenever he returned, he brought this daughter wonderful gifts. The shelves in her bedroom were populated with beautiful dolls from his travels. Her mother was a homemaker, and the girl observed and learned her mother's daily routines, so she could dutifully and ably help tend to the household tasks, including caring for her younger sister and older brother. There was no question the girl was devoted, smart—special. Her father never doubted she would rise to great success despite any challenges put before her. Even the name he had given her implied an enduring destiny: "Chiyoko," a title that meant "child of a thousand generations." She was, figuratively, and in life, the forever girl, who made a lasting impression on all who met her. Everyone recognized that she was a person of rare and intrinsic value. And so no one, other than Chiyoko, was surprised when her father sold her into a life of virtual slavery.

"She told me that Mariko was her professional name."

Harold is talking about the revelation that gave him his first glimpse behind the smoke and mirrors of the geisha's life, adding, "She said all the top geishas took professional names, and Mariko was hers."

"Was it because she didn't want to use her family name?" I ask. "Was there a stigma attached to being a geisha?"

"God, no!" Harold exclaims, explaining that the opposite was true. "If a girl made the grade and became a geisha, it was a point of pride for her entire family."

He considers, "I suppose it's like when a movie star invents a stage name. They want something that sounds glamorous, that will be part of the illusion—a title for a persona that may or may not be representative of who they really are. I think that's why she called herself Mariko," he conjectures.

I have no doubt he is right. There were probably no greater cultural icons in postwar Japan than the most highly celebrated geishas. And as Harold was starting to comprehend, a geisha's prestige depended upon a well-cultivated mask of illusion.

"Then one day, out of the blue, she said to me, 'Mariko is not my real name. My name is Chiyoko—Chiyoko Okada.' And I thought right away that was a beautiful name," he insists. "I actually liked it better than Mariko! So from that moment on, she was Chiyoko to me."

The significance of the geisha sharing this information was not lost upon him. She had revealed something of her private self, a very unusual admission. He had not asked her about it, nor did she owe him this information. The only reason for Chiyoko to disclose such a fact is that she wanted Harold to know it—to know her. The geisha mask was slipping.

Since their first introduction, Harold had been intensely curious about the details of how and why Chiyoko had become a geisha. As their meetings progressed, and the language barrier dissolved, they grew more comfortable with one another, conversation was easier, and at last Chiyoko's story began to unfold.

"She told me that when she was very young, her mother had died," he says, "and that event is what set everything in motion."

I ask Harold if she told him how her mother died.

He nods. "She'd been sick for a while…I'm sure it was tuberculosis." Doubtlessly considering his own father's demise, he adds, "Like here, that disease was also taking a lot of lives in Japan. She said her mother had breathing problems, and grew weaker over time, until she was bedridden at the end. Chiyoko told me that she sat beside her mother's bed and watched her die, and of course, it was tragic for her because she'd loved her mother dearly."

Unfortunately, he tells me, the girl's troubles were only beginning.

"Throughout her mother's illness, Chiyoko had done her best to help care for the family, taking over more and more of the household responsibilities as her mother failed. After her mother died, even though she was still in elementary school, as the oldest girl, she assumed her mother's duties in the home: cleaning—including dusting and polishing the floors—and even the cooking. She was following her mother's example, and trying very hard to please *dear daddy*."

Harold practically spits this appellation, leaving little doubt about his regard, or lack thereof, for Chiyoko's father—and with good reason.

"She was very attentive to him, to her whole family," he continues, "and they all owed her a lot—but her father owed other people more." Harold's scowl intensifies. "He was a gambler, and deeply in debt."

"Was he a poor man?"

"No, he made good money! He had a skill—he was what they called a 'hooper,' a maker of wooden barrels. One of his specialties was building enormous storage kegs. He would get contracts to go different places and construct these large wooden vats for businesses. He'd get paid, then come home and gamble the money away." Harold says darkly, "His children suffered greatly because of it."

"Chiyoko said that?"

"Not directly, but she told me how her older brother had fractured his knee in an accident, and her father either couldn't, or wouldn't, spend the money to put him in the hospital to have it mended properly. The doctors probably could have fixed him up, but their father declined to pay, and so her brother was crippled his entire life. At the time she and I were meeting, her brother was barely eking out a living as a barber." Harold shakes his head disgustedly, "And that same tightfistedness with money is how she ended up at the geisha house. Eventually her father found a new wife, someone to take over the household chores, and not long after that, he took

Chiyoko and her little sister to the okiya, where he sold them for a good price."

It is a lot for me to absorb; it must have been overwhelming to a little girl. "Did she have any inkling this was coming?" I ask.

"I don't think she had *any* idea—her father had spoiled her! He always brought her gifts from his trips and had seemed genuinely fond of her. Then suddenly, *wham-o!* So of course she was shocked to be taken from her home by her father and sold to a place like that. At first, she cried herself to sleep, every night."

"How old was she?"

"Old enough to understand what had happened to her," he emphasizes. "Chiyoko was eleven or twelve. Her sister, Yoshiko, was nearly four years younger, and they were both devastated. For her part, Chiyoko had tried so hard to replace her mother and be of value to her family. But I guess her father decided that cashing in both girls was worth more to him."

"She must have hated her father for doing this."

"You would think that," Harold concurs, "but whenever she talked about her father with me, she never blamed him or put him down. And it was my understanding that he was never embarrassed that he had sold his daughters. In those days, it was not considered dishonorable, and he certainly never apologized to her for having done it."

His words suggest yet another dimension to the story that boggles the imagination. "Do you mean to say that after all this, she kept in touch with her father?"

"Not right away," he tells me. "She lost track of what was going on with her family during the years she was undergoing training as a geisha. The girls weren't encouraged to communicate with their families," he asserts, "so if she did, it was very limited. But by the time I met her, she had reconnected with her father and visited him quite often. In fact, I'm certain that well into her adulthood, she was giving him money."

I am not sure how to begin processing this. Harold has had a lifetime to sort it out, and his advice is to not even try. He shrugs, "It was one of those complicated father-daughter relationships that will never make sense to people on the outside. And perhaps it was a cultural thing as well." He notes, "Dedication to parents is deeply rooted in Japanese society."

Rather than dwell on the sins of the father, Harold prefers to focus on the adaptive aptitude of the brave little daughter. "I can't imagine, in my own mind, what it must have been like for a girl that age to be taken from the home she loved and to suddenly find herself in a strange place, where she's no longer allowed to attend public school or even roam in public. Instead, she's required to learn exacting new skills for doing even simple tasks…" Harold gives me an example: "Like serving tea. When a geisha serves tea, it's not just putting leaves and hot water in a cup. It's a ritual. There's a proper way to handle everything—the cup has to be turned just the right amount, the tea leaves added just so. This is all a skill, and it requires a great deal of practice. And almost everything a geisha does while entertaining her guests demands this level of artistry. These were the things she had to master to stand the test."

The pressures to succeed as a geisha were considerable, and not least because the consequences of failure were grim, as Chiyoko's sister learned firsthand. "Yoshiko didn't make it as a geisha," Harold reveals. He tells me how Chiyoko described her little sister as an awkward country girl who, try as she might, could not summon the elegance and sophistication that are the essential calling cards of the geisha. Inevitably, she was dismissed, but not to return home. "This was another low point for both girls," he murmurs, "because Yoshiko was sent to a house of prostitution, and obviously, an even more difficult life than at the okiya."

"And this, too, was legal?!"

"All above board," he huffs. "When the girls were sold, they essentially became the property of the person who paid the money." Harold is unsettled, and for once, it is not because his bladder or any of his other physical ailments are eating at him. This is a queasiness born of revulsion, an empathetic sickness roiling in the pit of his stomach. "When I heard about these things," he growls, "I thought this was about as rotten a thing as you could possibly ever do: selling children…of course, I still think that. But in Japan, during that period of time, this was not an uncommon practice. It happened to countless girls every year. Boys were labor for the family farm or business, the wife did the everyday chores, but a girl—she was just another mouth to feed. So men like Chiyoko's father," he glowers, "they sold their daughters."

"But at least it was to a geisha house…" I posit. I'm wondering whether her father might deserve some benefit of the doubt. In spite of how things turned out for Chiyoko's sister, and despite Chiyoko herself being forever bound to her employer by debt, a successful geisha enjoyed the company and comforts of the upper crust of Japanese society. "Is it possible," I wonder, "that her father did this terrible thing thinking that he might be giving his daughters a chance for better lives?"

Harold is not buying it. "They were pretty little girls," he growls. "He got the best price for them there."

With the growing intimacy between Harold and Chiyoko came a degree of physical temptation that would have snapped the will of a less sincere man like a balsa chopstick. For months, Harold had been on his best behavior: no attempts at foot play beneath the table (even though his legs were sticking straight out, maddeningly near her hips), no exploratory incursions with his hands between the folds of her kimono, and absolutely no lips, anywhere, other than framing his perpetually enraptured grin. But, as time passed and Chiyoko signaled increasing warmth toward him, there came a day—house rules, Oki-boy, and his own insecurities regarding women be damned—when Harold could no longer resist the urge to advance his position. At least he had the good sense to make it somewhat romantic.

"I kissed her."

This catches me off guard. "Tell me about that!"

He surprises me again by staring vacantly, saying, "I've got to give it a little thought…"

"Really?!" I am amazed the details do not reside forever in the same wrinkle of brain that houses his breathing and heartbeat and the other essentials that give him life. "This must have been a big deal!" I emphasize.

"Oh, it was…" He inhales introspectively, and I see then that his hesitation is no lapse in memory. Rather, it is about taking one last opportunity to savor the moment, through his mind's eye, before sharing it aloud. "It surely was!" he repeats. Then he swivels to face me. "I put my arms around her, and when that didn't offend, I kissed her. Incredibly, she responded in kind. I'll tell you one thing," he exclaims, doe-eyed, "it was another learning experience."

He is not just talking about the novel and delicious sensation of her mouth melting into his, or how his own blood astonished him by rushing through his extremities like heated water in the veins of a mineral spring. Even in the throes of this long imagined and highly anticipated act, Harold's mind was working overtime to absorb every thrilling opportunity it might afford. In Japan, the nape of a woman's neck is a highly erogenous feature to men, but his attention was wholly focused according to Western obsession. "I hugged her tightly, and it was more than was really necessary," he acknowledges, "but I was curious about something…I wanted to know if she had breasts! Because even when a geisha is informally dressed, she wears something underneath called a *chichi bando*—a wide strip of material used to bind her breasts. I didn't know anything about that at the time," he says, and his tone suggests he does not understand it to this day. "All I knew is that beneath the fabric of Chiyoko's kimono, I could never discern any breasts. So, the first time I kissed and embraced her, I put a little extra emphasis on the *squeeze*," he stresses, then grins broadly, "and all my questions were answered! After that," he enthuses, "kissing between us was routine. It was mainly either in greeting or good-bye," he notes. "We didn't sit around smooching one another," Harold sparkles, "but we may have thrown in an extra one now and then."

Of course, that was it. Harold had come to the end of the road in terms of moving his relationship with Chiyoko forward. As long as he was paying for her time, they were free to continue meeting and talking, sharing secrets, and even sneaking a few kisses, but he could never go beyond that, never risk taking things to the next level— even if that was something Chiyoko also desired. In her capacity as a geisha, sexual activity was forbidden, and because the business held her debt in perpetuity, she had no capacity other than as a geisha. Mama-san owned her, body and purse.

This frustrated Harold to no end. Not just because it meant there was zero possibility of ever realizing his lust—and by this time, with Chiyoko returning at least a degree of his affection, he freely admits that his libido now had a piece or two on the board. But beyond that, he adored her. He had come to care deeply about her well-being and her happiness. Though he did not recognize it or define it as such until much later, Harold loved her.

For all these reasons, he found the injustice of Chiyoko's situation untenable. To hell with *Shikata ga nai*, in the back of Harold's mind, an idea was beginning to take shape.

# Chapter 14
# RESOLVE
## 決意

"GENERAL DOUGLAS MACARTHUR changed everything." In the days since Harold first described to me the grim misfortune of Chiyoko's sister, Yoshiko—how, after washing out as a geisha, she had been reassigned to a brothel—I have not been able to get this unlucky girl out of my mind. Today, I've begun the interview with Harold by asking if he knows whatever became of her. Not only does he know her fate, he is happy to report that around the same time he was wooing Chiyoko, Yoshiko was delivered from her ordeal. He also knows that the person responsible for this was none other than the corncob-pipe-chewing Supreme Commander for the Allied Powers in Japan. Harold is offering up a little background on how this came about.

"After accepting the Japanese surrender," he tells me, "General MacArthur took control over every aspect of life throughout the country. Under his authority, a new constitution was drafted, one that included a guarantee of rights for Japanese women. No more buying and selling of girls," Harold notes firmly. "No more holding women against their will. Thank goodness, those days were over."

"Yoshiko was free?" I ask, "It was as simple as that?"

"Even the Emperor—God himself—answered to MacArthur!" he chuckles. "Yes, after the war ended, forced prostitution was outlawed. No one could legally constrain a woman, for any purpose. Her sister was free to find other work, which she did. She worked in the cafeteria at a department store."

This begets an enormously obvious question: "After MacArthur's edict, why wasn't Chiyoko also free to leave the geisha house?"

In fact, Harold informs me, she was. But as a geisha, the circumstances of her captivity were not so cut-and-dried, and the consequences of throwing off those chains were morally and practically complex.

"Chiyoko was bound by her debt," he explains, "beginning with the money that had been paid to her father—*especially* by the money paid to her father," Harold underscores, "and for all the years of training, clothing, and bed and board that followed. These were legitimate expenses the business had incurred on her behalf, and in the Japanese culture, you don't just walk away from debts. She could have," he notes. "*Legally*, she could have. But this would have brought lasting dishonor upon her father—who had accepted money for her that was paid in good faith—and by association, shame upon her entire family. Plus, she would have been penniless. If she left the geisha house, she'd leave with nothing. She would be free, but with no money and no livelihood, no clothing or possessions, and she'd have ruined her family's reputation, so they wouldn't take her in. A girl in that situation would have little choice other than turning to prostitution." Harold gives a little snort of disbelief, "It's hard to imagine," he says, "but the way things turned out, her sister was the lucky one."

"Was there any hope," I ask, "that Chiyoko might chip away at her debt over time?"

Harold shakes his head soberly. "Earning her freedom outright would have been impossible. By this time, she owed so much she could never begin to pay it all back." Plus, he explains, she was ensnared in a classic "company store" ploy: "Any personal income she earned as a geisha amounted to less than her living expenses, so her debt to the okiya increased every day. She was trapped."

I ask him whether she at least enjoyed being a geisha.

Harold considers this. "I don't know if it was enjoyment or pride..." he mulls, "probably a combination of the two. I know she had confidence in her skills, and was very proud that she had advanced to become one of the top girls in her profession. I'm sure she enjoyed that feeling. If you're asking me whether she would have kept working as a geisha if her debt was erased and it was her choice, rather than her obligation, I'd say *yes*. It wasn't at all unpleasant work. It was safe, honorable entertainment, and she was very admired while she was doing it—and besides, it was what she knew, what she was trained to do."

This circles back to something I have wondered about ever since he first described to me her years of arduous study. "How old was Chiyoko by the time she was ready to start entertaining professionally as a geisha?"

Harold is guessing, but he thinks around fourteen or fifteen. And then he drops a bombshell: "At whatever age her virginity was sold."

There is heated debate between historians, anthropologists, and even among former and present geishas about the extent, or even the actualities, of auctioning a girl's virginity as part of *mizuage*—a ritual ceremony marking a novice's coming of age and her transition to geisha. Whether this occurred in prewar Japan is not disputed. How often and whether it happened to legitimate geishas are contested. Some insist that the practice was widespread during that time and was commonplace for geishas-in-training, even those schooled at the finest and most exclusive houses. Others argue that where this custom was inflicted upon a girl, it was rare, localized, and reduced her to the level of a prostitute, disqualifying her from ever becoming a geisha in the purest sense. All Harold knows is that it happened to Chiyoko, who was held in the greatest esteem as a respected and successful geisha, and she was no prostitute. "Of that I was certain," Harold declares, "because during my negotiations with Mama-san, she had made it clear that road was firmly gated, and no amount of money was going to open it!"

Shockingly, one person had been handed this key.

"Chiyoko never offered details, other than to admit it was something that had happened to her," Harold recalls, adding, "but I'm sure it was the Gambler who took her virginity."

In his conversations with Chiyoko, she had revealed to him that from the start of her geisha career, she'd regularly entertained a very wealthy patron, a man Harold calls "the Gambler" because he habitually hired Chiyoko to accompany him whenever he visited gaming establishments. The Gambler believed she brought him luck. Harold speculates that this man's fixation with her as a talismanic object was rooted in a darker sense of ownership.

"One reason I think it was the Gambler is that in order for a person to possess her this way, it had to be someone with a lot of money. The exact price is negotiated. The girl's father actually has a role in that," Harold hisses, "and I expect hers probably did, but the owner of the okiya sets the final amount, and for a beautiful girl with great potential like Chiyoko, it must have been substantial."

Thanks to Harold, the differences between geishas and prostitutes, generally blurry among Westerners, has been clear to me—until now. Despite confusion wrought by street girls who marketed themselves to occupying troops as "geisha girls," I've understood that a fundamental division between the two is whether there is sex for hire. Sex equals prostitute. For this reason, the time-honored concept of the geisha as chaste artist, entertainer, and hostess seems incongruous with this business of auctioning virginity. Yet, as this odious chapter in Chiyoko's story reveals, the historical origins of the geishas are knottily entwined with sexual services, with a perverse remnant from ancient and feudal times still being practiced during the mid-twentieth century. If there had been any consolation for Chiyoko, it was that this was a onetime ordeal.

"She was never forced to have sex again," Harold stresses. "After that, she was a geisha—never again for sale in that way."

Of course, once is still barbaric, and although Harold does not presume to speak from a woman's perspective, as he opines on the subject, it is as though he is channeling Chiyoko:

"There are few things more sacred to a woman than her virginity," he asserts, "and to have it sold—that's a hard and traumatic thing. A geisha only has this gift to offer just that one time, and it's a treasured and intensely personal thing to her, as it is to any girl. To have other people negotiating a price on it and then being forced to sell it, as if "it" was something separate from herself, was degrading and humiliating—not to mention heartbreaking. Because she didn't have a choice."

"Chiyoko was never pressured to have sex with a client again after that," I ascertain, "even with the Gambler..."

Harold leans in to make the point. "I'll tell you something I learned from her about the Japanese: they're an up-front and honest people. Chiyoko told me, openly and without embarrassment, that for a period of time the Gambler had paid to have her live with him in a house he owned. But I believed her when she said there was no further physical intimacy between the two of them. He hired her to stay there because he believed her proximity brought him good luck, but there were no sexual demands made on her because, of course, by then, she was a geisha!"

He eases back into his chair. "She wasn't allowed to have a husband, or even a boyfriend." Harold smiles wanly, "Once again, I was breaking all the rules."

In fact, he was rewriting the rules, because if Harold wanted to continue seeing Chiyoko, he was going to have to change the game. For starters, he was shelling out a king's ransom just to be in the same room with her. "Paying to have these meetings was costing me a small fortune," he bemoans, "and at no small risk!" Harold's smuggling operation was now running at capacity as boxcar after boxcar with secreted shipments of cigarettes, sugar, and other illicit commodities rolled through the Yokosuka rail yard in order to finance his courtship with Chiyoko. "I was spending the money as fast as it was coming in," he says, "and with that level of illegal activity going on, it was only a matter of time until someone figured it out."

An even more pressing issue for Harold, however, was the injustice of Chiyoko's situation. The circumstances of her profession were a roadblock to advancing their relationship, but what had him seeing red was the idea of her enslavement by debt—an obligation she had no role in assuming, but she had no choice other than to honor. This, he could not abide. Someone other than herself had put her in debt, and now, he resolved, someone else would get her out.

"When I came to the realization that she was stuck there for life," Harold fumes, "I said, hell, I've got to do something about this!"

Brimming with optimism and youthful indignation, Harold believed he could drill through any obstacle by applying his resourcefulness (like when he had vandalized an empty house to escape a drudgery of dishes), his mulish tenacity (like when he had strong-armed his reluctant parent into signing off on his navy enlistment), and mustering help (like when he had convinced his best friend to lobby on his behalf in a Quixotic quest to date a cultural icon). Now, he was determined to redeploy this last asset a second time, in order to bore even deeper down the same well.

"I told Barney, 'I want to free Chiyoko from the okiya, and I need your help negotiating what it will take to pay off her debt.'" Of course, once again, Harold found himself confronting a wall of reasoned practicality.

"'But...' Barney told me, 'I've never heard of anyone ever doing anything like that!'

"I said, 'Never mind that. You're the only person who can get me the answer to my question. I need to know what it will cost me.'

"He said, 'I don't think—'

"And I said, 'Barney, I'm not asking you to think, I'm asking for your help finding out how much!'"

Barney's sigh of resignation must have rivaled the steam venting from Mount Fuji.

"He said to me, 'Alright, I'll try to arrange it.' So we made another trip to the geisha house, where again, he had to translate because of Mama-san's lack of English and my lack of Japanese."

This time, they were, in fact, nearly laughed out of the room.

"'Oh, no,' Mama-san grinned with amusement, shooing us toward the door, 'Not possible. Too much!' But I persisted by sending Barney back into the ring for another round. 'No, no!' she repeated, and she explained to us about all these expenses over the years. She said Mariko's education, boarding, costumes and clothing, all of that costs money, and it never goes off the books; year after year it adds up. Mariko had come to the okiya as a girl, and she had been building up debt every day since. Plus, she was one of the most popular geishas in the Tokyo area, much in demand, so her kimonos alone were very, very expensive. Mama-san was sorry, she told us dismissively, but this was not something somebody could just pay off."

Harold grits his teeth, "But by now I was set upon the fact that I was going to do what I was going to do! I said, 'Lady, you've got a golden opportunity here. Let me worry about the money. You just have to name a figure.'"

Mama-san frowned. This young sailor was not going to be dissuaded so easily, and she was a busy woman, with no time for such foolishness. His doggedness convinced her it would be more expedient to just give him a sum—astronomical though it may be. Better to let him discern the reality of the situation for himself and see the futility of such a ridiculous ambition. Then he would leave her alone.

Mama-san said a few words—if a number was mentioned it certainly was not part of Harold's vocabulary—and it caused Barney's eyebrows to rise nearly to his hairline, something Harold deduced as the equivalent among the well-heeled Japanese of a spit-take.

"What did she say?" Harold pressed him, "How much?!"

"She said, enough 100-yen notes to fill two bushel baskets," Barney intoned.

"Well, how much is that?!" Harold asked excitedly.

Barney, the numbers man, attempted a mental conversion, but this concept of money measured as volume was new to him, and the sheer quantity of digits slowed his thinking to a crawl. At last, he announced, "About forty thousand American dollars!"

If Barney was stunned, his pal was about to deliver a knockout punch. Lest Mama-san have a chance to reconsider or rescind the offer, Harold turned to her and nodded, "That'll work."

# Chapter 15
# THIEF
# 泥棒

AT THE END of the Second World War, the median income in the United States was just shy of $2,400 per year. The average cost of a new house was $4,600. A new car would set you back about a grand. Adjusted for inflation, forty thousand U.S. dollars from that time equals over half a million in today's money—over by about forty thousand dollars.

It is no wonder Barney nearly fainted.

Harold, on the other hand, had felt invigorated. Jubilant to know that there was a number, though a whopper, that would earn Chiyoko's release. He'd been spurred to action, as he is now, reliving that excitement. Clutching his cane, as he ushers me to my seat on the sofa, he is a bundle of gesticulating energy swathed in forest plaid. His shirt today is green—the color of money.

"I didn't know how I was going to do it," he bubbles excitedly, passing me the candy bowl, "but Mama-san had given me a price that would secure Chiyoko's freedom, and I was determined to meet it."

"Did you tell Chiyoko you were going to do this?" I ask, my fingers trolling for toffee.

"No," he says, "I held back. I didn't want to disappoint her, because I didn't know how, or when, or even *if* I was ever going to have the money. I'm sure Barney and Mama-san were both thinking, *good luck, kid!*—and with good reason. My black marketeering was netting me a lot of cash, but it was a pittance compared to what I would need to pull this off. I thought to myself, I have my own goddamn railroad. I can sell anything, but I could smuggle cigarettes from now till kingdom come and still not earn enough—so what else?!" Harold frowns, but there is a hint of "what else" playing out beneath the surface, nascent emotion tugging at the corners of his mouth, the beginning of a smile. "A few days later I was down in the yard, supervising the workers on the coal pile, wracking my brain about this when I happened to glance up at that tunnel. And a light went on."

When the Allies first occupied Japan, a top priority was the immediate and systematic dismantling of the Japanese war machine. To this end, the Seabees became *de*-construction battalions, responsible for rounding up and destroying Japan's fighter airplanes and other military hardware. At Yokosuka this meant sweeping every nook and cranny of the base for munitions and small arms, including searching a number of large, underground bunkers quarried into the rock faces adjacent to the rail yard. Harold had been a part of this detail, and during the hunt he had explored many of these subterranean chambers.

It was the one he had not visited that suddenly piqued his interest.

"It occurred to me that in the months since we had swept those caves, I was the only one from that crew still stationed at Yokosuka, and that was the one place I'd never been inside. I thought, I'm going to go and check it out because we'd cleared a lot of valuable stuff from those tunnels. I went in and groped around until I finally found the switches for the lights. I flipped them on—and I couldn't believe my eyes!"

Harold cracks open one of his albums and shows me a photo of the tunnel entrance. It is important to understand that what he's describing was not some dank passageway, but a concrete-lined portal large enough to accommodate entire railcars. In fact, this was the front door to an expansive underground complex, like an arch-villain's lair, designed as a place where submarine construction could proceed unhampered by Allied bombing.

"That whole damn mountain was *full* of machinery!" Harold exclaims. "Every kind of fabricating equipment you could think of: drill presses, lathes—large ones and small ones—anything you could imagine! Everywhere I looked, there were whole floors of this stuff." Harold wandered the aisles in a daze of incredulity and opportunistic intrigue that persisted long after he had finally switched off the lights and slipped back out through the tunnel. "As I lay in bed that night, I thought, *I wonder what I can steal out of there that I could sell for forty thousand dollars?!*"

He recognized immediately that whole machines would be too cumbersome and heavy to move. This was a pity because Japan was in the process of retooling and rebuilding. The country's industrial infrastructure had been targeted throughout the war, and as a result, a high percentage of factories, mills, and machine shops had gone up in flames. Any number of Japanese companies would have paid a premium for precisely the kind of equipment Harold had discovered.

That left stripping the machinery for parts and materials. Picking them to their bones would take ages, and most of the parts were too specialized to have significant value, but there was one common component of every machine that Harold recognized as an essential and highly adaptable building block for industry, not to mention loaded with precious copper wiring—electric motors. He decided to conduct a little market research.

"I needed an interpreter," Harold explains, "but I didn't want to use Barney because I didn't want him to know anything about what I was thinking. I wanted him free and clear, in case things went south on me. So I enlisted the help of Imai, the boy who had taught me how to do hip throws by tossing me down the coal pile. He understood English quite well. I sent him out to the main station, where I had him ask the guys I'd been dealing with there if they would come to the gate. I wanted to talk to them."

"Who were these guys?" I ask.

"My henchmen!" he smiles. "I had two Japanese fellows working at the end of the platform in the main station who took care of shuttling all my train cars in and out. When I had a shipment ready to go, all I had to do was contact them. They would move that car to a rail siding and then find a buyer for whatever I'd tucked inside.

After they sold it, they'd give me 80 percent of the money and keep the rest for themselves."

Harold was gobbling up quite a piece of the pie, I note admiringly, considering he never even had to get his hands dirty.

"Like I've said," he smiles, "all I touched was money! I had this kid arrange a meeting with these guys, and through him, I asked them, is there a demand for electric motors? If there was, I had a proposal for them. I told them I needed six hundred thousand yen—that was the equivalent of forty thousand dollars. I told them I could fill a boxcar with motors, but I needed that much money, no less, but no more either. I told them they could keep anything above and beyond that."

"And what did they say?"

"They said they would get back to me."

Harold may have been plotting the ultimate surprise for Chiyoko, but she was also capable of springing an occasional eye-opener on him. Nevermore so, Harold tells me, than the day she turned up for one of their meetings without a kimono.

"Excuse me?"

He shoots me a look of mock sternness. "It wasn't anything like that!" he scolds. "She wore this white cotton dress, and it was the first time I had ever seen her in Western clothes. It was summer, and it was hot and muggy, and she showed up in this light dress. Up till then, her figure had always been buried beneath the layers of her kimonos—not that day," he grins wolfishly.

Of course he has a photograph.

"Wow!" I can't help observing. "She really is beautiful." Noting the decidedly un-geisha-like cut of her sleek, short-sleeved number, I remark, "There's a lot of arm showing—and leg, too! What did you think when you saw her in this dress?"

Harold clutches one hand to his chest. "I was in a state of shock," he asserts, and he wanted more than a memory. "I had the woman who owned the house take this picture of us together."

They are a handsome couple, Chiyoko in her breezy summer frock nestled beside Harold, who is decked out from head to toe in his navy dress whites. "Why were you so formally kitted out?" I ask.

"That's what I had to wear any time I left the base," he explains. "Always in uniform. That was the regulation: no civilian clothing for servicemen when we went out. And that's why it was so important that Chiyoko was never seen with me in public—why we had to take separate routes to our meeting house. There was no mistaking me for anything other than an American sailor; being observed in my company would have torpedoed her reputation and her career."

It could have sunk him too. Despite the platonic nature of their get-togethers, the military police would likewise not have made a distinction between a geisha and a prostitute—especially when, as was the case whenever Harold met with Chiyoko, money was changing hands.

It was for that reason, on one memorable night, Harold found himself in a very tight spot.

"We were meeting as usual," he explains, "when suddenly the woman who owned the house came rushing into the room, talking excitedly in Japanese. She told Chiyoko the MPs were cruising the neighborhood and searching homes! During the war, this lady had also dabbled in reselling things that were in short supply. (Apparently everyone in Japan had a finger in the black market.) There was a small space underneath the floor where she had cached rice and other valuable foodstuffs. When they heard the MPs outside, the woman and Chiyoko crammed me in there! They hid me until the coast was clear. That was a twist…" he notes dryly, "me—stashed in a smuggler's hole."

Of course, selling a few bags of rice from under the floorboards didn't hold a candle to the intricate criminal web Harold had spun. And now he was preparing to dramatically grow the operation by trafficking stolen goods. The likelihood of being caught was significant, and the ramifications dire: a general court-martial, disgrace, prison. The scandal and punitive consequences would eclipse anything yet achieved by a member of the Stevens clan—and that was saying a lot.

I have to ask him, "Was there ever a moment where you thought, this is crazy, why am I doing this? Or, I should not do this?"

Before I have even finished asking, Harold is shaking his head. "Nope. I was going to do it."

"Was it lust?" I press, frankly. "You've said before, lust has driven you to make bad decisions. In the back of your mind, were you thinking, if I do this for Chiyoko, maybe I can finally move the relationship forward to a point where I can—"

Still shaking his head, he interrupts, "No, that had nothing to do with it." In fact, he tells me, it was the opposite. "I was doing it because I had such high regard and so much respect for Chiyoko. I'd never met a girl like her before, and never have since. After learning about everything she'd been through, I thought, my god, she's amazing—she deserves a better life."

As a thief, Harold's conscience was also clear. To his way of thinking, this would be a victimless crime, on par with smashing all those deserted windows. The underground machine shop was similarly abandoned, a forgotten relic of a conquered and disbanded navy. Like Robin Hood, he rationalized that if he could plunder these rich and idle resources and apply the money toward a noble cause, why not? Justice practically demanded it. Chiyoko deserved her liberty and all the freedoms that went with it, including the right to control her own life and make her own decisions—about everything.

And then he puts his finger on it: "Deep down, I did have hopes," he admits. "I loved that girl without even knowing it. So, yes, I guess maybe it was about me wanting her—but not for sex. Or, at least, not just for that. I wanted us to be able to associate freely, and to maybe have something more with her. I wasn't sure what that meant, or if she would even want me, but I hoped for the chance to find out."

Not long after he had put out feelers, Harold heard back from his cronies at the station. It was the best news he could have hoped for. "Yes!" he announces gleefully. "They said they would take all the electric motors I could get my hands on, and they had found someone who would meet my price!"

When I ask him who the buyer was, he replies, "I didn't need to know, and I didn't want to know."

"You must have been dumbfounded! Did you say to yourself, now what? How am I ever going to pull this off?"

"I had it all worked out," he says coolly. "What I said was, *Okay, here we go!*"

It is not a bit surprising to me that this sounds like something a person riding a roller coaster might say as the car crests its dizzying climb. Harold was about to take a plunge from which there would be no going back. As he begins detailing for me how he set in motion a straightforward, but precipitous plan—one that relied upon the brazen use of bribed accomplices and conspicuous resources—I settle in for the ride.

"I went and got two laborers from the work gang, and I asked them if they would like to make a little extra money. Well, of course they would!" he grins. "I explained that I had a job for them, probably a couple days' work. I would pay them well, but it was hush-hush!" Harold closes an imaginary zipper along his lips. "I said, 'You can't talk to anybody about this!' They mirrored this gesture and said, 'No worries, boss!'

"The next morning I loaded up a jeep with toolboxes, and I drove those two guys up the railroad tracks inside the tunnel. I turned the lights on, and I went down the line of machinery pointing out the motors. I told them not to worry about any of the big motors, but I wanted all the smaller ones. I said to them, 'I want you to take those off the machines, and I need you to put them in a line here, along the train tracks. Do you understand?' They nodded, 'Oh yeah, we can do that!' So I told them, 'Great. Here are the tools. Get started.'"

"Just a second," I interrupt. "How did you know how many motors you would need?"

"I had no idea," he replies, "so I had to get a lot. Those guys worked all day inside that mountain removing motors and lining them up by the tracks. The next morning, when the daily shipment of coal came in through the gate, I had arranged to have an empty boxcar on the end of the string. I was running the engine myself, and I backed that line right into the tunnel, where I unhooked the boxcar. Then I pulled the gondolas back out and over to the coal pile for unloading.

"I had my two laborers go in and load the motors into that boxcar. When they were finished, I said, 'Okay guys, good job, and remember, mum's the word!' I even paid them a little extra, and they went away putting fingers over their lips and nodding and just happy as hell…" Harold can't help but chuckle at how easily things seemed to be falling into place.

"That evening, when the coal cars had been emptied, I pushed them back into the tunnel, and I snatched that boxcar, pulled it out, and parked it in the yard close to where I was living. I opened the door a crack—just enough to check one last time that everything was in there and ready to go, and then I put seals on both doors."

"A seal—what is that, some kind of lock?"

"No," he explains, "but it adds another layer of security. It's a metal band—a numbered strip that loops through the latches on the doors. It's not strong like a chain or a padlock, but you do have to cut it off to open the door again. The important thing is that once a seal has been put on, only certain officials can remove it. It's to prevent things from being stolen," he says, smirking at the irony. "Everything is meticulously recorded, so if an inspector finds a seal has been removed prematurely, he knows there's been some monkey business, and he can track the shipment back to see where it was last reported as being intact."

Harold anticipates my next question.

"Those two seals were listed as 'lost.'" He shrugs coyly, "That's how it went in the record book, and that's the only time Barney had a finger in things—although he was in the dark about this whole operation. But it was his job to make the log entries, and so I told him there were two missing seals—presumed lost—and he recorded it that way. I never wanted Barney to know anything about what I was doing…"

"But surely he *knew*," I protest. "I mean, he was in the room when you'd committed yourself to amassing the riches of Solomon to free Chiyoko—and now you're shuttling strange boxcars in and out of tunnels, reassigning workers, security seals have gone missing…"

"He never asked, and I never told him." Harold cannot make this point often enough. "I wanted Barney to be clean. It wasn't that I didn't trust him. If I had told him, 'Here's what's happening, now keep your mouth shut,' he would have—but why put that on him? Barney was an honest man. Oh sure," Harold agrees, "he had to know I was pulling some kind of caper, and he didn't ask questions because he was a true friend." Harold grins cagily, "Or maybe it was out of fear that I would bump him off if he did! I had a .45 on my hip most of the time that I was in Japan, and he already thought I was a little crazy!"

The following morning, hitched to a long line of empty coal cars queued to roll out the gates of the Yokosuka Naval Base, there was one lone boxcar. According to Harold, the rest was duck soup.

"I called the guys who were down at the station to let them know I had a car coming out. Again, I moved it myself. I had an engine all heated up, and I took that string of railcars down to the gate and pushed them out. And that was it. I said to my co-conspirators, okay, it's all yours."

"Just like that?"

"Just like that," he smiles triumphantly. "And I never asked them what they did with all those motors," Harold marvels, "but they must have fetched a good price because about a week later another car came back in through the gates, and inside was a mountain of yen! Boxes of it! Barney's calculations had been right on the money— enough to fill two bushel baskets!"

"You'd actually pulled it off," I gape. "You had the cash to pay Mama-san and erase Chiyoko's debt! She was free?"

"Not quite yet," he informs me. "I had the money, but I couldn't pay it all at once. I still had to get it off the base, and I could only smuggle out so much at a time. I paid in installments."

I ask him how on earth he managed to get all that cash past the guards.

"The same as when I'd started out moving cigarettes," he says matter-of-factly, "in my boots!" Harold elaborates, "On the old combat boot there was a wide horizontal flap with two buckles that closed the top of the boot around the leg. I'd stuff stacks of yen in there between that flap and my sock. Then I'd cinch up the buckles, blouse my trousers over the boots, and walk it right out." He smiles, "I could move a fair amount of yen that way!"

Something else occurs to me. "Where did you hide all that money while it was still on the base?"

Harold pumps his eyebrows furtively. "I stored the main hoard above the Hot Room…" but his grin fades at the memory of that hellish place. "This was a large, indoor bay where we did maintenance on the trains," he frowns, "and the locomotives idled in there the whole time. There was so much smoke that all the windows and doors were permanently thrown wide open! Up above this work area there was another little room where nobody ever went because you'd be gassed to death from all the fumes, and that's where I stashed the money. Whenever I was ready to move some, I'd climb up there holding my breath, grab smaller amounts, and transfer that to a footlocker I kept under my bed…and then I'd walk it right out the gate."

"And where did you take it?"

"Straight to the geisha house."

"Mama-san must have been stunned when you started showing up with all that money—and stuffed in your boots!"

He nods, and the satisfied smile is back, big as life.

Over and over again, like a swashbuckling picaroon, Harold sidestepped the military police and snuck into the okiya, where he unbuckled his boots, and presented Mama-san—her eyes agog—with fat wads of oddly sulfurous-smelling cash. Then he melted away again into the night, one practiced step ahead of the law, back to Sherwood Forest.

# Chapter 16
# BLISS

## 至福

"WHAT HAPPENED when Chiyoko found out you were paying off her debt?"

Listening to Harold recount the details of his great train robbery, I share Mama-san's slack-jawed amazement. Even so, it is a challenge to imagine the bewildering blend of shock and joy that the geisha herself must have experienced upon learning that her young sailor had somehow amassed the fortune necessary to erase pages of red ink extending all the way back to her childhood. It must have been something beyond belief. According to Harold, that pretty much sums it up.

"She didn't think it was true," he concedes. "She knew I was determined to help her—to gather money to make her life better…but paying off her debt? No. That was unimaginable to her."

"Alright then," I allow, "tell me about when and how she realized you were determined to help her."

"My plan was to not say anything about any of it until I had made payment in full," he replies, "but circumstances forced my hand. One day while we were meeting at the house, her brother showed up…"

This was an unexpected visitor. Harold knew that Chiyoko's surviving family—her father, brother, and sister—all lived in the

Tokyo area, but he had never met any of them, and why would he? Whenever Harold and Chiyoko were together she was technically working, and they were sequestered in an out of the way neighborhood. But one evening there was a knock at the door, and everything Harold had learned from his own clan about the resourcefulness of relatives was confirmed: there is no escape from family—especially when they're looking for a handout.

"Her brother had tracked her down," Harold rumbles. "Chiyoko's father had sent him to ask her for money! When I got wind of that," he glares, "I couldn't hold back!"

With pronounced indignation, he explains to me that this was during the time when he was making payments on Chiyoko's behalf, impossibly large deposits that would eventually free her from the yoke of servitude placed upon her by her father's greed. So when her brother turned up, at their father's behest, asking for cash—and she actually gave him some of her meager earnings—Harold blew a gasket. "It all came out! I explained to her in great detail what I was doing for her. I told her that soon she would have no obligations to anyone—not to the okiya, not to me, and certainly not to her father. Whatever her life was going to be, it was going to be *her* life to live. She would be free to make her own choices—but giving money to her father..." he splutters, "after what he'd done? I told her that's where I drew the line. I was risking everything to get all this money for her, I didn't want a single yen going into his pocket!"

Harold eases back into his recliner, although relaxation is still some distance down the road. "The fact that I was paying her debt," he crabs moodily, "this was definitely not something I'd wanted to spring on her in anger."

By forcing his hand, Chiyoko's father had managed to rob Harold as well.

"And what was her reaction?"

"Like I've said," he shrugs, "it didn't register. It was inconceivable to her that I'd ever possess enough money to actually do that. Little did she know, I was already well on my way to paying it all off! But I'll tell you what," he brightens, "she was ignoring the signs. She actually caught me one time with my boots full of money!" Any lingering anger erodes, and he laughs, "I was taking my shoes off to enter the house and a couple fat bundles of yen fell out! My pant leg was raining money! She must have thought I was the richest man in Tokyo—but even then, buying her freedom?" he shakes his head, "That was too much to believe."

I ask him when did she finally comprehend the full extent of what he had been doing.

"When I turned over the final payment. We were at the okiya—"

"Chiyoko was present?

He nods, "But even then, I don't think she fully understood what had happened. I said to her, 'That's it, kid...your debt is paid. You're free!' Then Mama-san explained it to her in Japanese, handed her a receipt—and finally it started to sink in."

"What did she do?"

Harold almost looks embarrassed. "Japanese women don't faint easily..." he chuckles.

Even before Chiyoko was a free woman, she and Harold had begun sleeping together. "Sleeping" as in getting some shut-eye, and "together" meaning in the same room, but in separate beds. It was an innocent arrangement, born of practical necessity. Omori was a far and circuitous trip from the naval base. To get to their meeting place, Harold had to take the train up to Yokohama, then on to Shinagawa via an express line, a distance of over thirty miles, before backtracking four miles to the Omori station. Their rendezvous often continued well into the evenings, and if it became too late, he found it more expedient to simply overnight there at the house—he had already paid for the room—and then catch the early train back to Yokosuka in the morning. The landlady provided additional incentive by cheerfully spiking his morning tea with whiskey. In time, however, as Chiyoko got to know Harold and feel safe with him, she also elected to sleep at the house rather than walk back to the okiya late at night. From the moment she first announced she would be spending the night there with him, it was a wonder Harold slept a wink.

"I very much anticipated getting ready for bed," he grins wolfishly. "I wore a cotton kimono, and she put on silk. But a geisha can change clothes right in front of you and you'll never see skin," he grumps. "She was a master at the art of decorum!" He found the sleeping arrangements equally frustrating. "The woman who owned the house made up two beds for us. These were futon mattresses, side by side, but with space in between." When he did sleep, he dreamed of bridging that chasm.

"She was so close to me that if I extended an arm, I could touch her," he sighs, "but I didn't do that for a long time. I just wasn't the kind of person who charged ahead with a woman."

"You had that fear of rejection…"

"That was it," he affirms, "and I never wanted to do anything to frighten or offend her. So it took me months. But eventually, I found the courage to edge over closer to her bed and slide my hand under the blankets—"

I have to interrupt, "Where the heck was Oki-boy while all this was going on?"

Harold answers, surprisingly, "If Oki-boy stayed there—and he didn't always—he slept in another room. As long as he felt reassured that Chiyoko wasn't going to run away, he didn't care what we were up to."

"And what was that?" I ask pointedly. "Where did those fingers end up?"

"At first she pushed me back," he admits, "but eventually she let me hold her hand while she slept."

As an indentured geisha, with no concept of what Harold was doing behind the scenes, even this had been a bold concession on her part.

Now, however, things were very different. Chiyoko was her own woman, no longer subject to the scrutiny of a chaperon or the dictates of an overseer. If she decided to remain a geisha—and that was something she would have to consider—she would still need to observe the proprieties of her profession while in public, but she was free to indulge a private life, including a relationship, if that was what she wanted.

On the night Harold settled her debt at the okiya, the couple retreated to the house on the hill for what he describes as "an intimate conversation." Chiyoko listened, finally comprehending as he once again (and in a more measured tone) explained his motivations for freeing her, how he had done it, and what his expectations were now—the gist being an assurance that despite his obvious affection for her, there were no strings attached.

"I did my best to make her understand that what I had done was to give her the freedom to choose. I went over that quite a few times trying to explain it to her. I said, 'I'm not asking you to commit yourself to me, and you owe me nothing,' but I obviously had strong feelings for her."

I ask whether the word love was mentioned.

"God, no!" he erupts. "I had just turned eighteen years old! I didn't know what love was! I was a crude, young man with no brains and even less romantic experience. A person like me never talked about love! I came from a family of lowlife ruffians," he snorts. "I would have been more comfortable punching someone in the nose than saying the word *love* out loud..." Harold's face relaxes, and these strident declarations about his younger self give way to sager perspective. "Of course I did love her," he reflects. "I just didn't recognize it yet. I knew that I cared for her—just look at what I'd done for her! I'd have fought a pen of wild dogs for that girl, but saying, *I love you?*" He shakes his head, "That would have taken more guts and maturity than I had then."

That night, after they finally went to bed, when Harold's hand slid beneath her blankets, it ventured into unexplored territory. As his fingers passed beyond Chiyoko's wrist without protest or rebuff, he felt the thrill of a voyager approaching lush and uncharted shores. He slowly traced her arm, then across her shoulder, where he involuntarily shivered, as did she, as his fingers transitioned from the cool, sensuous silk of her kimono to the luxurious heat of bare skin. His hand circled down her chest, fingers working reverently, caressing, massaging. "Finally, I reached her breast," he tells me, "and to me, it was..." he raises both palms ecstatically and his eyes roll upward, "I mean it was..." he sighs and slumps into his chair. For the first time since I've met him, Harold Stevens has no words. "I'll tell you what," he finally breathes, "it was an *adventure!*"

But that was as far as it went that night—as far as Chiyoko would allow it to go. With so many heady and competing emotions surging inside her, she desired nothing more than to be caressed, reassured, and held. Harold, to his great credit, was attuned to her needs and did not press or angle for advantage. True to his word, he respected her newly granted freedom to consider and savor her choices—and to control them.

"This was the beginning of our intimate relationship," Harold tells me, "and a few days later we were back at the house. Again, we were both staying the night, and I noticed this time that the beds were made up with the mattresses pushed together—it wasn't two single beds anymore!" The meaning was unmistakable. The prospect excited him beyond words. The reality was more sobering. "Being an awkward kid and knowing very little about the art of seduction," he confesses, "I didn't have a clue about how to advance things physically with a woman, never mind a geisha who was renowned for her practiced poise and sophistication! My approach," he mopes, "was drawn-out and very clumsy."

What he calls clumsy seems to me the natural trepidation of a man suddenly graced with the intimacy of a woman he has long desired, but always considered beyond his reach. In fact, Harold's infatuation, coupled with his inexperience, made him the ideal lover for Chiyoko. "Remember," he reminds me, "her virginity had been sold—sex had not been a pleasant thing for her. She'd been handled very roughly." With Harold, the pendulum swung to the other extreme. "Now, here I was, probably the most inept guy that was ever in bed with a woman because I was more afraid of hurting her than anything! She was a delicate girl," he explains, "no more than five feet tall, barely one hundred pounds, so I was consciously very gentle with her. That, and my deep fear of offending her and embarrassing myself, meant that the way I touched her was overly cautious and very tentative."

Thankfully, just as on the first night he met Chiyoko—when she had so expertly buoyed his confidence by walking him through unfamiliar and intoxicating terrain—she would help him relax and find his way.

"She was very patient with me. She knew more about how I should handle her than I did, so I let her guide me. She showed me that I didn't have to be afraid of her body, but you don't just start grabbing—there was an art to touching her. I began to investigate with my hands, fondling and caressing her breasts, and I wasn't rejected. Then the kissing started. Of course, we had kissed one another before—even hotly, but this was more drawn out and what I would describe as very passionate. Again, she did not reject me. Eventually she allowed me to explore below her waist, and once we got that far—" he smiles, eyes moist at the memory of their tender consummation, "she welcomed me."

This was a far cry from the selfish backseat groping that Harold had previously equated with sex, and based on Chiyoko's reaction, it bore no semblance and thus carried no ill associations with her previous trauma. It was a wonderful and transformative experience for them both—and they both wanted more.

"After that, we made love quite regularly," Harold says, telling me candidly that each time they did his joy and awe were compounded, even after the act. "When we were being intimate, we used to leave a lamp on. It was a very dim little lamp. And afterward I used to love lying there alongside her, watching her sleep…watching her breathe. I can still think of it—her beside me there, in that subdued lighting. She slept flat on her back so I could see her chest moving up and down, and I could admire her beauty. It was exhilarating for me. It was hard to imagine how I had come to be with her. I felt *so* lucky. To be there like that, with the most beautiful woman I had ever encountered. I felt that way about her from the moment she first stepped through the door on the night Barney and I visited that geisha house…" Harold shakes his head, rapt with wonder, "and I never got over it."

For Harold and Chiyoko, it was a fairy tale beginning. It was also the beginning of the end.

In order to secure her freedom, he had put his own in terrible jeopardy. The way Harold had obtained the money to pay off her debt, though nobly conceived, was recklessly illegal and would inevitably be traced back to him. The crime itself might have been as fine a piece of planning and as cleanly executed as any crackerjack military operation, but it had more loose ends than a moth-eaten sweater. Eventually, someone would discover all the stripped machinery inside the tunnel. An investigation would quickly conclude that the only way such a cache of valuable motors could have been smuggled off the base was by using the trains, and that would point to the guy running the railroad—the same guy the Marines already knew as a resourceful black marketeer. With all the circumstantial evidence, including the various accomplices and other witnesses to Harold's shenanigans, it was only a matter of time before everything unraveled.

Of course, Harold had known all this from the beginning. Not for a moment had he entertained the possibility he could pull off such a caper without the chickens coming home to roost. But he also did not plan on going to prison—not if he could help it. Even as he had determined to steal military property to pay off Chiyoko's debt, he knowingly accepted a terrible irony: after she was free, he would not be there to share in her new life.

As soon as he could arrange it, Harold would have to quit the navy, and leave Japan.

# Chapter 17
# PARTING
## 別れ

THE BRIG AT YOKOSUKA had the reputation for being the hardest jail in Asia. Lying on the concrete floor of his tiny cell—there wasn't even a bed—the prisoner couldn't argue with that. Four steel walls surrounded him. There were no windows, just one thin slot for ventilation. The highlight of his day was getting a little salt for his bread, the only food on the menu. No talking was permitted between inmates; men sentenced to hard labor worked silently, their shovels mixing gravel and cement to make concrete blocks—then used sledgehammers to break them back down into rubble, and started all over again. Lying night after night on a slab stained with sweat and other things he did not want to think about, the prisoner had ample time to contemplate his predicament. He had no one to blame but himself. He had been pushing his luck without getting caught for so long that he had come to feel above the rules, and as a result, he'd gotten cocky. Stupid. Caught. Now he was paying the price. They had locked him up and forgotten about him. This was not an exaggeration. As far as the warden was concerned, Harold could rot.

For our meeting today, he is back in blue, dressed in a distinctive white and navy plaid. The stark, grid-like pattern of Harold's shirt reminds me of cast iron fencing. Or prison bars.

"The only time I ever felt ashamed of myself in uniform," he mutters, "was when I was in that brig on bread and water. That was utterly humiliating to me."

Our discussion is centered on Harold's waning tenure in Japan. He puts it plainly, "As a result of my illegal activities, things were heating up there. I knew I had to get out—and soon." This urgency was compounded when he suddenly found himself sentenced to hard time for a relatively laughable infraction: nineteen hours AOL— Absent Over Leave.

"I was supposed to report for morning roll call," he explains, "and I wasn't there."

"Where were you?"

Harold's randy smirk answers the question before he does. "Where do you *think*?" he says. "I was with Chiyoko, at the house in Omori. I was due back at the base, but I said, to heck with it. I'm just not going in."

Maybe it's his tone, or the fact that I have gotten to know him over these weeks and months, but my confidence is high when I suggest he had done this before.

"*Hell,* yes," he laughs, "and without ever getting into trouble."

"What happened this time?"

"You remember when I told you about my lieutenant—the one who never came down to check on me? Well, he finally did. When I missed that morning roll call, he came looking for me. Of course, I wasn't there, and there was no way Barney could cover for me. Nineteen hours later, when I finally showed up, that lieutenant put me in front of a deck court-martial: five days, bread and water."

Harold accepted the judgment. He had been caught flouting the regulations, fair and square. "So I gave them the old salute," he says, giving me the old salute, "and I took my punishment. With a Marine guard on each side, I marched right up to the brig. I went in, served my time, and at the end of five days..." he frowns, "nobody came to let me out. At the end of six days, nothing! Seven days—still there. You can understand that I was starting to get concerned!"

Indeed I can.

"Well," he breathes pointedly, "believe it or not, the Marines that had walked me into jail were two of the guys I was dealing with on the sly with my black market activities. One of them finally went to the warden's office and said, 'Stevens is supposed to get out!' The warden, who was a grouchy old coot, told him, '*You* get the hell out—and mind your own business!' Thank goodness those Marines took it upon themselves to go up to fleet headquarters to get to the bottom of things. It turned out one of the clerks there had buried my release papers and forgot all about 'em! They had to get the duty officer to dig them out of the files, and finally those Marines hip-hopped me back out of jail. Boy, was that a relief—if it wasn't for those two guys, I might still be there!"

Of course, there is a coda. "Naturally," he says, without a speck of conscience, "I went right back to doing what I had been doing before I got caught..." But, he explains, he did buy himself a little insurance. "I took a bottle of booze to the master-at-arms and told him, from now on, whenever you call the morning roll," he winks, "I'm here!"

It seems Harold could not help living dangerously—even when he was trying to play it safe. For example, he reasoned another way to ensure he wouldn't be late again after a night with Chiyoko was to not leave the navy base in the first place. She was the first thing he ever tried to smuggle *in* through the fence.

"I snuck her in!" he crows. "I had her right there in the coach where I was living—" he bares his teeth in a pained expression, "and that time she and I *both* nearly ended up in the brig! And it wasn't because of some flunky lieutenant," he notes gravely. "It was the commanding officer of the base who nearly caught us!" Harold explains, "The CO was making a survey of all the facilities, and it just so happened that the morning after she stayed over, he was checking out the rail yard! It was just dumb luck that I looked out the window and saw him coming—I nearly had a heart attack! I had about thirty seconds before he knocked on my door. I really had to scramble to hide her."

"Where—"

"I stuffed her under the bunk!" he interjects, and for the high-class geisha, it couldn't have been more undignified than it sounds. "I shoved her underneath and put my footlocker in front of her, and then I buried her under a bedroll. Oh!—and I quickly splashed a little shaving cream on my face to make it look like I was in the process of washing up." He winks, "I didn't want the CO to think I was slacking off in terms of living up to navy standards! Thankfully, when he arrived, he just stood in the doorway and looked things over from there, rather than coming inside to poke around."

I wonder if Harold's commanding officer was surprised to find him living there in the rail yard.

"That subject did come up," Harold concedes. "In fact, he told me, 'I think it would be a good idea if you moved up to the barracks with the rest of the station.' I said, 'Yes sir!'"

"And did you?"

"No sir!" he laughs. "I stayed right where I was. I knew he wouldn't be back to check on me, and besides," Harold acknowledges, "my days there were numbered."

Harold is leafing through an album of photographs from his navy career. The most well-worn pages—sheets with hinges so tender from repeated thumbing that I fear they might break loose at any moment—are pictures of Chiyoko. He points to one of her smiling in a lovely summer dress standing in a garden. "I think here she was just showing off," he opines. The images range from candid, casual moments like this, to artfully posed photos she had taken special for Harold, featuring her in elaborate geisha costuming, heavy facial makeup, and propped out with musical instruments and other tools of her trade—including one where she's wielding a formidable sword-like weapon! Today, as he has throughout the ensuing decades, Harold lingers over these pages, contemplating everything he was giving up by fleeing Japan.

I ask him how he could bear to leave her.

"It was a sad and difficult decision for me," he remarks, "but I really didn't have any other choice. I had to get out of there, and I had to go then because my hitch was up."

Like the great majority of navy sailors, Harold was inducted as part of the Navy Reserve. Because of the war, he had been on active duty since day one, but now he was scheduled to be returned to the States and separated from naval service. He had already managed to

extend his duty in Japan by ninety days to spend a few more precious
months with Chiyoko. "But if I wanted to stay longer than that,"
he explains, "I would have had to commit to going full navy—four
years." He shakes his head, "With all the illegal things I'd been fooling around with, that would have been the end of me. I knew I had
to put as much distance as I could between myself and Japan before
everything hit the fan." He also harks back to the promise he made
to himself during his come-to-Jesus moment aboard a pitching transport amidst a raging typhoon, that he and the navy must part ways,
adding, "Plus, I never wanted to be on an LST again. Ever!"

As he has said, however, the decision to leave wasn't easy. Harold
considers those final months in Japan among the very best of his
life. His happiest memories are of the days and nights he spent there
with Chiyoko. At the time, his bliss was tempered by the fact that he
would soon be saying good-bye to her, certainly for years, probably
forever. Even if he and Chiyoko somehow found a way to reunite in
the future, their lives and situations, and the world itself, would un-
doubtedly be much changed from what it was then. And that made
his heart ache because the way things were at that moment in time
was magical.

"I was there for three months after she gained her freedom,"
Harold tells me, "and during that period, we traveled several times to
the town of Ito, near Atami, on the Izu peninsula. This was a secluded coastal town facing east into Sagami Bay. For us it was a secret
hideaway. We went down there and stayed in a little hotel, and it was
in Ito where we could finally be together in public."

"Why was it okay for you to be seen there?" I ask.

"Anonymity," he replies. "No one knew her, or that she was
a geisha, and there was no military presence there, so no MPs to
bother us..." His words drift into an idyllic contemplation of how
they relished the simple freedom of moving their relationship beyond
clandestine meetings and out from behind closed doors. "We were
free to walk," he recalls happily, "like an ordinary couple, exploring
the shoreline and the forest trails. We walked until our feet were tired
and then we dangled them in the river. In the evenings we strolled
the beach, hand in hand, just talking to one another."

"Is that where you told her that you were leaving?"

He nods. "I did. I explained to her I would be going soon, and why. She understood—of course she was sad, crestfallen, but she didn't want me to get into trouble, especially because of her."

They also talked about Chiyoko's future and what she would do after Harold was gone. "There was one very important thing I wanted her to understand," he stresses. "I said to her, 'You have your freedom now to do whatever you want to do. You're not obligated to anyone any longer. If you decide to continue as a geisha, that's fine. But you *must* stay out of debt. Your continued freedom depends upon it. I've done all that I can do—now that's in your hands.' Then I told her that if she still wanted to work in the geisha house, she should make a booking arrangement with Mama-san and pay her for that service, but Chiyoko must insist upon keeping the lion's share of the money she earned for herself."

"Would Mama-san be open to that?" I wonder. If *I* were Mama-san, I think, such a proposal might seem to me a humbling—bordering on humiliating—reversal of their previous professional arrangement.

"She was a businesswoman," he asserts, "and Chiyoko was a top-notch geisha, in very high demand." Fearing he may have given me an unfair impression of Mama-san, Harold assures me that even when Chiyoko was duty bound to serving the okiya, the woman had treated her well. She was never cruel or unjust (although by Western standards, the act of selling a girl's virginity seems to me the height of both). "I was actually very grateful to that lady," he insists, "for the opportunity she allowed me to earn Chiyoko's release, and for the freedom she gave us to meet before and during that time. She was very lenient. Of course," he considers, "she was also making a goddamn fortune off of me!" But even so, Harold liked Mama-san, and she apparently liked him. "She used to make me vegetable beef soup," he tells me. "She made pretty good soup, that woman, although..." He hastens to add that he regarded her cooking cautiously, "I always checked to make sure it was beef, just in case the neighborhood dog had gone missing. This was Japan, after all!"

Harold and Chiyoko spent every free moment together at the house in Omori or at the hotel in Ito, as gradually, inexorably the weeks and days until his departure counted down. The evening before he was scheduled to board a troopship for the voyage back to America, they met at the little house on the hill for one final romantic encounter. Then Harold walked to the Omori train station for the last time, and Chiyoko accompanied him there, in public, for the first time.

"That night was the only time we'd ever walked those streets together," Harold says, explaining that nature itself provided enough cover so they could be with one another to the last second. "There was a typhoon blowing in from the south, thunder and lightning, and the winds were already so strong they were tearing sheet metal off the buildings and shacks, sending it flying down the streets. We were ducking and dodging debris all the way to the station."

Nevertheless, the greatest risk, Harold tells me, was that someone would see them. By this time, Chiyoko had decided she would remain a geisha—she had taken Harold's advice and come to an agreement with Mama-san that would allow her to continue living and working at the geisha house and still make a good profit. For this reason, as before, it was important she wasn't recognized while in his company. Chiyoko was determined, however, to stay close to him for as long as possible. She had tied up her hair to alter her appearance, and she and Harold walked the back alleys to avoid other people, but they need not have bothered. Thanks to the turbulent weather, the streets were empty.

The moaning wind and bawling sky provided an apt backdrop for what I anticipate was a cinematic farewell. "We finally reached the station," Harold says, "and there was only one other person on the platform, an Australian soldier, who, after gibbering at me for a few minutes, finally got the message and left us alone."

*Perhaps we'll leave that out of the movie*, I think. "And then what happened?"

"We were only there for about ten minutes before the train arrived."

"And then?"

"I kissed her, and I told her, 'I can't promise anything. The world is what it is, but I will probably be back in Japan some time.' Those were my last words to her. I got on the train and the doors closed."

I admit I am disappointed. Considering all that had passed between them, from their improbable romance to his epic sacrifice, such a noncommittal good-bye falls a good distance short of the impassioned declarations I expected to hear. Specifically, I wonder, "Why on earth did you tell her 'probably' rather than assert you would *definitely* be back?"

"Because I wasn't sure!" he says. "I was going home to quit the navy; how the hell was I going to get back to Japan? In those days, you couldn't just visit Japan, the only way was to be stationed there by the military, and I was getting out. I didn't know what was coming next. I just knew I didn't want her waiting around for something that might never happen."

"*Really!?*" I exclaim, still struggling to grasp how, at such a climactic moment, he could pull his emotional punches. "In your heart, didn't you want to shout your affection and plead with her to wait for you?"

His face softens, and he uncaps a well of sentiment, "Her life was starting over. She was out of debt. She could operate independently as a geisha. She was free—and I wanted her to stay that way. Free from debt, but also from any obligation she might have felt towards me. True, I had done something for her that nobody else probably would, or could have done, but she didn't owe me anything. In my heart," Harold says, inhaling deeply, "I wanted her to have a good and happy life."

I finally get it. Such selfless devotion is the truest measure of perfect affection. Harold may insist that he never understood love until he was older and wiser, but even as a young man, he surely and instinctively knew how to give it.

Harold's attention has returned once more to the book of photographs spread across his lap. Now, however, as I look at him, I see a man contemplating the face of the young woman who inspired him to grow beyond the aggression and defiance and self-interest rooted in his genetics. I cannot help wondering, on that bygone and tempestuous night, when they looked into one another's eyes before parting, who owed whom the greater debt?

I have one last, inevitable question about those final minutes on the platform before the train pulled in beside them, but as is his knack, Harold beats me to the punch.

"I told her I loved her," he says, looking up from his album with wet eyes, "or at least, I made her feel it. I can't be certain that I used those words—but I believe I convinced her that I cared for her so deeply, and I would do everything in my power to come back to her. She could take that information and do with it what she wanted. That was the best I could do…"

And with that, Harold closes the book on Japan.

# ALBUM, PART ONE

ROOTS:

Father's funeral                    Mother

Young Harold

Brothers: Harvey -- Lorin
        Howard - Harold

im on MY WAY WEST!

Teenager

Truck driver ID

NAVY:

Mom & new recruit

Seabee

Hawaii

Truck driver, Tinian island

JAPAN:

Yokosuka Naval Base

Sunken ship in Tokyo Bay

Welcome to Japan!

SEABEES

Returning Japanese soldiers at Yokosuka Station

Barney Nozaki

Harold and worker (Imai)

Fleet landing gate

MARIKO:

In her Geisha costuming...

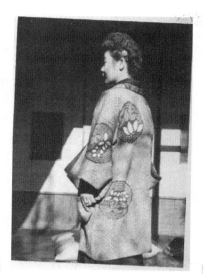

Traditional dress

Western dress!!

With Oki-boy

THIEF:

Coal yard
locomotive

Tunnel entrances adjacent to coal yard

# Part Two
# Debt Owed

千代子

# Chapter 18
# INTERLUDE
# 幕間

M Y WIFE AND I are hosting a dinner party, and Harold is the guest of honor. A few of our close friends are eager to meet the man who freed a geisha. It is late spring, the ice is long gone, and with it any trepidation that Harold will skate to his doom off my stoop. I haven't considered that the evening breeze might affect a similar disaster, but when he arrives Harold is toting an enormous piece of Styrofoam poster board, and glancing out the window, I am alarmed to see him nearly go over the edge as he battles like a windsurfer trying to stay on course. Rushing to his rescue, I am acutely aware that this is the second time a man who has survived a knifing, a typhoon, and two wars has nearly bought the farm on my stairs.

Once I have lowered his sail and we have him battened down in a comfortable chair, it isn't long before my wife and our friends are captivated by a firsthand accounting of Harold's postwar escapades in Japan, including his criminal antics, and subsequent star-crossed love affair with Chiyoko. Of course, he is a masterful storyteller and perfectly at ease entertaining strangers, but beyond that, he's brought the Big Board upon which he has mounted a collage of select photographs from his albums to add some visual spice to his anecdotes. Needless to say, throughout drinks and dinner, Harold owns the room.

It is the question mark at the end of the romance that really hooks the crowd. As he wraps up his tale with the gut-wrenching farewell on a storm-swept railway platform, nobody wants to believe it was the end. What everyone, myself included, is eager to find out is *what happened next?!*

"When I left Japan, I couldn't imagine how or when I would ever see Chiyoko again," Harold tells us, "never mind the fantasy that one day she might be my wife—"

"But, you did…and she was," my own wife interjects. "Chiyoko is the woman you married, right?" she asks hopefully.

Harold surveys the expectant faces gathered around the table. "Nobody was more surprised than me," he says, reaching for his wine goblet, "when only a few months later, I was engaged to be married…" he pauses for effect and raises his glass, "to Shirley."

I am speaking for the entire group when I spontaneously cough out a mouthful of Cabernet to ask, "Who the *hell* is Shirley?!"

Harold is the first to admit that after returning home from Japan he was not acting rationally.

"I was kind of lost," he tells us. "I was drinking more than I normally did. I bounced around from job to job, mostly driving for different trucking outfits. Two of my friends had been discharged from the army around the same time I left the navy, and whenever I had a payday, we would party until the money ran out—and then I'd have to find another job. I was living pretty fast and dangerously…"

That is putting it mildly. Descriptions of his exploits during this period are peppered with disquieting phrases like, "I was dating the wife of a friend…" or, "I had no idea when I beat the guy up that I'd hurt him so badly!" Initially, Harold lived with his mother, but she had strong opinions and hard rules about drinking and catting around, so it wasn't long before he moved out and took a room in a low-rent hotel—someplace where he could indulge himself freely without condemnation or restriction.

Enter Shirley.

"My older brother Harvey and I were having a few beers at a dance hall," Harold explains, "when he spotted her out on the floor. Shirley was somebody I had known since we were kids; we had gone to school together. She was a nice looking girl, and Harvey teased me, saying, 'I think I'll go dance with her.' I told him, 'Not if I get there first!' I scooted right out there and asked her to dance with me. A month later, I bought a ring and asked her to marry me."

Again, it is left to me to tactfully put forth the obvious. "A month! Harold—what were you *thinking*?"

"I wasn't thinking," he quips. "If I'd have thought about it, I wouldn't have done it!" But then he offers up an explanation we can all accept. "I was insane," he declares. "Look, I liked Shirley and we had fun. She was A-okay. She offered me companionship...and I went a little haywire."

"You didn't marry her, though, did you," my wife says. It is a satisfied statement rather than a question, but don't call it a woman's intuition—it isn't just the women at the table who are rooting for true love, and it doesn't take psychic powers to predict Harold's relationship with Shirley was destined to go down in flames.

"It was a terrible ending to a good friendship," he confirms. "Like me, Shirley had a temper, and she proved it one night during a heated argument when she threw a shoe at me—a leather shoe with a really hard heel. She hit me square in the back, and it hurt like hell! So I picked it up and threw it back at her...and then the ring came bouncing off the wall, and I knew the engagement was over. And do you know what?" he proclaims. "I was relieved. I didn't know what I wanted to do, but I realized then that getting married to Shirley wasn't it." Plus, he reasons, if the two of them had stayed together, they would have surely ended up killing one another. "Because when I picked up that shoe and threw it," he stresses, "I was aiming for her!"

Our guests are not satisfied. The prevailing sentiment is still perplexity over how he could propose marriage to another woman only a few months after leaving Chiyoko. According to Harold, it was an act of self-preservation.

"I didn't have the same feelings for Shirley that I did for Chiyoko," he admits, "but there's a wall you put up, and you have to quit thinking about what's on the other side. You're trying to get something out of your system..." he sighs, "but I never did. Chiyoko was always on my mind. I had my pictures of her, and I'd get those out often and I would study them. When I dated other women during this time, I found myself making comparisons. I thought about Chiyoko, and how great it would be if she was here instead. I didn't want to look down on American girls, but..." Harold considers his words, adding generously, "for me, *nobody* else could have measured up. I just didn't see a way for me to get back to Japan to be with her. So I tried to block her out. I don't mean any disrespect toward Shirley when I say that she was a port in a storm I was weathering."

It occurs to me that there was something else missing from Harold's life, another positive influence that had been a constant throughout his transition from a knockabout boyhood. After he returned to Duluth, Harold was acting out his melancholy and his frustration in a number of imprudent, self-destructive ways. In fact, he was reverting to conduct that typified the lives of his boorish siblings: undisciplined behavior, impulsive carousing, and entering into relationships and marriages of convenience (or, in the case of every one of his brothers, obligation after a pregnancy). For the members of Harold's family, this was the unfortunate but inevitable path, one it seemed he was also destined to follow—until he had joined the navy.

"It's too bad," I observe, "that you'd had to leave military service. It seems to me that had been a good thing for you." I'm thinking of the structure the navy imposed, the daily regimen of expectations and consequences, not to mention the *esprit de corps* he had found while serving. Without that sense of pride and a framework of strict regulations to check his natural tendencies, Harold was spinning out of control.

He agrees with me. In the same way Chiyoko had made him a better man, he thinks the navy helped him to focus his thinking and measure his decisions and behaviors. "Back here, I was directionless, self-centered, and I found myself regularly getting rowdy and drinking too much," he reflects, "and I rarely did that in Japan."

"If it was Chiyoko and the military that had kept you out of trouble," I reason, "it seems like you needed to get back to one, or the other—or both."

Harold smiles knowingly, "Funny you should say that..."

It was a chance meeting during a blind date that turned the tide. The girl had failed to ignite even a spark of interest in him, and so

Harold had determined to skip out on her in the middle of dinner. He wasn't a complete cad—he had paid the restaurant bill before ducking into the kitchen, intending to slip out the back door.

"There was a guy there washing dishes," he says, "and I knew him. He was an officer who worked at the army recruiting station in the post office. I kidded him that cleaning up the kitchen in a Chinese restaurant was pretty glamorous duty for a 1st lieutenant. He explained that the owner was a friend of his, and he was lending him a hand. Speaking of favors, I joked about what the army could offer me in terms of postings in Japan. He told me to drop by the office and we could talk about it."

The next day Harold went to see him.

"After eleven months in the States," he explains, "I decided I had to get back to Japan. My thinking was that if I enlisted as an army soldier I could start over with a clean slate—I hoped my navy history would be filed under 'Sailor Harold Stevens' and remain locked away in some forgotten cabinet."

The recruiter made Harold an intriguing proposition. "First, he told me he could get me in as a regular army corporal—that was equal rank and pay to the 'fireman first class' designation I had when I left the navy. I said to him, 'If you can get me to Japan, I'm all for it.' The recruiter said, 'Well then, what about becoming a paratrooper?' Although he couldn't make me any promises about my ultimate station, he told me the 11th Airborne Division was based on Hokkaido, the north island of Japan. I thought about it for a day—"

"What the heck was there to think about?" I interrupt.

"I had a pretty good job by then," he says, feigning indignation. "I had been hired by the Western Electric Company to solder wires onto the backs of telephone switching panels—something I was damn good at, by the way! Plus I was working the swing shift, which meant I could still make it to the bar before closing time!"

This may all be true, but he is fooling himself if he thinks anybody here believes that making switchboards—or last call—was going to keep him from moving a step closer to the girl imprinted on his mind and in his heart. "That boss of mine at Western Electric cried on my shoulder when I told him I was quitting to join the army," Harold grins.

As we serve dessert, Harold tosses out this morsel: "I wrote to Chiyoko shortly before I enlisted." Suddenly everyone at the table is hungry for more than pie. "I told her my plan was to join the army with hopes of returning to Japan. It wasn't specifically a love letter, but I wanted to let her know that I still cared about her, and I was trying to get back to her."

"Had you written to her before that?" I ask.

"I had sent her one other letter."

"Did she write back?"

Harold nods. "I only got one letter from her during all this time, and I was surprised to get that. Although she had gotten pretty good at speaking English, she didn't know the first thing about writing it. But somebody there must have helped her because I did get that letter. It was composed in broken English, basically thanking me for the things I'd done for her and for our time together." To appease the romantics, he adds, "The word love wasn't used, but there were sentimental things written,"—though he does not elaborate. "I think we cared for each other, but we were both afraid of investing too much of ourselves in something so indefinite. Who knew if I would be able to get back there?"

My wife asks whether he ever considered trying to bring Chiyoko over here.

He shakes his head, "That wasn't possible. We'd have had to have been married before I left the navy, and the military wasn't allowing marriages between servicemen and Japanese nationals at that time."

"Your only option was joining the army," I remark.

"That's *why* I joined the army," he confirms. "I was going to try like hell to return to Japan, and to her. I was playing a long shot, but it was the whole reason I enlisted."

Harold explains to us that since he was technically re-enlisting, he did not have to repeat the whole boot camp ordeal. Instead, the army sent him to a three-week refresher course at Fort Ord in California, and it was there that his plan to go Airborne failed to take off.

"I fell in with some older soldiers who were also re-enlisting," he tells us, "and when I told them I was signing up to become a paratrooper, they sized me up and said, 'Well, we thought you looked kind of dopey when you first walked in—now we know for sure!

Smart people have enough brains to know you don't jump out of a perfectly good airplane!'"

Going all the way back to his time with the Seabees, Harold had looked up to more seasoned GIs. He respected their experience, and their opinions carried a lot of weight with him. The old-timers at Fort Ord may have been having a little fun, but their barbs got him thinking. What good would it do Chiyoko or himself if he made it to Japan, only to end up cratered in some field, drowned in a lake, or shot out of the sky while floating helplessly under a canopy? "I went to personnel and told them, 'I don't think I'll go Airborne after all.' The officer there asked me whether I wanted to go to OCS, and I didn't even know what that was. He said, 'It's Officer Candidate School. You're a corporal now. If you pass a test, we'll make you a sergeant and then you can go to OCS and make 2nd lieutenant.' I thought, *You're going to promote me to sergeant just to go to school?* 'Sign me up!' So I went back, proud as a peacock, to those older guys and announced, 'Airborne is out. I'm going to OCS!'—and they just rocked with laughter. They told me, 'Boy, you *are* crazy! Don't you know that all the crap rains down on the 2nd lieutenant? That's the bottom rung on the ladder!' By the time they were done talking, I had firmly determined I would not be attending OCS. But now I didn't know what to do."

Because Harold's navy service record showed he'd had railroad experience (apparently the army and navy *did* share files!) the decision was made for him. "I ended up at 'diesel-electric locomotive maintenance school' at Fort Eustis, Virginia, for sixteen weeks. I graduated with full honors from there as a certified locomotive mechanic, but," he chuckles, "in accordance with standard military efficiency, the army would spend the next few years bouncing me around doing every damn job imaginable with trains, except that!"

Furthermore, he lets us know that anyone at our dinner party who has been waiting to hear about how the army shipped him off to be reunited with Chiyoko, will be going home disappointed.

"My duty station was not Japan," Harold says caustically. "It was Korea."

# Chapter 19
# RETURN

帰り

JOCKEYING FOR TERRITORY and influence at the end of the Second World War, the Great Powers carved up whole nations like Cornish hens. In Korea, the two hungriest eaters split the carcass down the middle; each grabbed an end of the wishbone and pulled. Everything north of the 38th parallel went to the Soviets, while the U.S. occupied the South. In 1948, the same year Harold enlisted in the army, the two halves proclaimed separate governments, each in the style of its sponsor. The northern Democratic People's Republic of Korea was none of those things, ruled by the opportunistic and repressive Kim Il-sung as a totalitarian communist state. Meanwhile, to the south, the fledgling Republic of Korea was being nursed along by the United States as a beachhead for Western-style constitutional government.

At the time, however, the South was a long way from becoming a gleaming city on a hill. Even before the war it had endured centuries of turmoil, mainly due to the expansionist ambitions of its neighbors. Throughout the first half of the twentieth century, Japan had occupied the troubled peninsula and roughly abused the Korean people—a subjugation that climaxed during the Second World War when Korean men were conscripted as laborers or into the Japanese military, and Korean women were forced to "provide comfort" to the troops. By the time Harold arrived as part of the American occupation, the fate of the South Koreans was no less uncertain as this haggard, impoverished population grappled with political instability and economic chaos. Put simply, the country was a mess.

"It was the stinkin'est place I had ever been in my life," Harold says frostily, and he is not just speaking metaphorically. "Every time I left Korea, it took me a week to get the smell out of my clothes."

He and I are back in his apartment. June sunlight is streaming gloriously through the broad picture windows, blanketing the recliner where he sits soaking it up like a cat. Today's ensemble from the Stevens Collection is khaki pants paired with a short sleeve, lilac and periwinkle (plaid) shirt. Although he may be dressed for the summer solstice, Harold's tone is pure ice.

"When I first arrived there, my ship dropped anchor at Inchon," he mutters sourly, "and I'll never forget the stench of that place!" his nose wrinkles disparagingly. "From my first whiff of it, I did not have any liking for Korea."

The smell was a pungent blend of the sulphurous coal burned in hearths and industry, human manure used to fertilize rice paddies, and fermenting kimchi—the cabbage-based, cradle-to-grave staple of the Korean diet. But it was not just the odor that made Harold want to keep this country at arm's length. The beggared plight of the Korean people had made them notorious opportunists. "We were warned," he says, "'When you go ashore, whatever you do, don't let go of your bag. Sit on it! If you don't, someone will snatch it and run.' And they were right! God, how those Koreans could steal!"

After landing at Inchon, he witnessed firsthand the desperation and ingenuity of the natives as exemplified by the curious spectacle of five people simultaneously working a single shovel: two on each side manipulating the handle via rope tethers, while one in back steered the spade. "This was a form of public works," he explains. "The government was giving people a way to earn a little money. If you worked, you got paid, but there were more workers than jobs." And, apparently, more workers than shovels.

From Inchon, Harold was handled more like a package than a passenger, as he was abruptly shipped out on a train with no seats or windows to a receiving and distribution camp. The toilet on the train was a hole in the carriage floor that emptied onto the tracks. Once he arrived, he found the camp itself was barely a step up—just a complex of crude wooden buildings in a muddy field. "Those barracks were rough," Harold says. "The beds were bare springs! The Koreans had scavanged every bit of fabric off the mattresses!" He spent three days there doing manual labor (laying a cement footpath amidst the clawing mud) before his unit mercifully picked him up and delivered him to Seoul.

"I was assigned to the 3rd Military Railway Service," he tells me. "They staffed all the trains in Korea, from Pusan in the south all the way up to the 38th parallel. Military railcars were hitched to the ends of the regular trains," he explains, "and those carriages had army conductors. That was my job, starting out."

But not for long. When a small, southern unit suddenly found itself short an auto mechanic, the higher-ups extrapolated that a guy schooled in locomotive maintenance ought to be able to keep four wheels turning, "So they detailed me down to Taegu to maintain a motor pool: one big truck, one little truck, and a jeep," he mutters, "—some pool!"

Eventually, he was recalled to Seoul and put to work again on the trains. Back and forth—that is a fair description of Harold's entire yearlong deployment in Korea. "Mainly, I was a short-run conductor," he says. "I would ride down to Pusan, spend the night there, and then take the morning train back to Seoul. That left the rest of the day with nothing for me to do." This freedom afforded Harold an opportunity to observe a defining moment in the country's history. "I got to take in the festivities when General MacArthur came to South Korea and they declared their independence. There were speeches, parades, and flags flying throughout the capital."

By 1949, in the wake of South Korean autonomy and an American assessment that occupying the country no longer served any strategic purpose, the U.S. began pulling out its troops. For Harold, the stars finally began to align. Whenever he had visited Pusan on the southeast coast he had stared pensively across the Korean Strait toward Japan, a mere 120 miles away. Now, with the order to evacuate, came the best possible news: "They told me they were sending me to the 1st Cavalry Division in Tokyo! Well," he grins, "I thought, *things are looking up!*"

The landlady at the little house in Omori regarded the stranger warily. She had answered the knock on the door to find a very official-looking American soldier decked out in a class-A army uniform on her stoop. Visits from U.S. military personnel were infrequent, and even more rarely a good thing. She listened guardedly as the soldier attempted to communicate with her, but he was not making things any easier by speaking just about the worst Japanese imaginable—a tentative jumble of Japlish intermingled with a few harsh coughs of something else. But, as he spoke, something about him aroused in her a sense of familiarity—and finally recognition. And she nearly doubled over with laughter.

"I'd been assigned to the combat engineers of the 1st Cav," Harold explains, "stationed on the north side of Tokyo. As soon as I could get a pass, I went to the house in Omori where Chiyoko and I used to meet."

By this time, Harold had no idea whether Chiyoko was still living and working at the okiya, or, for that matter, if she was even in Tokyo. If she was employed at the geisha house, he could not just show up, for all the old reasons. During his navy days, she had taught him how to ask for her so expertly on the telephone that the other girls at the okiya had no idea they were speaking to an American, but now, two years out of practice with the language, a garbled phone call would be an exercise in futility (and might start tongues wagging). In desperation, he had come to their former meeting place, looking for information or advice about how to track her down. But first he had to figure out how to converse with the woman there.

"My communication skills had gotten a bit muddled," he acknowledges. "My Japanese was rusty, and in Korea I'd picked up some of that language working on the trains. Korean has similarities to Japanese but there's a lot of this," he says, startling me by clearing his throat as if there's a fish bone lodged in his windpipe. "It threw me off in terms of my Japanese," he notes. "Between that and the fact that she had only ever seen me in a navy uniform, when the lady who owned the house answered the door, she had no idea who I was or what I wanted. But I kept mentioning Chiyoko's name, and it finally dawned on her that it was me, and she broke into a big grin and started laughing."

I ask him what it was that she found so humorous.

"She couldn't get over the fact that I had swapped uniforms," he remarks. Apparently, for his former landlady, the sight of a sailor in army issue was as novel and amusing as a chicken's head on a cow's body. Nevertheless, she happily ushered him inside and set the tea kettle to boil.

"She didn't know if Chiyoko was still at the geisha house or not, but she offered to make a call there to find out. Lo and behold," Harold beams, "she quickly handed me the phone, and guess who was on the line?"

Harold recounts this long-awaited reconnection with Chiyoko: "I explained to her where I was and asked whether she might be able to meet me there—"

"Wait a minute!" I interrupt. "You hadn't spoken to her in two years! What was it like, just to hear her voice again?"

He smiles thoughtfully. "She sounded—I don't know…excited, and I think there was also some nervousness. But I'll tell you what," he emphasizes, "she said she would come, and I don't think it was even thirty minutes from the time I hung up the phone until she knocked on the door!" He reminds me that, in that time, she'd had to cover a distance of twelve blocks, and all uphill. Clearly enthusiasm had trumped nerves.

"When she came through the door, I stood up. Just as with the landlady, my army uniform was disorienting for her. She immediately hesitated, with an uncertain, puzzled look…but once she saw my face, and this head of hair," he says, pointing to his trademark mop, "she recognized me instantly. She came to me, and I hugged her and gave her a kiss on the cheek, and then she stepped back and looked me up and down."

Surveying him appraisingly, Chiyoko's first words to Harold since the blustery night two years prior, when train doors and the opportunity to grow their relationship had closed between them, are something he has never forgotten: "You went away a boy," she said, *"and you've come back a man."*

Over the course of the next few hours the couple talked, sipped tea, and got reacquainted. It was a joyful, if measured, reunion for them both. They did not launch themselves into one another's arms. There was no heated kissing or impulsive tangling of bodies, no outpouring of souls or impassioned declarations. The conversation was more or less innocuous chitchat, much as it had been when they first began meeting in this same house, years earlier.

"I asked her how she had been," Harold says, "how she was getting along at the geisha house, and she asked me similar things. It was a lot of talking and a lot of giggling. Just…friendship."

"Friendship?!" I am nonplussed. After all they'd shared and meant to one another, is he really telling me that he and Chiyoko were essentially back to square one? Unlike their early encounters, Oki-boy was not present, but in his place they now shared the room with a rather imposing elephant. How long, I wonder, could they dance around it, engaged in friendly patter, before somebody tripped over those formidable tusks? "What about your *relationship*?" I press. "You must have discussed it! Where did you both stand?"

"We didn't really get into it at that meeting," he answers. "It wasn't the time for commitments or confessions. Obviously, she had continued working as a geisha for the past few years, but whether or not she had a boyfriend, then or now, I didn't ask, and she didn't volunteer. She was a very desirable woman, and I had placed no demands on her, so it was not at all beyond the realm of possibility…"

Noting my dissatisfaction, he exclaims, "For chrissake, I had gotten engaged! Who the hell was I to judge or question her about any of that?"

"But you wanted to be with her," I insist.

"Of course!" he remarks. "Absolutely. But the practicalities of that were still very uncertain. I was stationed in Tokyo, but some distance from her—clear across the city—and for how long, who knew? I didn't even know my own schedule at that point. No," he declares stoically, "I had to find a way to make my situation there more secure, to be more accessible to her, before I could even consider asking her to be with me. And I think she was feeling the same way."

With Harold's return to Chiyoko, his "better man" had resurfaced. Rather than being ruled by a preoccupation with short-term satisfaction, he was determined to make a relationship that would work for them both. In the meantime, Harold was content with the fact that, at long last and against all odds, he had managed to see this beautiful and beloved girl again, and enjoy her company. Whether they would rekindle their love affair, or if she even wanted that, time would tell. But there was cause for optimism. "All I knew," he twinkles, "was that she had practically run up the hill to that house to see me again."

# Chapter 20
# TAURA

タウラ

AFTER GENERAL MACARTHUR famously declared to the people of the Philippines, "I shall return," it took him two and a half years to fulfill that oath. Harold's more measured declaration about Japan ("I will probably be back...") took only two. MacArthur relied upon the full weight of the American military to help him get reestablished. Harold had Barney Nozaki, but that was enough.

"One of the first things I did when I got back to Japan was to head down to Yokosuka to see if Barney was still there. And sure enough," Harold declares gleefully, "he was!"

Even though Barney was still in the same place, doing the same job, his life had changed. Most significantly, Barney was now married. In fact, his engagement had been announced even before Harold quit the navy. "When Barney found out I was leaving Japan," Harold remembers, "he was very sorry that I wouldn't be able to attend his wedding. It was a big disappointment for us both." Nevertheless, before his departure, Harold had met Barney's intended bride, and he'd given her the thumbs-up.

"Her name was Flora," he tells me, which I find surprising—like Barney, this sounds more like someone born to West Duluth rather than Tokyo. Nevertheless, Harold informs me, Flora was a native, upper-class Japanese girl, and, by the way, very much his type. "Frankly," he confides with an impish squint, "if it hadn't been for Chiyoko, I might have run her husband off! She was a very attractive, wonderful lady, and I liked her *very* much." He grins, "She had a special nickname for me. Flora called me 'Bomb-san.' Mr. Bomb!" He explains (unnecessarily), "I had a short temper when I was young. It didn't take much to set me off, and I would explode! So I was always Bomb-san to her; that's how she addressed me my whole life. Whenever I called on the phone or knocked on their door, she would greet me, '*Hello, Bomb-san!*'" He muses, "Maybe I'd flown off the handle one too many times in her presence, but for whatever reason, with her, that name for me just stuck."

I am thinking he'd also dropped quite a shell on his pal. "What was Barney's reaction when you suddenly reappeared after being gone for several years?"

"Shock!" he grins, "but he was very happy to see me, and in no time at all it was just like old times." This was undeniably true, if for no other reason than, once again, Harold needed Barney's help wooing Chiyoko.

"I explained to him that I was working toward getting back together with her, and I asked whether he might be able to help me find a convenient place where she and I could meet regularly—some place away from Omori, where we wouldn't have to worry about being seen together." Harold smiles broadly, "It so happened that Barney knew an elderly couple who lived just down the road from him in Taura, a neighborhood just outside the naval base. This couple had a larger, very nice house, and Barney said he would talk to the woman there about renting me a room. Barney knew I would respect a Japanese home; that's something a lot of American GIs *didn't* do, but he would put in a good word for me."

Meanwhile, Harold concentrated on freeing himself from the uncertainties of the 1st Cavalry Division. "I was assigned to a combat engineering outfit, and I wanted nothing to do with that," he says, only partly in jest. "Those guys fight the wars!" The more immediate concerns, however, were that his duties had him working nights and stationed in the far northern reaches of Tokyo—both of which threatened to drain voltage from his plan to jump-start a relationship with Chiyoko. To keep the spark alive, he would need to make changes, and for the first time ever, Harold was grateful for time spent in Korea.

"Based on my Korean experience," he explains, "I requested a transfer to the Military Railway Service, located in Yokohama—midway between Omori and Taura. Normally, it takes some time to process a transfer request," he boasts, "but with my locomotive schooling and work history, they pushed it through, and in just a few days I had orders to report to Yokohama as a military railway conductor—one of my luckiest days ever."

"You were so much closer to Chiyoko now," I observe.

"That too!" he remarks, because there was an even more pressing reason he was happy to be making a quick exit from the 1st Cav. "I'd spent the previous night replacing a huge sprocket on a piece of heavy tracked equipment. It was a big job; I had to use all kinds of gear pullers to get the thing off, but I finally got it undone and got the new one installed. I tightened every bolt on there until it was really secure—and then I stepped back, surveyed my work, and I thought, *uh-oh*... It dawned on me that I had put the damn thing on backwards!"

I ask him how he knew.

"It was clear to me the minute I finished. I could see it was out of alignment, and I realized I had it reversed. The sergeant in charge was going to murder me."

"What did you tell him?"

"*Tell him?!*" he leans forward with a frown of puzzled incredulity. "What part of 'murder me' don't you understand?" He snorts, "I didn't say a word to anyone! Thankfully, that morning I got my orders to report to Yokohama, and I was out of there like a shot. If he's still alive, that sergeant is probably still carrying a rope and looking to string me up!"

A day or two after their meeting at Yokosuka, Barney called to tell Harold the couple in Taura was amenable to renting him a room. Harold had Chiyoko's phone number, but he'd been reluctant to contact her again until he had something positive to report. Now that the pieces were falling into place, the time had come to let her in on the plan.

"I told her I had transferred to Yokohama, and I was now working for the railroad. It would be easy for me to meet with her, and I also had a line on a place where that could happen. I still wasn't sure where she stood in terms of her desires toward me, but I was ready to find out. I told her I wanted to start seeing her again, to see if there was anything between us—"

"I hope you didn't say it like that!" I interject.

"I'm not sure how I said it," he remarks dolefully. "I had a hard time expressing myself. It was that old fear of rejection and those feelings of inadequacy. I had never quit loving this girl, and the emotions were in here," he taps his heart, "but it was difficult to make them come out here," he says, drumming his lips. "Somehow I managed to spit out the fact that I wanted to see her again—and, I hoped, on a regular basis."

Despite his stammering insecurities, Chiyoko readily consented to resuming their courtship.

"I think when I showed up out of the blue, it was a shock for her," Harold reflects. "I had no claim on her, and there had been no guarantee I would ever return—now suddenly, here I was! So she'd been dealing with all that. Thank god," he sighs relief, "she'd decided she wanted to be with me too."

Harold never asked Chiyoko whether she'd had other suitors during his absence, but his gut says no. I wonder if the reason is because he believes she was holding out for his return. "Do you think she'd been waiting for you," I ask, "or had she given up?"

"Neither," he decides. "I think she had been doing just what I had hoped—enjoying her life." As proof, he points out how successful she had been at marketing herself as an independent geisha. "In fact, she showed me a very complimentary letter she'd received from the Inspector General, thanking her for entertaining the brass at Eighth Army headquarters. You don't get a job like that," he remarks, eyebrows ascending, "or a note of commendation from the top man unless you're the cream of the crop."

In terms of their relationship, Harold believes Chiyoko had taken his parting entreaties about that to heart as well. After he left Japan, she hadn't been paralyzed by loss or fixated on perceived obligations. Instead, she had boxed up her thoughts and feelings for him and tucked them away in her mind. Whether that box contained only treasured memories, or something deeper and worth revisiting, is something Chiyoko had been purposefully ignoring in his absence. Now that Harold was back and his intentions were clear, the lid was off the box.

All they needed now was the love nest.

"I asked her to come down to Taura," Harold tells me, "which was just a small burg on the main line. We made arrangements to meet there, to visit the home where Barney's neighbors had a room available." Their tour revealed the accommodations to be lovely and spacious, and the landlords were a novel pair. "Unique characters," Harold observes. "The husband trapped and sold songbirds! He showed us how he used a branch with some kind of stickum on the end; he pushed that into the bushes, and when the birds perched on it, they'd get stuck. Then he would put them in little cages he made. The woman was also friendly, but she wore the pants. We made our arrangements with *her* to have the room available for us whenever we could meet."

And so they did. In his new posting, Harold typically got a day off from working on the trains after each two-day run. As an independent geisha, Chiyoko controlled her own schedule, so there were ample opportunities for them to rendezvous. "She and I got together there whenever we could arrange it. We would meet in Taura," Harold says, adding dreamily, "and spend the night."

Mr. Nosy takes the bait. "So, was it in Taura that you and Chiyoko became intimate again?" I ask.

"Yeah," he says, demurely, not because he is shy or embarrassed by the question, but because, once again, Harold is time traveling. "I remember walking with her," he recalls happily, "exploring the neighborhood, and looking at all the beautiful flowers in the yard around the house…just soaking up the beauty of it, the beauty of her, and the pure and simple joy of being with her. As evening came on, we went inside to our room, where the lady who owned the house had made up our sleeping arrangements, and it wasn't two futons. It was one big mattress…"

"It must have been a dream come true, falling into bed with her again, after all that time."

"Honestly," he nods, "I think it was the happiest moment of my life..." he pauses, then reiterates earnestly, "the most wonderfully satisfying moment of my life. And I believe she was as happy as I was. I even think the word 'love' was used once or twice..." he smiles raptly, "or three or four times."

"You were finally mature enough to say that word, and understand what it meant?"

"I was," he nods. "I did."

"Did she say it too?"

"Yes."

Unable to resist scripting the scene, I ask, "Did she also say to you, *I knew you would come back!*?"

"She never said that, but I could tell from the first time we made love again, it was what she had hoped for. She was as hungry for me as I was for her. I think she had known that we'd had something special together, but like me, she'd tried to block it out of her mind. Now that we were together again, her memory came back. She could let it come back."

As a military railway conductor, Harold staffed multiday trips north from Tokyo to Sapporo, as well as the line running southwest from Yokohama all the way to the city of Fukuoka on the south island. One of his regular stops on this southern route fascinates me. It was a significant industrial port during the war, sheltered behind a warren of channel islands that had made it nearly impregnable by sea, but an unmistakable target from the air. Hiroshima.

"I used to buy oysters in that town."

I admit, this is the last thing I expect to hear about a city that, just a few years earlier, had been a literal hotbed of radioactivity. But now that he's brought it up, "Were they safe to eat?!"

He shrugs, "Well, I'm still above ground." In fact, he explains, when he visited Hiroshima, the oyster business was thriving, and radiation never crossed his mind. "My train would make a stop there going each way, and on the return trip I'd always bring back a quart of those fresh oysters, fished right out of the bay, so we could fry them up." His eyes narrow, "Unfortunately, the woman who owned the house in Taura also loved them, and once I got those oysters home, that container never seemed to produce as many as it should have. I think the old lady was sneaking them raw!"

But my interest in Hiroshima extends beyond shellfish. Today, it is once again a thriving and verdant city, with almost no visible scars (other than those purposefully preserved for posterity) of its tragic history as the first casualty of the Atomic Age. But Harold was there only a few years after the A-bomb detonated. I'm wondering whether the landscape he witnessed then was one of rebuilding, or was it still post-apocalyptic. According to him, it was predominately the latter.

"Wide open spaces. No trees, no buildings…" he planes both hands outward smoothly, "nothing. You could see just a couple of the concrete buildings that had withstood the blast, but other than that, it was flattened."

I ask him whether he ever walked among the ruins.

"No, I was only there for fifteen minutes at a time while the train was stopped, so I never left the area around the station—where, by the way, there was some reconstruction going on. But if you got in the right position on the platform, you could look out across the whole damn area, and all I could see was destruction. It had to be just a horrible thing for those people."

I note his use of the then-present tense. Even going on five years after the bomb had dropped, the inhabitants of Hiroshima were still suffering.

"I could see people who were scavenging and moving about," he says quietly, "picking up whatever they could find in the rubble. And I saw people who had been badly hurt, but not killed—there were even some who were strong enough to be doing jobs in and around the train station. A huge source of injury had been the burning, and I witnessed many people with bandages on, including those with wrappings over their eyes, who had to rely on someone else to help them along. It was a pitiful thing."

Harold felt a great empathy for these A-bomb survivors, collectively known as the *Hibakusha* in Japan. All the conflicted emotions he had once held—for Pearl Harbor, for the Japanese people, for the war itself, including the thrill of relief he'd experienced at Tinian when news that this very bomb piloted from that very island had spared him from a prolonged and perilous siege—those feelings were long gone.

"We'd been fighting a war," he breathes, "planning an invasion, and a lot of people will argue we had to do this, to prevent that. But once we were past the fighting, you couldn't help but pity what we caused with that bomb. I never talked to anyone in Hiroshima about it—I didn't feel it was my place to do that. And they never showed me any anger because I was an American, although I'm sure there were many who had those feelings. On the other hand..." He pauses to reflect on an aspect of that culture we have touched on before, resignation that many things—including these horrors—are beyond a person's control. "The Japanese have that perspective about fate," Harold muses. "If the first atom bomb hadn't dropped on Hiroshima, it would have dropped somewhere else. But it had happened there, and there was nothing the people of Hiroshima could have done to change that. Many simply accepted that they were the ones who'd had to endure this terrible thing that was the end to war."

It was the perfect setup for Harold and Chiyoko. On the arranged days, they would meet at the station in Taura and walk together to their rooming house, passing Barney and Flora's home along the way. The Nozakis had an upstairs apartment with an observation area and windows that would slide open, and if Flora happened to be there and saw them walking, she would call out and wave to them. It was a luxury just to be recognized together in public.

Taura was a haven—a place where their separate lives fell away and, for a day or two, they could live a combined existence, almost like a married couple. By this time, Chiyoko's English was nearly perfect, and they reveled in the day-to-day domesticity of routine conversation and simple tasks like cooking and gardening. Harold made pot roast. They kept pet rabbits. At Christmastime they hosted a boisterous, sake-soaked holiday shindig for Harold's old navy friends. When they could string together more than a few days to be with one another, they would escape to their favorite getaway at the secluded beachside hotel in Ito, or climb up into the mountains where they strolled the lush hillsides gathering greens for their rabbits. Wherever they were, the act of being together, whether making love or just walking, had taken on a familiarity and permanence that transcended mere courting.

In fact, Harold admits, "I had pretty much decided I was going to marry this girl," he sighs, "and then the damn Korean War started, and ruined everything."

# Chapter 21
# WAR

# 戦争

IT WAS AN unmitigated disaster, and nobody saw it coming. The United States military had spent the previous year withdrawing from the fledgling democracy of South Korea, so in June, 1950, when eight divisions of the North Korean army suddenly swept across the border, the only resistance they encountered was woefully ill-equipped southern troops and a relative handful of American advisors. The northern forces, armed with Soviet-made tanks and artillery, rolled down the peninsula like snowplows—burying any opposition with overwhelming might and numbers. It took them just three days to capture Seoul.

The sad truth is that virtually none of the world's governments rushed to the rescue of South Korea purely out of concern for that country's sovereignty or its people—but wars are rarely so simple. Despite the North's justification of "Fatherland Liberation," the invasion was a brazen act of communist expansion, and in those early days of Cold War, the broader implications are what provoked a United Nations resolution to swiftly counter with force. Fresh on the heels of having turned out the lights, the U.S. scrambled to return troops to Korea. The 24th Infantry Division, garrisoned in Japan, was first to arrive, and it was practically a suicide mission. Their orders were to muster whatever resistance they could to slow the

North's advance and buy time while more U.N. troops were rushed to the country. Korea was a shit-storm all right, and Harold was in the thick of it.

"I was on a thirty-day leave when the war broke out," he informs me. "Chiyoko and I were down in Ito, and when I turned on the radio one morning, it was blaring the news: *The North Koreans have crossed the 38th parallel and are advancing on Seoul. All American military personnel are ordered to immediately report back to their units.* I said, well…(he pantomimes turning down the volume) I didn't hear that! I still had ten days left on my leave; I'd be damned if I was going in now!"

The man's brass never ceases to amaze me. "You just chose to ignore the start of the Korean War?" I stare.

"*Darn* right!" he stresses. "Because I knew exactly what it meant for me. My commanding officer in Japan was a guy I'd also served under in Korea, and I knew he would be looking to send anyone with previous Korean experience over on the first boat. I *knew* what he would tell me when he saw me—and I was right! When I finally got back from leave, the sentry on the gate said to me, 'The Old Man wants to see you!' And someone must have tipped him off because as I got closer to the barracks, I could hear the tippy-tap of shoes following behind me. Before I could even throw my things on the bunk, the CO stepped inside and said, 'Corporal Stevens, don't bother unpacking your bag. I have a little trip planned for you…' In no time, I was on a ship—a goddamn LST!—headed for Korea."

"Were you at least able to get word to Chiyoko?" I ask.

He shakes his head. "Not before I left. As soon as I could, I sent her a letter and let her know I was in Korea. But when we'd parted, I'd told her that was almost certainly where I was headed. Of course she was sad—although this time when I left, she was more confident that, as long as I didn't get myself killed, I'd be back. We had gotten pretty serious…but fate has a way of stepping in."

Fate indeed. Harold was attached to Eighth Army headquarters as part of a transportation unit. He explains to me that the railroads in Korea, built by the Japanese during their occupation, were a vastly safer and superior form of travel compared to the country's confused network of narrow, muddy tracks that passed as roads. Thanks to the job he'd had with the Military Railway Service, I assume Harold was a shoo-in for being detailed to those trains. Not so, he tells me. The army made him a truck driver. Of course, there's more to this than meets the eye.

Shortly before the war broke out, Harold had been removed from his posting as a railroad conductor. It was the result of an unfortunate altercation with a drunk and disorderly passenger who repeatedly disrupted an entire sleeper car. After a protracted struggle to quietly remove the offender, Harold saw red when the passenger called him a "son of a bitch," which he took as a personal affront to his mother. Bomb-san took over, and he broke the passenger's jaw in two places. A special court-martial had severely docked Harold's pay (he had narrowly escaped prison) and he was reassigned as a driver for a counterintelligence outfit. When his boots hit Korean soil, truck driving was the natural, unfortunate segue.

Dispatched by train to help support the 24th Infantry Division in Taejon, Harold quickly discovered, at that moment in time, there was probably no worse place on the planet to be a truck driver. He arrived in Taejon to find the army in full rout.

"That was the front line," he exclaims, "and it was collapsing. The 24th Infantry was the only division we had there, and they were fighting a losing battle. They were being overrun!"

"My god…what did you do?"

"We were retreating, so I beat it out of there; I turned right around and took the same train back out. And it was a good thing I did because I had been on the last train into Taejon, and it was also the last train to make it out!" He explains, "The city was under attack from three directions and the 24th had evacuation convoys moving out, but they had to go up and over a mountain where there was a tunnel for both the train and the road. Shortly after my train went through, the North Koreans knocked out a two-and-a-half-ton truck and an ambulance and blocked the tunnels. The convoy couldn't make it out," he says soberly. "Those men had to take to the mountains on foot."

The Americans regrouped seventy miles southeast at Taegu, where the Eighth Army was headquartered. Harold has vivid memories of watching survivors from the Battle of Taejon straggle in out of the hills—days later—more dead than alive.

"They were stumbling into camp with no weapons and their clothing in rags. Some didn't even have shoes…it was a pitiful thing to see. I met one guy who had carried a wounded friend on his back some great distance. When he finally arrived, he discovered his buddy had died while he was carrying him."

At least these sacrifices were not in vain. While the 24th Infantry fought desperately to stall the enemy at Taejon, other American divisions were landing at the southern port of Pusan and establishing a fortified line along the Naktong River, creating the so-called Pusan Perimeter around that city and Taegu. It was just in time. After the fall of Taejon, the North Koreans controlled all but a tiny toe of the peninsula, but that zone now contained a stalwart concentration of fresh U.N. troops. Despite vicious and repeated assaults on the Perimeter, the invasion was halted at the Naktong.

Like most combat veterans, Harold is reluctant to offer up much in the way of specifics about his wartime experiences. Instead, he prefers to paint in broad strokes, such as when I ask him about what he did during those first weeks of the war. "After they backed us down to the river," he says, describing the bloody defense of the Perimeter, "there was virtually nowhere left to retreat to—it was fight or die. At that point, so many things were happening so fast that it's very difficult for me to recall specifically what I was doing. Hell, I was hauling bodies a lot of times—and not all dead. We would take ammunition forward, drop it off, and load stretchers on the truck to take back to the rear. We did whatever had to be done at the time, and more often than not, it seemed like nothing was going according to the plans or the regulations."

Even as the Allies struggled to hold this last bit of ground, the news outlets tended to downplay the withering onslaught, and instead, report from the rosy angle that the communist advance had been stopped by the timely intervention of U.N. forces. The simple reason for this is that most members of the press corps—doubtlessly out of self-preservation—were relying on information (propaganda) provided by the military. Journalists who did brave the front lines

quickly discovered that war in Korea was a new kind of hell. The
treacherous terrain, oppressive heat, lack of communications, and
the enemy's embrace and proficiency at sniper and guerilla tactics
made firsthand reporting of the conflict as arduous and fraught with
danger as any war in history. It was also Harold's personal nightmare
because he had finally been given a specific assignment—he was the
press' chauffeur.

"I was detailed to the Public Information Office," he says, "as
an escort for war correspondents—people like Hal Boyle, Randolph
Churchill (son of Winston), and Marguerite Higgens (who would
win a Pulitzer Prize for her Korean War reporting). My job was to
drive them up to the line units so they could interview and photograph the frontline soldiers. Everybody thought I had a plush assignment, but for the first three or four months it was a *damn* dangerous
job! For one thing, I wasn't allowed to attend the briefings, and the
correspondents didn't know the first goddamn thing about where
they were going!" Harold was armed to the teeth with an M1 rifle,
a .45-caliber sidearm, and a 9 mm pistol in a shoulder holster. "And
I eventually ended up firing every one of them!" he tells me. But in
terms of moving safely around the countryside, the correspondents
themselves were his worst enemies. "Because of them, I would end
up driving right onto the front lines where the infantry outfits were
dug in—and dug in for a reason! Or worse yet, I would find myself
*behind* enemy lines! At this rate, it wasn't a question of *if* I'd get shot
or blown up..." Harold huffs. "So I finally went to this major that
I worked for and said no more! I told him that if he wanted these
people delivered alive, I needed to be in those briefings!"

I ask him why the briefings were such a big deal.

"That's when they went over the maps and overlays showing
where they were going and how to get there! But I'd been relying on
these correspondents, and they didn't know anything about reading
Korean maps and signs. They would steer me right into a hot zone
and not even know it! Anyhow," he sighs, "after I complained, the
major let me in the briefings, and at least then I knew the situation.
I'd take them up so far and say, 'Okay guys, the front is about fifty
yards up there. Get going—I'm going the other way!' But even then,
the briefings were not always accurate. Sometimes they didn't know

exactly where the lines were, and you never knew where the hell the enemy was because they were constantly infiltrating behind the lines. Hell, I might have a whole squad of North Koreans behind me by the time I got there!"

"Did you ever come under fire?"

"Right in the middle of lunch!" he snorts. "I was coming back after dropping a guy off, and I stopped for a little bite. I was sitting in the cab, eating my ration, when a bullet hit the metal stay that holds the canvas on top of the truck—just inches above my head!"

"I'll bet you never put a truck in gear so fast in your life," I laugh.

"Whoever the hell put me in his sights had me cold," he flashes a grim smile. "Luckily, he wasn't much of a shot."

In mid-September, in perhaps the crowning achievement of a storied military career, General MacArthur landed 75,000 troops halfway up the peninsula at Inchon and severed the enemy's supply lines. The North Korean army began to wither like a flower with a broken stem. U.N. forces broke out of the Pusan Perimeter and pushed the invaders northward, right into MacArthur's lap. Seoul was liberated as the North Koreans were driven back across the 38th and the 1st Cavalry chased them all the way up to the Yalu River on the border with China. In a month, the strategic situation in Korea had completely reversed.

Harold also moved north in pursuit of the story—or at least in the company of those who were. In ravaged Seoul, where he rigged up a power source from his jeep so Irving R. Levine could run his tape recorder, Harold wondered if this was the same city where he had once watched happy citizens gaily parading through the streets. "It was all destroyed," he notes sourly, "except for the concrete government buildings and just a few areas of houses and shrines. I don't know how the North Koreans missed them." Sadly, they would get another chance.

In late November, MacArthur got a dose of his own medicine when China intervened by flinging three hundred thousand secreted troops at U.N. forces. Harold was on his way to the northern capital of Pyongyang. He arrived to find the army in retreat, barely one step ahead of the North Koreans and the Chinese.

"By the time I got to Pyongyang at the beginning of December," he tells me, "we were blowing the bridges and burning rations."

"Burning rations?"

"Destroying all our supplies," he nods, "so the Chinese wouldn't get them! And then we hightailed it back south."

Back and forth. For Harold, the familiar rhythm of Korea. Throughout one of the most brutal winters on record, the opposing forces seesawed south and north. Seoul fell again—and then was liberated again. By late spring, the two sides had more or less stalemated in territory surrounding the 38th parallel. The conflict was far from over, but the dramatic, sweeping drives up and down the peninsula were done. Instead, the opposing armies dug in for a war of attrition, right where it all began.

# Chapter 22
# BLOSSOMS

THE SQUAD OF nineteen men materialized from a gray drizzle in the blink of an eye. One second they weren't there, and then they were: spectral forms with pale ponchos billowing below their knees, accentuating the ghostlike effect. The moment Harold discerned these trudging figures framed in dreary mist, he felt his pulse quicken with something akin to cold panic.

"They were right in front of me," he tells me, emotion surging to the surface. Harold stares, but it is not me he's seeing, and he's waving both hands as if to ward off something—in this case, an affecting memory. "I just...I couldn't handle it." A deep breath or two later his focus returns to this place, his living room, and his narrative. "It's a group of GIs on patrol, and they've gone to great lengths to make them look realistic. Each soldier is seven-foot tall and they're spread out in the form of a squad. If you come upon them from the front, they're headed right at you. Without even thinking about it, you have a tendency to put yourself in their place..." He rubs at his forehead pensively. "That's what got to me."

It is a scene from the Korean War he is describing, but it was not in Korea, or during wartime. This was his own country and many decades later when he visited the Korean War Veterans Memorial in Washington, D.C. But as soon as Harold glimpsed that eerie, lifelike procession of steel men, it stopped him in his tracks and a sudden, jolting echo of the past transported him back to a cold and miserable war—the last place or time on earth he ever wanted to revisit. Harold turned around right there, and he never looked back.

There have been two changes of plaid shirts since we first started talking about his experiences during the Korean War, and we're barely halfway through. There is no doubt that the man put in his time—back-to-back combat tours. The army had made provisions so nobody would ever have to do that, but as always, Harold—by then Staff Sergeant Stevens—marched to his own drummer. Like every soldier in Korea, he was sick of the war—the unceasing misery, the horrific toll in human life, the seemingly fruitless ping-ponging of the battle lines; and yet Harold didn't want to go home because he did not want to leave the Far East. The woman he loved was in that part of the world, and he could not risk leaving her behind again. Not even if it killed him, which was a distinct possibility.

The army did finally manage to extract him—briefly. After sixteen months in the field, he had earned enough service points, including his time spent in prewar Korea and Japan, to put him—willing or not—at the head of the line for rotation back to the States. He ended up at Camp Atterbury, Indiana, in a sort of placement limbo, as the division there struggled with a roster of thirteen sergeants and where to put them all. When Harold learned they were gearing up to deploy him to Europe, he played his ace. It was the same card he had laid by smashing windows when he'd reasoned the best way to effect change was to get himself arrested: during a three-day pass to visit Duluth, Harold went AWOL and stayed out for nearly a week.

"They stood me in front of yet another court-martial," he says glumly, but with a hint of defiant satisfaction (that's his third time in the dock, by my count) "and some major tried to give me a speech about how I better watch my step or I might end up in Korea, and to trust *him* when he said that I didn't want to go there! I told him, 'I don't need that from you. Let's just get this over with!' Of course, the major didn't like that one bit—but it was true!" he glowers. "I'd just come from a year of combat in Korea, and I wasn't in the mood for someone to tell me what it was like, especially someone who didn't have an overseas insignia on his uniform!" Harold softens, "That guy was just doing his job, but I wanted out of that outfit." The major didn't know it, but he had given Harold an idea.

As punishment, Harold was busted down to a regular army corporal. Unlike their surplus of sergeants, corporals were a rank his division wouldn't have any trouble getting rid of—they could be sent anywhere. So Corporal Stevens went to personnel and demanded, "Get me the hell out of here, and I don't care where you send me!"— knowing full well where they would send him. There was a war on, he was a pebble in their shoe, and they were only too happy to rid themselves of the irritation by plucking him out and casting him off to Korea for another tour.

I admire his bravery, his resourcefulness, and his devotion. "You were thinking, this is my way back to Chiyoko!" I smile.

"Of course," he nods, "and I also figured that if I got sent back to Korea, maybe I would get R&R in Japan. The next thing I knew, I was on a troopship bound for East Asia," he notes with satisfaction, "and, lo and behold, I did get a few days in Tokyo!"

Chiyoko had been down this road before: a caller from out of the blue, an apparent stranger, yet something familiar about the man…a dawning realization, a flood of emotion and a joyous reunion—but this time was different. This person did not even remotely resemble Harold. The formidable mustache, unkempt hair, civilian clothing—even though she hadn't seen him in over a year and a half, she was sure this character was someone else, and that caused her heart to skip a beat. The sudden arrival of a Westerner, perhaps one of his army friends, could not herald good news.

Throughout their long separation, Chiyoko and Harold had written one another many letters. Her ability to read and write in English was still a work in progress, but in this regard, Barney and Flora had been of invaluable service, translating their letters both coming and going. Knowing their correspondences were looping through friends may have put a damper on expressing their most intimate sentiments, but the arrangement provided Chiyoko with regular updates on Harold's whereabouts and reassurances he was safe. However, she had not received a letter from him in some time, and now, here was this strange, disheveled man...

"While I was gone, Chiyoko had finally moved out of the okiya, and had taken a room in Shinjuku," Harold explains. "That's in western Tokyo. Of course I'd never been there, but I had her address. I got a cab and the driver had knowledge of that area, so it didn't take us long to find the house. When I knocked on the door, an elderly lady answered, and I asked to see Chiyoko."

He pauses for an important sidebar. "While I was away, I'd grown a long handlebar mustache—it had become a sort of signature thing with me in Korea. Add to that I had not had a haircut for a couple of months, and that she had never seen me other than as a very well-groomed serviceman in uniform..."

He continues, "So when Chiyoko came down the hall, as she got closer to me she moved slower and slower until finally she just stopped, staring at me. She had no idea who I was until I spoke to her. Even then it took a while to sink in! When she finally understood and accepted that it really was me, we rushed together and there was a lot of happy hugging and words of affection—but after we made it to her room, she nearly skinned me alive for having changed my appearance so much. I'd scared her to death!"

Soon enough, however, all was forgiven as the young couple reveled in their long anticipated reunion. "Our lovemaking that night was slow and very tender," Harold tells me, his eyes simultaneously dancing joyfully and puddling with nostalgia. "Every memory and every feeling I'd had for her was confirmed. She was still the most wonderful, beautiful girl I'd ever seen!"

At Chiyoko's insistence, the first thing he did the next morning was visit a barber shop. "I felt rather naked on top," Harold confesses, "but being clean-shaven was also a good feeling after so many months in a combat zone, not to mention a couple of long ocean crossings. After that, we walked together in one of the large parks in the Tokyo area—and it was heaven."

Or the closest thing on earth: cherry blossom time. At the dawn of the growing season, like an exuberant impressionist painting, the parks and hillsides throughout the islands of Japan are a riot of colorful gladiolas and other bulbs, but there is nothing amidst all the lively flora—perhaps no part of the islands' iconic geology or distinctive fauna either—more evocative of Japan or beloved by the Japanese people than the cherry trees in spring. It is a short-lived but glorious spectacle when the trees hold back their leaves in favor of dense pink and white blossoms and the landscape is a fairyland of aromatic cotton candy boughs.

As Harold and Chiyoko strolled across glowing, bubblegum carpets of strewn petals, he was struck by the similarities between these trees and the girl on his arm. Like them, she was almost too beautiful to be real, a heaven-sent reminder that sweetness and grace were still present in the world, despite the proximate ugliness and brutality of war. Unlike the oak and other trees that cling to their leaves miserly, the cherry releases its blossoms freely to the breezes, brightening every nook and cranny of its surroundings—just like Chiyoko, Harold thought. He has described to me how, whenever she entered a room, it was like the sun burning through a cold mist, as every heart was suddenly cheered by her warmth and her luminous smile. On this day, it was not hard for Harold to imagine that the park bloomed with even greater intensity, in partnership with his radiant companion.

"People were lying around on blankets and having picnics," he says of the idyllic afternoon, "just soaking in the scenery. As Chiyoko and I walked, we talked about so many things, but mostly about our past times together. We had so many happy memories of Taura and also from when I was a young sailor in the navy, when we'd had to be so careful not to be seen together. Of course, we still did, but on that day, with the cherry trees in their full glory, nobody was paying any attention to us. It was a day made for the two of us, and we made the most of it."

Despite the spectacular surroundings, Harold only had eyes for Chiyoko, and he again allowed himself the luxury of contemplating a future together with her—not just as lovers, but as man and wife. Yet, even in this romantic setting, it was not time for a marriage proposal. "There was no one else for me," he insists, "no one who could so utterly captivate me and smooth the roughness that had defined my growing up. I knew that I wanted her beside me for my whole life. But I also knew that I was headed back to the war. Whether I would survive it, who could say? I accepted that, but I didn't want her bound to me under those circumstances. Nevertheless, I very much looked forward to returning to her, so we could continue our journey together."

All too quickly his R&R was up, and Harold had to report to Camp Drake, near Tokyo, for redeployment to Korea. "Once again," he sighs, "parting with Chiyoko wasn't easy, but we said our good-byes, tough as it was."

In the dark months that followed, he would be sustained again and again by the memory of their afternoon in the Tokyo park when they had wandered hand in hand through a pink and fragrant snow.

In Korea, almost nothing had changed, and yet, for Harold, everything was different.

The U.N. forces and the Chinese were still faced off in the rugged terrain surrounding the 38th parallel, where victories for either side were no longer being measured according to captured provinces or cities, but by individual hills. To this end, the Chinese fought fiercely, with an almost insect-like tenacity, for every inch of ground they could garner.

"The Chinese were determined," Harold tells me, "to continually improve their position while peace talks dragged on in Paris. They threw thousands of troops against the fortifications we had on the high ground. Our machine guns would cut down the advancing wave, but the unarmed men following behind would just pick up the weapons of the fallen and keep pushing forward—again and again. It was a slaughter, but just by their overwhelming numbers they would manage to take these key hills. To this day," he notes, "the North Koreans still hold a number of those strategically important hilltops, where they can look out and observe the entire area."

Harold's assignment was also much different this time around. His days of operating independently as a driver for Eighth Army headquarters were over. For this tour, he was detailed to another outfit—and a very big one: the 25th Infantry Division.

"How in the world did you end up in the infantry?" I wonder.

"Too easily," Harold grunts. "Some clerk probably said, *This guy's been having it good. We'll fix him!*" He rolls his eyes, "I was a diesel-electric locomotive mechanic, but there wasn't a single diesel locomotive in the whole damn country, so they figured with my mechanical experience, I could look after their vehicles. They made me motor sergeant—but not for long." In fact, he never even had time to change a spark plug.

Harold explains, "There was an older guy there who'd been a master sergeant, but was busted down to PFC for some infraction, and they wanted to put him someplace where he might eventually be able to get promoted back to some rank. So they gave him my job and sent me down to help load at the number one gun position."

"What's that?"

"Artillery!" he says, one eyebrow raised. "Howitzers: 155 millimeters. I didn't know the first thing about goddamn artillery, but a week later, I was gun chief on the number six position!"

# Chapter 23
# GUNNER

砲手

THE FIRST THING about goddamn artillery is cover your ears. This is not something you need to be taught. It's either instinctive or, as Harold discovered, forever ingrained in your brain about two seconds after the gun chief yells, *Fire!*

"There was no such thing as earplugs," he mutters. "The first time that big gun went off, it nearly deafened me!"

Despite being defined in millimeters, the 155 Howitzer is a massive cannon. Twenty feet long, with a twelve-foot barrel and weighing in at more than twelve thousand pounds, it can lob a shell up to nine miles downrange. In Korea, there were three batteries with six Howitzers each, and ten to twelve men working a gun. As soon as Harold arrived at his emplacement, a corporal gave him a crash course in artillery, explaining in detail how the various members of the crew worked as a tightly choreographed team to aim, load, and fire the weapon. Harold does the same for me.

"The artillery batteries are dug in some distance behind the front lines," he explains. "Whenever the infantry was stalemated, they'd call for artillery fire to soften the enemy's positions. There's a forward observer—a member of the artillery unit—up on the line with the infantry to identify targets. His job was to transmit the information by phone or radio to the fire direction center, where they charted the coordinates, and then calculated and relayed the firing instructions—range, elevation, charge, the type of round—all this was sent to the gun chief in about thirty seconds."

Harold tells me that the key to aiming the gun was two red and white striped stakes, located between twenty-five and forty yards out. These were the reference points the gunner sighted to plot the firing coordinates. As soon as the target was dialed in, the gun crew shifted into high gear. The breach swung open and the projectile was loaded and rammed, followed by bags of gunpowder. A trigger unit with a lanyard was screwed into place. The gun chief, who was directing and overseeing the operation, gave the fire command, the gunner yanked the string, and the organs in every chest and belly rippled as a concussive blast tore the air sending a hundred pounds of fused death and destruction winging toward the enemy lines.

"How accurate were these guns?" I ask Harold.

"It all depended upon the information we got from the forward observer," he replies, noting that after each round, the observer would call in corrections, if necessary, to zero in on the target. Sometimes, however, you just got lucky.

"We had one fire mission where we were targeting an enemy mortar position," he recalls. "We got the coordinates over the phone and gave them to the gunner. When we were all sighted in and loaded, we gave the fire order and away that projectile went… The forward observer almost fainted up there. We had completely missed the mortar position," he reports gleefully, "but hit a damn tank! Nobody even knew that tank was there, it was so well camouflaged."

I imagine that must have been quite a sight.

"We were positioned a long way back," he chuckles, "so I didn't see a thing. But the forward observer saw it. He radioed, 'Man! A direct hit on a tank!' I said, 'What *tank?* What the hell happened to the mortar?!'"

Even sequestered in an artillery battery, well behind the front lines, Harold was at risk of losing a lot more than his hearing. The gun emplacements were themselves prime targets for their enemy counterparts. The very first night he was there, the Chinese came knocking. Harold was asleep in little more than a fortified trench when he was shaken from his cot by a thundering rain of hellfire and hot, exploded metal.

"Everything around me was blowing sky high," he says, and this is not a figure of speech. "One of the big guns got hit and just lifted right up in the air, killing most of the crew. Below us there was a maintenance tent and a couple of ammo trucks. The three guys operating out of that tent all dove for the same foxhole. Only the first one in made it out alive," he intones soberly. "When those trucks got hit, the two bodies on top shielded the bottom guy from the shrapnel." Meanwhile, up on the firing line, the 1st sergeant got hit, prompting in Harold newfound empathy for the kitchen crew. "The mess sergeant had to take over," he says, "and when we got orders to counterfire he shouted at us, *'Get out of those holes you bastards, or I'll shoot you all!'*"

"What about your gun crew?" I gape. "Was anybody there killed?"

"Not that time," he remarks, significantly. "We were all in a sandbagged parapet we'd built up around the gun, scrambling to return fire. But we had casualties. There were three officers in that battery, and all three got taken out—not killed," he emphasizes, "but wounded."

Whether it was this abrupt lack of qualified supervision or in recognition of Harold's innate, no-nonsense competency for taking charge and getting things done, he suddenly found himself with his sergeant's rank reinstated and promoted to gun chief on the number six gun. As it turned out, the army could not have picked a better person to hammer a group of men into a cohesive unit. The mess sergeant had nothing on him; the crew did whatever Harold said—or else.

"As gun chief," he boasts, "I ruled the roost. I was a strict sergeant, no doubt about it, but never brutal..." He reconsiders, "Oh, every once in a while I'd lower the boom. If I had problems with somebody or if someone got smart with me, I'd pull him off to one side and say, 'Okay, there's nobody looking. Are you ready for this?'"

I blink. "Are you saying...you would fight them?"

"*Damn* right I would!" he glares. "I'd tell 'em, 'Friend, you've got a lesson to be learned, and school is in session!'" His face relaxes, "It didn't happen very often, but if I had to hit someone, I made sure he knew it—and why. But you know," he reflects, "I don't think it was the hurt that got 'em. I think it was embarrassment. I was small, and some of these guys thought they were pretty tough." Harold chuckles wryly. "I could whip anyone in the battalion! I was an expert fighter by this time. I had taken my knocks as a kid, I had picked up some tricks from the Japanese, and I'd learned from the Koreans, who fought very violently—none of this bowing or defensive posturing… a Korean would start right out by crushing your nose with his forehead! And because I was a smaller guy, I'd studied and learned every trick in the book. As a gunnery sergeant, I wasn't afraid to apply a little physical persuasion to command discipline and respect."

"And that worked?"

"You better believe it," he grunts. "When I barked, my men moved! We could get off a round every twenty seconds—and safely," he stresses. "No cutting corners; we swabbed the tube for sparks between every round and still managed three shots a minute. One night we fired over five hundred rounds and warped the barrel—it got that hot!" He smiles with evident satisfaction, "There's no doubt that I had a top-notch gun crew. I was always proud of that. And so were the men."

If Harold ran his unit like a hard-boiled coach grooming a well-oiled team, it must have felt about right to the half dozen members of his squad who were, in fact, college football players. These oxlike draftees impressed him by forgoing the rammer's staff, and deadlifting the hundred-pound shells out of the loading tray and stuffing them up the barrel with their knuckles. The fact that Harold could physically intimidate these gorillas is further proof of his own prowess with his fists.

But the war was neither sport nor a game. It was a deadly serious conflict in which the lens of battle magnified personalities and intensified interpersonal bonds and conflicts. The forward observers who scouted targets for Harold's battery exemplified the two sides of this coin.

"I had a real good forward observer," he tells me, "and then I had one I wanted to murder…"

Oh boy. "Tell me about the good one," I suggest.

"He was one of the nicest guys we ever had come into the unit," Harold extols. "Friendly…a real gentleman. Forward observers were typically officers and he was a 1st lieutenant, but he always had time to stop and talk to the guys, and he was very respectful toward me. 'Sergeant' was always my first name with him…" Harold's face clouds, and he murmurs, "But being a good guy is no insurance in a war, and sometimes it's the opposite. On his first trip to the line as a forward observer, the infantry needed someone to help with fire direction for one of our tanks. So this guy got up in the turret and started giving directions to the crew, and a sniper popped him right out of there. Dead—first trip up! One of the best guys you'd ever hope to meet. He wasn't even supposed to be in a tank…he was doing them a favor."

I remark that being a forward observer must have been as dangerous a job as there was.

He nods, "Often, if the infantry was dug in on the line, the forward observer was prowling around out beyond them—in other words, in enemy territory. It was a good way to get killed," he affirms. Still, to Harold's mind, that didn't give the forward observer license to be a son of a bitch.

This brings us to the second guy, the one Harold wanted to murder, and he means it quite literally. He assures me that if he'd had the firing coordinates, he would not have hesitated to dial in on this lieutenant's position and personally yank the lanyard.

"Why?"

"His attitude toward the men," he mutters. "He was not respectful. For no reason at all he would make disparaging comments about my gun crew—and he only had to do that once!" Harold scowls icily, "I really did want to kill him…but he beat me to the draw." Again, Harold is not just turning a phrase.

"I was looking to have one of my men promoted to corporal," he explains, "a guy who was always taking on extra work without being asked, like cleaning the weapons and equipment, and he was also, by far, the best track-vehicle driver in the entire organization—that was how we towed the cannons," he enlightens me. "Well, we had a vacancy for a corporal, so when this lieutenant was in camp, I went to see him about giving it to this very deserving soldier. The lieutenant was in his bunk, and I told him that I wanted my guy promoted, and I asked for his recommendation. And this *schnook*," Harold spits, "he gave me some crap, like, 'What the hell makes you so smart, thinking that you want this and you want that!'"

Knowing Harold's temper, I am already adding yet another court-martial to the tote board, but this time, he narrowly escaped much worse. Harold's measured tone defines understatement when he says, "About then I flared up a bit…" He continues, coolly, "I started reaching for my .45, because I intended to shoot him, and at the same time, he put his hand under the pillow and he came out with his own pistol, and he said, 'I wouldn't do that if I were you!' So I turned around and made my exit." Harold looks mad enough to eat nails. "That might have been the only time in my life I made a good decision while I was angry," he chews, "but I'll tell you what, that guy escaped death that day! I had every intention of shooting him!"

"Did he…make it through the war?" I wonder tentatively, unsure if I really want to know the answer—or the details.

Harold nods, his lips twisted with annoyance at what he clearly considers to be an oversight of Divine Providence. "I saw him several times in later years at reunions," he grumbles, "and I walked right past him. I'm sure he could still feel the heat coming off me. But then he stopped showing up, and I don't know what happened to him…" His eyes blaze wickedly, "Maybe somebody else did the world a favor and finished the job!"

According to Harold, the hardest thing about artillery was the downtime. "Between fire missions there was a lot of sitting around doing nothing," he informs me. To busy themselves, the crews filled a lot of empty hours, and even more sandbags, improving their fortifications. "In one place," Harold notes, "we dug a hole and built a bunker, and you could have parked a truck in there, it was that big! We lined the walls with logs and put more across the top, and then we sandbagged that sucker in…" Harold cracks open one of his albums and shows me a photograph of this dugout palace. It's captioned, *The Hilton*, although a self-respecting hotelier would likely bristle at the association since the amenities for guests included bunking on a dirt floor, while lazily stabbing with their bayonets at rats between the logs. Anything to kill time.

Of course, such lulls also afforded Harold ample opportunity to contemplate Chiyoko, and he missed her terribly. "We wrote back and forth," he tells me, "and she even sent me some care packages…" he rolls his eyes, "although she did the damnedest thing one time. The Japanese grow a sweet grapefruit that she knew I liked, so while I was in Korea, she sent me a parcel, and in it, she put a couple of those grapefruit along with some liquor-filled candy. Well," he chuckles, "the mail coming into a combat area is subject to all manner of abuse, so, of course, the damn grapefruit got smashed flat, and the juice soaked through the package and everything inside. Her heart was in the right place," he grins, "but that grapefruit wasn't very good…and come to think of it, after marinating in that mess for a week or two, neither was the candy!"

In truth, however, the hardest thing about artillery is not the waiting. It is something Harold is understandably reluctant to discuss, but eventually, my badgering for details about specific battles and wartime glories wears him down, and he goes off on me like a cannon.

"Let me explain something to you," he says sharply. "Whenever a forward unit called for artillery support, we had to fire all these explosives into that area. Sometimes it was a military target, other times it may have been a group of buildings or a village where the enemy was quartered. When you have a battery of six guns, or all three batteries of eighteen guns, pumping shells into one of these places, you cannot help but create a lot of collateral damage…" He swallows. "One six-inch round throws fragments up to fifty yards. As long as you don't go forward, you don't have to see what you've done…but remember, the infantry is always advancing, and you're moving up behind them…" Harold clears his throat again, his tone softens, and his eyes well, "And then you see what's left behind… the damage that you've done. I don't have much trouble seeing dead bodies—soldiers. But I will never, in my life, get over the sight of mothers, either dead, or picking up the pieces of their children. This is…this is the one thing that has affected me my whole life. I don't suffer from battle fatigue, and I'm not debilitated by these memories, but I have never forgotten them." His tears are flowing freely now, but Harold is unapologetic; he embraces the sorrow, because it is the only honest reaction to such horrors. "I try not to dwell on the war to the point that it consumes my mind…I know if I do, I'll be a brother to all the guys who suffer with these things day and night…" He stares past me, at clouds floating silently beyond the window. Whether he sees in them a reminder of cannon smoke or the handiwork of an all-powerful, yet sometimes inexplicably absent God, I can only wonder.

"I don't know if this is something that you want to hear," he sighs heavily, "but these are the things that happen in war—not just Korea, but every damn war there is. The hardest thing in the world is to see the little children who are innocent victims. If you can't feel sympathy for them…" he swallows, "then you've got a pretty rotten heart."

Big as they were, the howitzers were mobile pieces of field artillery. When the march order was given, the crew jumped to unweight the long trails extending out behind the gun and swing them together—like closing scissors—into traveling position. The 155 was a six-ton cannon balanced on two wheels, so even this task required considerable care and coordination by the crew to avoid accidents or injuries.

"We had moved out of our permanent position and were supporting a Turkish unit," Harold says, recounting one such maneuver, "when suddenly we started taking incoming rounds. When that happens, the best thing to do is get the hell out of there—sure enough, word came down to us to close station. That meant, *Get this damn gun ready to move!* I had a couple new kids in my gun crew, and they were working to remove the weighted spades that anchor the ends of the trails. A spade is quite heavy. It takes two people to lift one into position, but these guys were taking it off, and that procedure is a fairly simple one: knock out a wooden wedge and it drops free, but you always have to be careful when you're monkeying around with that kind of weight. I had just briefed these guys and told them, 'Watch your damn feet,' but when I looked over, one of them was standing with his foot right under that trail spade!"

Harold leaped up, sprinted across, and pushed the kid out of harm's way, just as the wedge came out and the hundred-pound blade of steel came smashing down—right onto Harold's foot.

# Chapter 24
# HUSBAND

夫

THERE IS A HOLE on Harold's wall. Not a crack in the drywall or a cavity from an old nail, not even a literal hole, but a place where something should be, but isn't. There is a framed collection of his military insignias on display here. It is a myriad of colorful service ribbons and medals he has earned throughout his navy and army careers, everything from a Seabee patch to the Army Good Conduct Medal ("It only took me nine years to finally nab that one," he announces drolly). But for a man now hobbled and bent from injuries suffered during military service, it seems a glaring omission that among his decorations there is no official acknowledgement of his physical sacrifices. No Purple Heart.

"After my foot was crushed in Korea," Harold notes, "I was in the hospital alongside a guy named Harvey Klinger. He was a company clerk from the 25th Infantry—my same outfit. Klinger had been doing some typing when we started taking incoming fire. He jumped in a foxhole and chipped his elbow. He got the Purple Heart. Me?" He smiles wanly, "Nothing."

The iconic Purple Heart is reserved for American servicemen and women who have been wounded or killed in action. There is some discretion and interpretation regarding the criteria for being awarded a Purple Heart, and injuries due to noncombat accidents are not eligible, but Harold had been in the thick of it. The fact that he sustained this injury pulling one of his men out of harm's way probably should have qualified him for the Army Commendation Medal as well. But he never received any honors or recognition, and the likely reason seems to have been a typo.

"One of the doctors," Harold sighs, "I don't know where the hell he got the idea, but he wrote 'training injury' in my medical records. I thought, *Training?! People were trying to kill us!*" For all his playful irascibility on the subject, Harold is acquiescent. To his mind, there are others who deserved the Purple Heart a lot more than he did, and he has never sought to put the record straight. To my mind, it is the definition of insult added to injury.

When the trail spade crashed to earth, it pulverized the bones and tendons in Harold's foot from the big toe back to the arch. Even though the pain was excruciating, it took a while for him to admit (or even realize) he had been seriously hurt. He hopped around trying to do his job until a medic insisted upon removing his boot and found a pulped, swollen mess that looked like a heel attached to a burst potato. Harold was swiftly evac'ed to the nearest field hospital.

"The pressure from the swelling fluid was nearly unbearable," he mutters, noting how every throbbing heartbeat felt like a hammer blow pounding beneath the well cap of his toenail. "I begged a nurse, I told her, 'Lady, you've got to open up this toe!' but she said there wasn't a doctor available to do that." Harold didn't need a doctor so much as a trenching spade, so he took matters into his own hands. "I started excavating at the cuticle with my fingernail until I'd gouged out a pretty good hole. When I finally got under that nail, the blood erupted like a fountain! The nurse came back in to check on me and I was bleeding all over the canvas cot. She said, 'Oh my god! You shouldn't have done that!' She was pretty excited, but all I could think was, *boy…that feels better!*"

From the MASH unit, Harold was sent to a hospital in Kobe, Japan, where the nurse there didn't know what to make of him either. By this time he had regrown his trademark handlebar mustache, and combined with his shaggy, black hair and sun-darkened skin, she assumed he was a Turk. "Can…you…understand…English?" the nurse asked him slowly and with marked enunciation. "Yes ma'am!" he startled her, speaking in flawless Midwestern parlance. "I understand English just fine."

As soon as he was able, Harold called Chiyoko to tell her what had happened to him and where he was. "She was concerned to learn I was in the hospital, but I told her it wasn't too serious and that she shouldn't come right away because I was confined to bed. We weren't married, so I knew it was unlikely she would be allowed to visit me." Nevertheless, Chiyoko did come to Kobe, and when the hospital guards would not admit her, Harold went on an unauthorized walkabout.

"I actually had an ambulatory pass," he notes defensively, "but I had to be back at a certain time. Of course," he winks, "I stayed out all night, and damned if they didn't court-martial me and bust me down in rank!"

I wonder out loud if there is any limit to how many times one person can be court-martialed.

Harold smiles broadly, "Well, this one didn't count!"

"How's that?"

"When they finally discharged me from the hospital," he explains, "they gave me a train ticket for Tokyo and all my records to take up there to Camp Drake—the damn fools! As soon as I got on that train, I unsealed the file, and I took out the documentation for that court-martial, tore it in half, and..." he makes a casual fluttering gesture, "out the window! So that disciplinary action was never officially registered."

"You were able to keep your rank?"

"Damn right! I never took my stripes off. I was a staff sergeant and I wasn't going to give that up—not if they were dumb enough to put me in charge of the paperwork that demoted me!" He grins smugly, "In fact, there was another guy, same rank as me, in the same hospital ward as I was, and he showed up about two days later at the holding station in Tokyo without his stripes. I asked him, 'What the hell happened to your chevrons?'

"He said, 'I got busted, so I had to take 'em off.'

"'Where are your records—did they give them to you?'

"'I got 'em.'

"'Give them to me,' I told him. I went through his records and I found his court-martial…" Harold pantomimes ripping paper in half. "I said, 'There. You're a sergeant again. I just promoted you. Now put those damn stripes back on!'"

While he was still convalescing at the hospital in Kobe, Harold and Chiyoko went for another memorable walk. There were no cherries in bloom, no greens gathered for pets, no meditations about how to mint enough money to ransom a woman's freedom, but something else was coined—a lifelong nickname for Chiyoko. Company clerk and fellow invalid Harvey Klinger, typist-of-the-Purple-Heart, with his bumped elbow cradled in a simple sling, joined them for a stroll. Harold needed a crutch *and* a cane.

"The three of us were meandering down the street in Kobe," Harold remembers, "just looking at the stores and shops, and Klinger kept glancing at Chiyoko and asking me, 'What's her name?' I said, 'Her name is Chiyoko.' I'd limp ten more steps, and he'd ask me again, 'I forgot, what's her name?'" Harold groans with exasperation. "He did that until I was about going crazy! Finally, after this had gone on for a period of time, he said, 'What's her name again?' and I turned to him and snapped, 'Oh for god's sake, just call her Mike!' So that's what he did. From that moment on, she was Mike."

I ask him what Chiyoko thought about that.

"She got a kick out of it," he insists. "In fact, she really liked that name, and pretty soon everyone, including me, started calling her Mike."

"*You* called her that?" I exclaim. "Mike?"

"Until the day she died," he nods, wistfully. "And she thought that was pretty great."

Mariko, Chiyoko, and now, Mike. She was a woman of many names. And there was one more Harold was determined she would have: Mrs. Stevens.

Now that Chiyoko—Mike—had Harold back in Japan, I can only imagine how badly she wanted to keep him there. Upon that goal, Harold was equally fixated, and ahead of the game. Even before being injured in Korea, he had put in for an intertheater transfer to

Japan. If granted, this would commit him to another two-year tour, but with the guarantee that he would serve that time in Japan.

"My application had gone all the way up through the Eighth Army channels and came back approved," he tells me. Unfortunately, after his accident, his unit decided to withdraw the request and ship him back to the States. "I said, hell no!" Harold states flatly. "So I went to see the Inspector General—the office that assesses complaints and recommends appropriate action—and told him my story. The IG said, 'Your intertheater transfer was already approved, so don't worry. Go back to your barracks and you'll hear from us.' The next thing I knew I had orders for Hokkaido, the scenic northern island of Japan, and there was never a happier soldier on earth!"

Once again the army had reasoned that Harold's mechanical expertise with diesel locomotives was a skill perfectly aligned with fixing cars. He was put in charge of the Exchange garage at Sapporo's Camp Crawford, where all the civilian vehicles on the island of Hokkaido were serviced. At long last, Harold was at a place and time where he could act upon his dream of securing a legitimate and lasting future for himself with Chiyoko. She also sensed the timing was right. He was barely there long enough to secure lodging in a rented room owned by yet another war widow, when he got a phone call from Chiyoko. "She said, 'Come get me, I'm at the train station!'" He marvels, "She'd packed her bags, unprompted, and left Tokyo, relinquishing her life as a geisha. She'd come to Hokkaido to be with me!"

There could be no surer sign of Chiyoko's commitment to their relationship than giving up her lifelong vocation—one that in many ways was also her identity—and relocating to join Harold on the northern island. It was a decision that he has never taken for granted, and her sacrifice still moves him to this day. "She was a top geisha, so to do that," he reasons, "to leave something she had studied so hard and for so many years to become, and that she was so *damn* good at..." There is no other way to parse it: "I guess she loved *me* more than being a geisha," he sighs thankfully, exhaling a lifetime of undiminished gratitude.

"Sounds as though the ball was in your court," I smile.

"There were restrictions on American servicemen marrying Japanese nationals," he notes. "It was allowed, but only during short windows of time—three or four months at a pop. In fact," he admits, "that's part of what had delayed me from getting married to her before, because every time the application period was open, I was in goddamn Korea! So when I finally got assigned to Japan for that two-year tour, and the opportunity opened up again, I meant to do it! I put in my papers to get married…" he grins, "and I made her a very memorable proposal."

After all they had been through to be together—from his audacious smuggling caper that paid her debt, through the years of repeated and agonizing separations and reunions due to war and other circumstances—I can only imagine the romantic heights that Harold might have climbed to finally declare his intentions to the girl of his dreams. I fully expect to hear about a proposal that culminates with him scattering cherry petals upon the summit of Mount Fuji. I'll have to be content with him perched on a high point in their tiny apartment.

"I was sitting on the arm of the couch," Harold tells me, "where she was watching television. She wasn't even paying much attention to me until I said to her, 'You know, we've known each other for almost eight years now. Don't you think it's time we got married?' *That* was my proposal," he laughs heartily, "and for an unsophisticated character like me, I thought it was magnificent!"

I am not so sure. "Was she at all…" I hesitate, struggling with how to ask the question tactfully. "Did you have any sense that she was…underwhelmed?"

"No," he scoffs. "In fact, she thought about it for a moment or two, and then she gave me her answer. She said, 'Well…I suppose so.'" His laughter redoubles, "It was the perfect reply to my very romantic proposal!"

If it is possible, their wedding was even more of an anticlimax, but there was still a fair bit of twisting road that had to be negotiated until that bridge was crossed.

Before she could marry an American soldier, Chiyoko had to submit to a thorough medical examination, including being injected with six *million* units of penicillin (a quantity more reasonable than it sounds, but what was unsettling, not to mention disparaging, was the purpose: to eradicate any venereal diseases) and she had to undergo an extensive background check. Various acquaintances and employers were queried, and all submitted glowing letters of recommendation. They included Barney Nozaki and Mrs. Fusa Suda—aka Mama-san—the woman who owned the geisha house, and who, for most of Chiyoko's life, had owned her as well. (Chiyoko's former position in the business was recorded on the forms as "resident maid.") It normally took up to six months to process a background check, but Harold had done a kindness at work by prioritizing repairs on a long-idled car belonging to the wife of a counterintelligence officer, and he believes it likely that this favor was repaid when Chiyoko's review was expedited and completed in just a few weeks. The verdict sounded like Harold had applied to buy a dog rather than take a wife: *She is docile in nature and her conduct is excellent. There are no unfavorable remarks from the neighbors.* No mention was made of Chiyoko having been a geisha. Indeed, to the army's way of thinking, they found her character in lockstep with what they considered the ideal wife: *Since she has no interests in politics or political parties, she is recognized to be ideologically sound.* However, there was one red flag. The investigation revealed that in 1946, Chiyoko had been questioned at the Omori police station on a charge of illegal possession of U.S. government property. She had been caught carrying a bar of American soap through a checkpoint. The investigators let it slide.

The couple also had to sit for an interview with a chaplain. This was standard army procedure for interracial marriages, partly to determine if a serviceman marrying a Japanese girl was making an impulsive decision he might later regret, and also to ascertain whether the woman seeking entry to the United States was merely an opportunist. "That chaplain almost fainted!" Harold chuckles. "He asked me, 'How long have you known this lady?' I said, 'Oh, only about eight years.' Harold does a double take to indicate the officer's shock. "'Well then,' the clergyman said, 'I guess I don't have to tell *you* what you're getting into!'"

"What about your wedding?" I wonder. Again, my imagining of their long anticipated nuptials trends toward romantic, sentimental vows made before an effusive and teary-eyed assembly of their closest friends and relations.

"The ceremony?" Harold laughs. "On our wedding day we went to the American consulate and filled out a pile of paperwork. They gave us a little sheet of rice paper, as thin as an onion skin, covered with Japanese writing, and at the bottom there was a blank line. The vice-consul handed me that piece of paper and a couple of other forms and said, 'You'll have to go over to city hall to sign this.' So we trudged over there, told *them* we wanted to get married, and produced these documents. The clerks took everything and worked through it all. Then they pushed that little piece of rice paper at me and told me to sign on the line. I did that, and they said, okay, now you can go back to the consulate. So, back we went again to see the vice-consul...and I'm standing in front of his desk waiting to hear what's next while he's looking over the papers. Finally he said, 'Do you have a ring?'

"I said, 'Yeah, I have a ring.'

"'Well,' he said, 'give it to your wife. You're married now.'"

# Chapter 25
# HOMECOMING
帰省

HAROLD HAS ANOTHER photo album open on his lap, and he has wedged himself onto the couch between me and the throw pillows so we are sitting elbow to plaid elbow as we peruse his pictures from Hokkaido. At the moment, we're contemplating his wedding day photo, in all its monochromatic glory. It is a wonderful picture, but as a wedding portrait, it's unconventional to be sure. Harold is wearing his class-A uniform, perched on the arm of an overstuffed chair. Chiyoko is seated in the chair and decked out stylishly in a crisp dress suit, accessorized with a silken floral corsage and netted gloves. Although neither of them is smiling, they both look serenely confident and exude 1950s-era glamour.

"Good looking couple," I remark, honestly. (In fact, so photogenic, the Coca-Cola Company in Japan had asked them to pose with bottles of Coke for an advertising promotion.)

"Thank you," he says, though in his mind the compliment is directed squarely at his bride. "I was the proudest guy in the world on that day. She really knew how to dress up, didn't she?"

She certainly did. Even in black-and-white, Chiyoko is radiant. "What color was her dress?" I ask.

"Oh god!" he frowns. "How do you expect me to remember that?"

"It was your wedding day!" I rib. "Do you mean to say you don't remember what color dress your wife wore?"

"In a word," he glares playfully, "no! But I know what color my outfit was—army green!" His gaze returning to the photo, Harold remarks, "We went straight from the consulate to the photographer. I told Mike, let's get some pictures taken because I won't look this good again for a long time!" Again, I suspect it had more to do with preserving an image of how beautifully put together Chiyoko was.

"And the next thing I did was make a telephone call to my mother," he continues. "She knew that I'd been associating with this girl for many years, and she had never approved of us just shacking up. I think one of the happiest days in Mom's life was when I managed to get a call through to her to let her know we were married. I put my new wife on the phone and they chatted for a few minutes, and when I got back on the line I said, 'Well, I hope you're satisfied. I made it legal!' She said, 'Don't be smart young man or you'll get a cuff from me the next time I see you!' And I probably did."

Married life agreed with Harold.

Even if the act of getting hitched had been something of a letdown (though they had apparently thrown one heck of a party afterward, as evidenced by an album photo of countertops covered in empty sake bottles, captioned: *Everybody seems to have had a good time!*), Harold found that being wed to Chiyoko was everything he had hoped it would be, a ticket to new heights of domestic bliss— not to mention a step up in living quarters. As husband and wife, they now qualified for family housing at Camp Crawford. "For years we'd been living in just one or two rooms," he says, "squeezed in here or shoehorned there; now, suddenly we had a whole house! Upstairs and downstairs! I had a lounge where I could sit down and read, even the dog had its own space…"

"The dog?!"

"We had a cute dog," Harold nods. "A mutt, but a smart little thing." He explains, "A friend of mine came into work one day and said, 'I've got a dog that needs a home. Can you take care of it over the weekend?' So I said, 'Mike, we've got a dog for few days.' Of course, it didn't take any time at all for her to decide it was now our dog." She named the pooch Buffy; clearly, in her new role as an American housewife, Chiyoko was having no trouble fitting in.

For their honeymoon, they traveled to the hills around Mount Fuji, stopping over for a few days in Tokyo to visit family and friends. There, the couple reveled in the newfound freedom of visiting their old haunts without the worry of being seen together.

"We went to parks and restaurants and all the places where we could never be in one another's company before. Now I could walk with her anywhere I wanted," Harold says, savoring the memory, "and we could do all these things together."

I can only imagine how wonderful and liberating that must have felt, I tell him.

"It did," he emphasizes. "Everything was so much better as husband and wife."

I am curious whether their euphoria was shared by her family. "What were the feelings amongst Chiyoko's relatives," I ask him, "to have an American soldier as a member of the Okada clan?"

"They were fine with that," Harold attests. "Being around the members of her family was not a bad thing for me." He starts down the list. "Her brother and I got along just great. We stayed with him while we were in Tokyo. Despite his disability, as a barber he had prospered through hard work, and now owned the building with his barbershop. We had a good visit there with his family, strolling the pier and walking along the river."

"What about her sister?"

"Mike's sister, Yoshiko, also liked me...in fact," he pumps an eyebrow, "I think she was in love with me!"

"Really!"

"Let's just say I always had a hard time getting free from the hugs and kisses whenever she saw me!"

"And, her father?"

Harold's smile recedes. "I never respected her father," he says coolly. "Not solely because of what he had done to her when she was a child, because selling a daughter to a geisha house was acceptable in that culture at that time. But in the years since then, her father continued to sponge off Mike and her siblings. He had the ability to work, but he preferred to laze around and be waited on, hand and foot!"

As an example, Harold tells me how when they visited him, Chiyoko's father would bark at his diminutive wife: *Ocha!* which was his way of demanding that she serve him the Japanese green tea. When she was not being worked to the bone by her husband, Chiyoko's stepmother was expected to bring what little money she could into the household by sweeping and doing other odd jobs.

"Suffice it to say, I didn't like him," Harold says, his eyes hardening. "The few times I had to socialize with him, there wasn't much communication between us. Of course, he didn't know English, and I didn't speak much Japanese, so any conversation had to go through Mike." He glares, "For all I know, every time he spoke to me he was telling me to kiss his ass—and I felt the same way about him!" Harold sighs, his temper evening. "But I never expressed that in front of her. That was taboo for me." He admits, "I made a disparaging comment about him one time, and she admonished me, saying, 'You'll not talk that way anymore!' So I never did...but I insisted that she wasn't to give him any more money." Harold squares his jaw, "It's no wonder he didn't like me. By freeing her from her debt, and then marrying her, I'd taken away his meal ticket!"

"Did anybody in her family ever know how much you'd paid to buy her freedom?"

"No, I don't think they ever did."

"But they knew you had released her from debt..."

"I'm sure she'd had to answer questions about that within the family, and whatever she decided to tell them, that was her business. I never talked about it with any of them."

"So no one in her family ever thanked you for what you'd done for her?"

"No," he smiles, "but I got the prize."

Even without his narration, the photographs in Harold's album tell the story of the newlyweds' happy and routine life on the north island of Hokkaido: pictures of Harold puttering off to work on the scooter he assembled from boxes of parts; photos documenting heavy winter snowfalls and summer dips in icy mountain lakes; snapshots taken during various parties they hosted for friends and coworkers (including one showing Chiyoko entertaining their guests by adeptly plucking the strings of a shamisen, in what Harold remembers as her farewell performance with that instrument). And, of course, pictures of cherry blossoms—nature's precious springtime gift to the people of Japan, blooms that Harold will forever associate with his wife and the walks he took with her in perfumed parks beneath branches heavy laden with blushing velvet petals. Life on the northern island of Japan was good, and the couple spent two wonderful years there. Eventually, however, Harold's tour was up, and he received orders for a new posting and a return to an old profession: training artillerymen at Fort Sheridan in Chicago, Illinois.

It was time to take his bride home.

The entire Okada family gathered at the pier to see them off. "Oh yeah," Harold notes, "they were all there. Her father, brother and sister, aunts and uncles, cousins…they had a whole crowd assembled to say good-bye. Her sister and her father were in tears," he remembers. "The sister because she was going to miss Chiyoko so much, the father because, despite my wishes, I believe she was still sneaking him money!" Harold throws up his hands in resignation. "Dedication to parents…" he mutters.

"The two of us (sadly, Buffy the dog had to remain behind in the care of friends) sailed on a troopship, and so we were separated. I was below deck and Mike was above in a stateroom. I could only visit the upper deck during the day—"

"But you were married," I interject. "Why were you separated?"

"Because that was the billet I had coming home!" He shrugs, explaining to me that there is a big difference between an army relocation voyage and a cruise. "The officers, they got staterooms, but I was just a sergeant, so I rode in steerage with the other enlisted men. During the daytime hours we could go on the upper deck to be with our wives, but at night, that was off limits."

"So this was not a romantic tour of the South Seas," I laugh.

"No," he chuckles. "No hanky-panky! They had guys on watch to keep us out of there at night. The wives shared staterooms, so even during the day we couldn't go up to their rooms. It was…" he grunts, "damned inconvenient. I was very glad when we finally arrived in Seattle."

"That was where your wife first touched American soil?"

"I have a picture here somewhere…" he says, rifling through the album pages, "of her coming down the gangway." Of course he does.

From Seattle, the couple boarded a Great Northern Railway passenger train, bound for Chicago with a stop in Minnesota. Needless to say, on this leg of the journey, Harold happily paid extra for a private sleeping compartment.

Throughout the trip, Chiyoko was amazed at the seemingly deserted, open spaces of the American West. She kept insisting, "All of this land is wasted!" Harold tried to convince her that much of what she perceived as idle soil was grazing land, but from her perspective, as a native of a densely populated island nation where people practically lived one on top of another, the United States was inarguably a territory of vast empty spaces and untapped potential. Of course, training eastward across the forlorn plains of Montana and North Dakota, where Harold had once dropped to his knees in mud to slake a desert thirst, he understood that they could not have picked a more desolate route across this country.

Despite the dense canopy of the Stevens' family tree, Harold and Chiyoko were met in Minnesota by a considerably smaller delegation of relatives than had seen them off in Yokohama. This was entirely by design.

"When we got off the train at Union Station in St. Paul," Harold tells me, "only my mother and my sister Floy, with her husband and two children, were there to greet us. I'd sent a message ahead that they were the only people I wanted in that station when we arrived." He explains, "I had a real fear that if a whole bunch of my brothers and sisters were there to welcome me home with my Japanese bride, one of them was bound to make an inappropriate remark, and then I would have to kill someone."

It was a legitimate concern, born of years of interfamilial brickbats and backstabbing. "My family was the *damnedest* crew," he asserts. "They could be the nicest people in the world, but they could also be just terrible…ridiculing others, not to mention one another! I mean it," he emphasizes, "they could find fault with the angels! My brothers especially, never having been exposed to Asian people or that culture, they worried me—particularly my older brother Lorin. I felt certain that if he was in that train station when we arrived, there was the distinct possibility he would say something crude or racist to offend my wife, and I would go to fist city with him right there!"

"What about your mother?" I ask, mindful that perhaps she might have judged Chiyoko to be a woman who had led her son down the sinful path.

Harold considers. "I can't say for sure what my mother was feeling," he tells me, "but I think she was okay. She greeted my wife warmly and with lots of hugs and kisses. I didn't see any animosity at all. And of course, she quickly came to regard Mike very highly. They all did."

"Even Lorin?"

He nods, "The whole family. It was something of a miracle. A couple days later we made a side trip up to Duluth where the extended family got together and threw us a big party. That night..." he takes a mental step back to expand the view, "in fact, throughout our entire marriage," and then Harold repeats something I remember him saying during our very first interview, "I never heard a bad or insensitive word said by any of my family about my wife. And if something had been said, it would have gotten back to me because they all liked nothing better than to tattle on one another. But to my knowledge, none of my brothers or my sisters ever spoke ill of her. And in a family like mine, that's really saying something."

"It does seem remarkable," I concur. "A lot of people, especially in those days, held strong opinions about interracial marriage—some still do."

"It made me proud of my family," Harold says, his eyes suddenly filling, and for a moment, I consider that his siblings collectively managed to do at least one thing that moves him. But, of course, his tears are for her. Always for her. "My wife had a personality that could win people over like nobody else. In fact," he marvels, "my brother Lorin absolutely adored my wife. He just thought she was the greatest, and he became one of her favorites out of the whole family. I never would have believed it," Harold swallows, "but that was Mike. You couldn't *not* love my wife."

# Chapter 26
# CHICAGO
## シカゴ

B Y ANY MEASURE, Chicago should have been a high point for Harold. He was back in the Midwest, near enough to Minnesota that his mother could visit, a proximity that would give rise to the proudest moment of his army career. He was based in a large city, where his newly transplanted wife, who had spent nearly all her life in a great urban center, felt at home and at ease. Astonishingly, their best friends on earth were living just a stone's throw away. But in the end, the negatives would far outweigh the good, and the repercussions of his time in the Windy City would howl and echo throughout Harold's life, leaving his conscience so troubled that this surpassed even the war in keeping him from ever again knowing real peace.

Things had started out so well. In fact, Harold's posting to Fort Sheridan almost seemed fated. That's because only a short time earlier, Barney and Flora Nozaki had also moved to Chicago.

"It was where Barney was born," Harold reminds me. He is standing, framed in his enormous picture window, staring out at a driving rain. His gray and white flannel shirt is perfect camouflage against the leaden downpour. "Ever since the end of the Second

World War," he says, loud enough to compete over the rowdy precipitation, "Barney had wanted to return to America."

Glancing toward his favorite chair, Harold is similarly focused on a familiar place to land. Flaps down, he lines up on the recliner and greases in for a practiced, three-point landing. "But when Barney applied to come back here," he continues, settling back, "he couldn't get a visa because of his service in the Japanese military. Eventually, his wife, Flora, immigrated to the States, where she petitioned for him to join her. This time, his application was approved—in fact, he was officially designated an Asset to the United States Government." Harold has no idea what had changed, or what that even meant, but he cannot help being impressed. "You had to know that Barney was a pretty smart cookie to be let in with that status!" he asserts, a fact that was confirmed not long after his friend arrived on American soil. "Barney sent out his résumé, and the Hotpoint division of General Electric snapped him up. They put him to work researching vacuum refrigeration, and Flora became a translator—and, by god," Harold marvels, "they had settled in Chicago!"

It is hard to reconcile the coincidence. "So it was simply by happenstance that you ended up assigned to the very same place in the world where Barney and Flora were living?" I ask, with amazement.

"Completely by chance," he affirms. "I'd kept tabs on Barney, so I knew he was there. When Mike and I arrived in Chicago, we drove straight to his apartment," he laughs, "and we surprised the hell out of him!"

In fact, Barney and Flora lived only a short distance from Harold's duty station at Fort Sheridan, where he had been assigned as an instructor for the installation's battery of 120-millimeter anti-aircraft guns. Harold had zero experience with anything other than field artillery before arriving in Illinois, but prodded by Cold War urgency (this was a time when defensive artillery batteries were located in and around major U.S. cities) he got himself up to speed quickly. Soon, he was training both army and National Guard units to rake the skies of any Russian bombers intent upon raining nuclear destruction on America's Second City. His firing range was the open expanse of Lake Michigan, but the deafening sound of the artillery shook both land and water. "Boy," Harold exclaims, working a finger in one ear, "when those long barrels fired, they really rang your bell!" It is a wonder that the Nozakis, living close by, got any sleep at all.

Chiyoko took to Chicago like a mouse in a pantry, sampling everything the city had to offer. Their apartment was located on the North Side, also near the base, but as a lifelong resident of Tokyo she was undaunted by the intricacies of public transit (in Chicago, they lived so close to the "L" tracks that a visitor remarked, "I didn't realize the train ran right through the bathroom!") and she soon found work in a Japanese restaurant near the Loop. She also had a full-time job attending to the cut of Harold's jib. "The whole time I was in service my uniforms fit me like gloves," he says, "because if they didn't, my wife tailored them to fit. In those early years, she made all those alterations by hand," he emphasizes. "Whenever I stood in front of a platoon, I was the sharpest damn soldier in the bunch. She made me that way."

With every feather neatly in place, Harold was a cock of the walk sergeant—and never more so than the time his family came to visit. He grins, "My kid sister brought my mother down to see us, and while they were there, the entire battalion was on parade. I'll be damned if the division didn't suddenly turn the whole thing over to me!" He notes that the responsibility for getting six hundred men organized and moving in lockstep, using just your voice, is not for the faint of heart. "You can very quickly make a damn fool of yourself if you screw that up!" he says. "But I took my position and I did the job. I formed them up, I marched them all over to the park, I marched them on parade, and I marched them all the way back again." Despite his crooked spine, Harold is sitting distinctly taller in his chair. "When I called cadence, you could hear me all over that park! My wife, my kid sister, and my mother saw me do that," he says, voice cracking, "and I was so damn proud!"

It is the thought of this last spectator that elicits such an emotional response. "I'd been a real problem child for my mother," he concedes, "defiant, self-centered, and constantly looking for trouble. Now, I wanted her to know that I understood she'd done the best she could by me, and I wanted to show her that I had turned out okay." Gulping sentiment, he remembers, "So on that parade field, I was really strutting my stuff!" Chin up, he smiles, "That day, I was the proudest SOB that ever walked in uniform."

When a cannon fires, the projectile is expelled by gunpowder undergoing something chemists call an exothermic reaction—it gives off heat. In its base form, a man's frailty is the same: feverish sexual desire that cannot be contained. "Lust takes over," Harold says. "It blinds you."

There is no easy way to talk about what went wrong in Chicago, so Harold simply lays it out, "While I was there, I was not faithful to my wife."

The impact of these words leaves me breathless and dazed, like a gut punch, or running headlong into a brick wall, except I would have seen those coming. Given all that has gone before—Harold's spontaneous and profound infatuation with Chiyoko (the very definition of love at first sight) and his obsessive pursuit of her despite the innumerable roadblocks and detours of money, culture, and distance, a quest that had finally, and against all odds, culminated in their happy marriage—the thought that he could jeopardize all of that by betraying her is a revelation that is shocking, heartbreaking, and, as Harold knows full well, it changes everything.

I am speechless, so in a voice nearly void of expression, a flat murmur of confession, Harold does the talking.

"In the summertime, the army would send me up to Camp Haven," he begins, "which was just on the other side of Sheboygan, Wisconsin. This was a place where we practiced firing anti-aircraft guns for two to three weeks at a time.

"In the basement of the hotel in Sheboygan, there was a lounge and a bowling alley. After work, a buddy and I would sometimes sit and have a drink in that lounge. One night while we were there, two women came up to the bar after bowling, and I thought one of them was particularly attractive. She was young, dark-haired, with a nice figure…" Although alcohol may have contributed to what happened next, Harold is not making excuses. He's just stating fact when he says, "I'd had a few drinks too many, and I was showing off. I waltzed over to her and I said, 'You know, if you play your cards right, you can probably have me.'"

He regretted it the moment he said it. It was not a serious proposition. He was over-served and trying to impress his friend, and when he heard the words come out, he knew they did not sound charming or smooth or funny, just stupid and rude.

"She could see I was obviously drunk and so she didn't say a word, and then she turned away. Feeling like a complete heel, I went back to my friend, we finished our drinks and we left. A couple days later we were back in the same lounge, and those two girls were there again. I told my buddy, I've got to go over and apologize for making a prize ass of myself. So I went down the bar and I said to the girl, 'I want to tell you how sorry I am for the way I acted the last time I saw you.' I said, 'I don't normally pull things like that, but I'd had a lot to drink...' She smiled at me and said, 'Well, in a way, I thought it was kind of cute!'"

Harold could have, definitely should have, walked away, but her comment switched off his brain and ignited something lower—an exothermic reaction. So instead, he uttered the fateful words that have marked both the beginning and the ruin of countless relationships: *Can I buy you a drink?*

"We introduced ourselves. She told me her name was Margaret, and after we had talked for a while, I invited her to go with me to another bar where we could get a bite to eat. There was a back room there with a jukebox, and we danced the night away. It started out as just two people having some fun...and we ended up back at her apartment. That's when the affair started."

I have found my voice. "Harold, why?! Just...*why?*"

He stares vacantly out the window, the pane drumming furiously with wind-driven rain. "How do you get involved in an affair..." he contemplates. I cannot help notice that he has switched to the second person point of view—perhaps, when discussing such things, it's easier to talk as if it is about somebody else. "You are blind," he concedes. "If you thought about it beforehand, if you thought about what the consequences might be, if you thought that your marriage might come crashing down because of it, you wouldn't have an affair—not if you loved your wife as much as I did. But you don't think about these things when lust takes over."

"As all of this was unfolding," I persist, "you must have been thinking—"

"I *wasn't* thinking," he underscores, with an angry flare of remorse. "I was satisfying my lust, and I had no reason to do that. My wife and I had a wonderful sex life. But this lady was attracted to me," he shrugs gloomily, "and I was attracted to her. We'd danced and had a good time…"

"And you had been drinking."

He is not taking the easy way out. A lesser man might be tempted to blame his behavior on the liquor, or even rationalize that adultery was in his blood—after all, cheating is what the Stevens boys did; infidelity was practically the family motto. But Harold waves a hand dismissively, accepting full responsibility for his actions. Furthermore, he wants me to understand this was not a one-night stand, or some tawdry tryst. "There was something between us," he avows. "When I saw Margaret in that lounge, instead of just apologizing and leaving it at that, there was a spark. So I asked her, would she like to go get something to eat, maybe have a drink or two. Socialize. And she agreed. I liked her. We could have been friends, but it went too far. I don't think either of us intended that in the beginning. I was married. I didn't make a habit of picking up women in bars, nor was she that kind of woman."

"Did you tell Margaret that you were married?"

"Oh, yes. I never hid that from her. But look," he says, generously, "she wasn't out to break up a marriage. And I wasn't out to wreck one. An opportunity arises, and you do something that normally you would never consider doing. Something stupid. Again, I'm not blaming anyone but myself, but it happens. I've known guys who loved their wives dearly, but one or two bad decisions later they were headed for divorce. They didn't stop loving their wives. They just made stupid mistakes. And their wives found out."

Ah. The crux for the repentant adulterer: whether to vomit the truth or swallow it, where it continues to bubble and gnaw.

"Did you ever confess any of this to Chiyoko?"

"No," he says, eyes filling, "It would have hurt her so deeply, and why would I put her through that? She had done nothing wrong, and I had no intention of leaving her and taking up with Margaret."

To spare his wife, this would be Harold's secret pain, his personal shame, but concealing the affair from her was also a desperate act of self-preservation. "No..." he considers, "I have little doubt that confessing this thing would have been the end of my marriage. And I loved being married to Mike," he insists. "I can't imagine there's a person who loved a wife more than me..."

Harold's regret is palpable, but I ask him about it anyway.

"Of *course* I regret it!" he practically wails. "Of course! Had I to do it all over again, I never would have spoken to Margaret in that lounge in the first place. But...when you're young, there's a multitude of mistakes out there, and they're all available for you to make. And what a person thinks he would do is not necessarily what that person will do when he's toe to toe with temptation. I'm not trying to justify my own ignorance or my behavior. All I can say is that I made a mistake along the way. I was never proud of it. Men who go through life—especially military life, where the husband is part of one world and the wife lives in another—and never make a mistake, I admire them. I envy their self-discipline and their morality. They're stronger and better people than I was."

"How long did the affair last?"

"Not long. I saw her several times while I was in Wisconsin. Then, after I returned to Chicago, she showed up there..."

"Did you ask her to come?"

"Absolutely not!" he insists. "That would have been the dumbest thing I could have done! No, out of the blue, she called me from the bus depot. I couldn't just leave her sitting there, so I went and picked her up and took her to a motel in the suburbs.

"So the affair continued in Chicago..."

"No," he says firmly. "I had broken it off when I left Sheboygan. When Margaret came to the city, I told her, 'I can't do this. My wife is here, and I will not risk my marriage.' The next morning I took her back to the bus depot and bought her a ticket home."

I want to ask him if he ever saw Margaret again, but he has moved on now, to Chiyoko and their relationship.

"I never wanted to spend my life with any woman other than Mike, but Chicago tested me with temptation," he says dejectedly, "and I failed that test. I'm sorry that it happened, but there's not a damn thing I could do about it after the fact. I was a poor husband in that moment, but I believe I became a better and more attentive husband because of it. I understood that I had risked everything. I knew how lucky I was to have such a wonderful wife, and I never took that for granted again. It was the only affair I ever had. Chicago taught me a lot of lessons…"

Again, I say, "What were you thinking…" although this time it is less a question than an articulation of my thoughts about the risks and potential consequences of such behavior. "I mean, what if Margaret had become pregnant—?"

Harold's plaintive expression suddenly collapses into an even deeper well of abject despair and guilt, and a terrible understanding jolts me as if I've inadvertently stumbled upon a live wire, a shocking strand hidden in long grass, which in a way, I have.

The trials of Chicago were not over.

# Chapter 27
# THUNDER

THE ELECTRIC REPERCUSSIONS of Harold's dalliance with Margaret have charged the atmosphere in this room, much like the progressing storm has outside, but like the weather, Harold is not quite there yet. He's building up to it. As he continues his narrative, I listen anxiously, knowing the wire is there, and that eventually, a bolt is coming.

Adultery was not worth the price of admission. This was Harold's miserable opinion in the immediate aftermath of the affair. Fleeting sexual gratification was a poor trade for what promised to be a lifetime of hidden truths and self-loathing. So he determined never to repeat such a blunder, and in the process, trite though it may sound, he discovered a pathway to a better life.

"Before my slipup," he says, voice flinty with resolve, "my goal had been to be a damn good soldier—and I was. But now I'd come to realize that my wife should be the center of my life. From then on, I determined that my achievements would be measured according to her happiness. It was important for me to produce a good life for this remarkable woman who had devoted herself so completely to me." Harold pauses to reflect upon this profound shift in his thinking. "I guess what I'm trying to say," he concludes, "is that I had woken up to the fact that I was a husband, and that Chiyoko deserved an honest partner and a good provider. And so at the ripe old age of twenty-six years," he manages a weak smile, "I decided that maybe education wasn't such a bad deal after all."

A decade after leaving Central High School via the rear exit, Harold sat for the General Educational Development Test (GED). These exams had been developed by the military as a way for servicemen like him, who had joined up before earning their high school diplomas, to prove they had the knowledge base required for securing jobs or pursuing higher education. "You can do it," Chiyoko had said to him, in response to his anxieties about taking the test. "Of course," she noted, quite practically, "you'll have to study." Despite his continued doubts and protestations, she just smiled and voiced unwavering faith in his potential: "Study, and you'll do it."

He passed with flying colors.

"Afterward, I thought, *that was easy*," he says, like a man who has picked his first lock with a single twist. "I decided I'd take a whack at the first year, college-level GED—and I aced that too!" He taps his noggin, "So I must have had some brains in here somewhere." Buoyed by these successes and by his wife's steady, almost obstinate confidence in him, Harold was seriously contemplating leaving the military to attend college when another door presented itself—one that would also require some jimmying and was too tempting not to try.

"While I was in Chicago," he says, "I had been farmed out as an advisor to National Guard units in Illinois, Wisconsin, and Michigan. During the course of these visits, I'd had a chance to observe the full-time army advisors stationed at those places, and it seemed like they had pretty plush situations." Specifically, he noted, unlike him, advisors did not work tedious, unpredictable hours; they were not constantly being saddled with problem recruits; and there were no junior officers breathing down their necks—in other words, they enjoyed duties free from all the usual army headaches.

Even more importantly, Harold explains, "These were very much professional positions, and to give my wife the kind of life she deserved, I desperately needed to shift gears." He fixes me with the honest frustration of a racehorse stuck in the gate. "Professionally,

I thought, *Why am I being held back? What am I doing wrong?* Because I knew gunnery: 120-millimeter guns, 90-millimeter, 75... you name it. If I knew all that, and enough to pass the GEDs, why was I trapped doing what I was doing, just training the knuckleheads? So I asked a couple of those advisors, 'How the hell do I get a job like yours?!'"

Basically, they told him to lie.

"They were pretty smart fellows," he chuckles, "full of sound advice about how to wangle my way into one of those assignments! They said, 'You're in a good position because you're getting near the end of your hitch. Go down to the advisor department at 5th Army headquarters and put in an application for one of these jobs. Then go back to Fort Sheridan and make those people believe you're getting out of the army—'"

"Hold on," I interrupt, "why would you do that?"

"To avoid being assigned to another damn artillery unit! I wanted out of serving another tour as a gunnery sergeant, but by now I had a Military Occupational Service number attached to my name that shackled me to artillery, and there's no doubt that's where they would send me—again. So I took the advice. At Fort Sheridan, I pretended like I was going to be discharged, and then, when the time came, I had the group at 5th Army re-enlist me for direct assignment to the unit I'd requested. Lo and behold," he beams, "they gave me a three-year stint as an advisor to the National Guard in Cloquet, Minnesota—just a twenty minute drive from Duluth!"

"You're kidding me!"

He shakes his head affirmatively, grinning, "We moved into an apartment just a few blocks from where my mother was living in West Duluth!" Harold sums up his satisfaction succinctly, "Being assigned to Cloquet was the best thing that ever happened to me in the army. It gave my wife and me...almost a normal life together."

"When you say you were an army advisor to the National Guard," I wonder, "what does that mean?"

"There were a handful of 90-millimeter anti-aircraft units scattered across northeastern Minnesota," he explains. "When they drilled, I had to be there to watch and report on their training. I had administrative duties too. I kept records, posted updates to the regulations, and verified payroll, among other things. So I was also getting an education by doing all that—not a formal education, but learning new skills and gaining confidence about what I was capable of doing."

Plus, for the first time in many years, Harold was home, enjoying the town and the environment where he had grown up. In the springtime he fished. In the fall he procured two M1 rifles and half a case of ammunition to go hunting with Lorin. The deer never had a chance.

Best of all, being back in Duluth gave him an opportunity to continue mending fences with his mother, to scrub one by one at the black marks he had accumulated throughout childhood. Harold stopped on his way to work every morning to bring her the newspaper. At night, if he saw her bedroom light was still on, he would pop up for a visit. Mainly they would talk about why people in the family were the way they were, but occasionally the conversation drifted toward more personal topics, like the reason she had never considered remarrying (she said it was because she couldn't bear the possibility of having any more kids).

For his mother's sake, Harold submitted to the trials of Stevens family gatherings and reunions, including one held at the city zoo—which was about right, he thought. The family even played a little baseball together; by now their roster included enough in-laws and outlaws to field an entire league of their own.

But perhaps the surest sign of Harold's sincere determination to make things right with his mother was when he started showing up at a place where wild horses could not have dragged him when he was a kid. On Sunday mornings, he accompanied her to church.

For her part, Chiyoko also enjoyed living in Harold's hometown, first and foremost because his new job allowed him to spend more time at home, although she was not the type to just sit around the house waiting for him. Unlike Chicago, there was not a Japanese restaurant within a hundred-fifty miles of Duluth, but she found other ways to busy herself in this modest city beside another Great Lake. In particular, she focused on furthering her own education. She applied for American citizenship, studied English and history, and found camaraderie in the company of other foreign nationals she met at night school.

And unlike Harold, Chiyoko looked forward to the get-togethers with the Stevens clan. These occasions were always brimming with children, with new ones swelling the family census every time the relatives flocked. Chiyoko was always on the floor with the little ones, playing games or reveling in their delighted laughter at the mouse puppet she inventively crafted from a handkerchief. She lived to entertain the little kids. It set her apart from the other women in the family. That, and the fact that she had no children of her own.

Chiyoko and Harold had been intimate more times than they could ever count, without a whisper of pregnancy. Before immigrating to the United States, she had undergone an extensive physical examination that suggested some abnormality in her fallopian tubes. The army doctors had responded by nearly drowning her in penicillin. Then, while the couple was still living in Chicago, she had occasionally experienced mild pain during sexual intercourse. An examination there clarified the problem—a tumor. It was benign, but, she was told, an impediment to ever bearing children.

"We should have asked more questions," Harold mutters, "done more digging, maybe gotten a second opinion. The army doctors never gave us options. They never mentioned the possibility of surgery or anything else..." He exhales a heavy sigh. "But I was changing assignments, we were moving between cities, and we both just got distracted. We never did anything more about it. We should have pursued it here in Duluth. That's one of my great regrets."

I wonder about Chiyoko, how this diagnosis affected her.

"Not much," he says, surprisingly. "It wasn't something that she dwelled on," he insists, "and it didn't make her outwardly unhappy. Maybe it was that Japanese attitude about fate, but she accepted it." Perhaps so, but Harold believes a family of their own was something Chiyoko would have welcomed—as he would have—and he should have pushed harder for it. "Later on, we discussed adopting a child or two from Japan, but the timing for that never worked out either. When you're in the military," he sighs, "and always going here and there, and switching jobs...it's difficult. I blame myself for this. I have guilt that I wasn't more aggressive in pursuing it. Because my wife loved little kids. She just loved them..." he muses, wistfully.

"My family was always sprouting children, there were new ones wherever we went, and she couldn't get enough of them. Maybe she could have had children, maybe not. I know one thing," he works his lower lip determinedly, "she'd have been a *damn* good mother."

Harold, on the other hand, had the potential to be as fruitful as any Stevens, past or present.

The proof is a high-voltage strand, crackling in the tall grass.

The rain outside Harold's window has been augmented with thunder, but curiously, no lightning. The brilliant flashes must be there, concealed within the growling folds of atmosphere. There cannot be an effect without a cause—although sometimes a consequence is so significant and enduring, it may seem that way. As the rumbling darkness spatters the glass, Harold gives voice to the perfect example, and it has nothing to do with the weather.

"I'm not sure how long I'd been in Duluth…"

He breaks off—until I wonder whether he is waiting for a response from me, but then, "…probably only a few months. My National Guard unit went down to Sheboygan for a firing drill, and I went along to observe…"

Another long pause, and it is clear to me now these delays are a brooding study; he will get to it, whatever it is causing this dark reverie. When he finally does, I understand his contemplation, and his mood. "While I was there, I happened to run into a guy that had been in my unit in Chicago…and he said to me, 'Did you know Margaret was pregnant?'

Staring out at the rain, Harold swallows, "I thought, *You've got to be kidding me*…because if this was true, I had a pretty good idea who it was that had made her that way. So I went to the bar where we used to meet, and I asked the bartender if he knew Margaret's phone number. He did, and I asked him if he would call her, tell her I was there, and see if she would come over…"

This time, it feels like minutes before he speaks again. It must have seemed hours to him, sitting in that tavern, waiting for Margaret to show up. In fact, she had come immediately.

"My friend had known Margaret was pregnant because she was so ballooned out, but when she walked through the door, she didn't have a trace of a tummy." Harold fixes me with a singular expression of anxious wonder, "She had delivered a baby boy three weeks earlier." His gaze shifts back toward the gray void beyond the window. The lightning has arrived. I imagine his memories are playing out there, as if upon a flickering screen.

"We greeted each other, and I immediately told her I knew that she'd had a baby, and why the hell hadn't she told me she was pregnant? She came straight back at me, saying, 'I was not going to break up a marriage!'

"I said, 'You're telling me the baby is mine?'

"She told me, yes, it was. My heart sank, and I felt like a goddamn heel because I hadn't known about any of this.

"I asked her, 'Could I see the baby?'

So we went over to her apartment. When I walked in, there was a crib there with little fingers and feet wiggling around inside it. I went over, bent down, and put my hands behind the baby's back and picked the little tyke up, and I stared right into his face. It was like looking at a reflection. There was no doubt in my mind that this child was mine. I kept asking her, why, why, *why* didn't you tell me? And she kept giving me the same answer: 'I was not going to break up a family.'

"I suddenly thought of her bus trip to Chicago—when she'd unexpectedly showed up there to see me—and I knew then that she'd come with the intention of telling me. But she never did. She never said one damn word about it. I asked her, 'Why didn't you tell me about this when you came to Chicago?' Again, her answer was, 'I made up my mind that I was not going to break up a marriage.' She just kept insisting on that.

"I said to her, 'What can I do now? Tell me what you want me to do.'

"'Nothing,' she said, 'I don't want you to do anything.' No matter how much I pressed her, she didn't expect anything, and she wouldn't take anything from me, no money, no promise of support, nothing. She wasn't angry with me, but she understood my dedication to my wife, and she knew that severing all ties would be the best way for us all to move forward..." Harold nods solemnly, "She was a very brave, very smart lady.

"To me, it didn't matter what *I* wanted," Harold says. "I felt I had no right to do anything other than abide by her wishes, so I told her, 'If that's the way you want it, when I leave here, you'll never see me again. That will be it. I won't try to contact you. I won't intrude into your life. If that's what you really want, that's the way it will be.'

"'That's what I want,' she said.

"So I put the baby down, and I never saw that child again."

Harold looks spent. Confession may be good for the soul, but it takes a lot out of a body, especially one that is nearly ninety years old. Even now, sitting, contemplating the storm, he is stooped like a penitent, which is right on the mark. He may be shrouded in sackcloth and ashes, but it is my role to delicately poke at the frazzled weave of this profoundly tragic admission.

"You must have been worried that at some point," I ask gently, "either this woman, or the boy, might suddenly come back into your life and upend the applecart of your marriage?"

"No, I wasn't afraid of that," he breathes out. "Because Margaret was so determined that it wasn't going to happen. She wouldn't have allowed it. She was very sincere in her desire to never cause me or my wife any trouble, and I trusted her."

I work another angle. "What if Margaret had been a different kind of woman, the kind who had said, 'I'm pregnant. Now what are you going to do about it?' Were you prepared to leave your wife if that's what she'd asked?"

Harold instinctively musters his twisted back against the doughy cushion of his recliner. "I would have lived up to my obligations," he asserts, "but no, I would never have willingly left my wife. I loved Mike. I idolized that lady..." he sags, and at last, emotion overwhelms him—it is a miracle he has held it back this long. But when the tears finally arrive, they are not for himself, or Margaret, or even his lost boy. "I would have given my life for my wife," he chokes. "The question is, would she have stayed with me?" Along with the sorrow written across his face, there is a vestige of relief that reads, *thank god I never had to find out.*

It seems unimaginable to me that Harold was never tempted to reconnect with his child, especially in light of how unkind fate had been to him and Chiyoko in this regard. "You and your wife weren't able to have children," I venture, "but you had a son. Somewhere out in the world you had a son. At some point—"

He cuts me off. "I never considered trying to contact him. Besides the hurt it would have caused Mike if she'd ever found out, trying to find him would have gone against my promise to Margaret. I owe her everything. Thanks to her, I had fifty-seven years of happiness with the finest wife I could ever imagine. It took one hell of a strong woman to do what Margaret did, to walk away and face what she faced, raising a child on her own. It's a debt I can never repay. So, no, I had no right to disrespect her wishes and intrude on her life, or the boy's."

Of course, that doesn't mean he did not want to find them. To find *him*. To know him. Harold stares disconsolately at the sullen skies through rain-smattered glass, streaked like the cheeks of this erased father. "I only saw him that one time," he muses, "when I held him for just a few minutes, but I never stopped thinking about that boy…my whole damn life."

Unanswerable questions press him like deep water.

"And every day…" he emphasizes, swallowing his tears, "since my wife died, I've sat right here and thought about him. Every day."

# Chapter 28
# LUCK

GODDAMN KOREA.

How Harold hates the memory of that wretched country. The stink, the rats, the ruin…he considered it a pitiful cesspool of a nation, defined by the ravages and miseries of war. He is embarrassed to say it, but he also had little regard for the native Koreans he encountered there. He remembers them as thieving opportunists, mired in poverty. He knows full well that, today, the South Koreans have pulled themselves up out of the muck. A few years ago he went there as part of a veterans' revisit program and was astounded at their progress, gaping with disbelief at Seoul's gleaming skyscrapers, touchstones of a thoroughly modern and prosperous society. During that trip, his heart was moved by the hospitality and gratitude of the people, including clean-scrubbed little schoolchildren who showered him with their thanks and kisses. But he considers that a different country. His Korea was an awful place—an opinion colored by three miserable tours and each one he had prayed would be his last. Then, after finally putting an ocean between himself and that place, and settling into the best job he had ever known, Harold was abruptly given orders to pack his bags. "Things couldn't have been going better for me in Duluth," he says, with a sardonic smile that plainly telegraphs the other shoe about to drop. "I was supposed to have a three-year tour of duty here, but after just eighteen months the army pulled the rug out from underneath me and they sent my fanny back to goddamn Korea. The war was done," he adds bitterly, "but that's one time I really wanted to kill somebody."

It is a new day—a sunny day. The storms of midsummer and the tempestuous events of Chicago are behind us, and Harold is sitting alongside me exhibiting renewed strength, a brighter checked shirt, and yet another photo album is spread open between us: Korea, round four.

"Why would the army do that to you?" I ask.

Because they literally had his number, he explains. "I was an artilleryman. I had that damn Military Occupational Service number following me wherever I went. I'd gotten free from it for a little while, but then somebody decided they needed another gunnery sergeant in Korea…" Harold shrugs.

"That must have been a bitter pill, being forced to leave Cloquet and suddenly being sent off like that—and back to Korea, of all places!"

"It was," he nods glumly, "and, of course, my wife couldn't go with me."

By this time, the Korean War was over, although not really. A few months after Harold's foot had been hammered out, so had a tenuous armistice initiating one of the most uneasy and long-lived truces in modern military history. For sixty-plus years and counting, there has been no peace treaty, hence no official end to the war. Instead, the opposing armies still glare and posture at one another across a demilitarized zone (a snaking ribbon of no-man's land that nearly replicates the same border *before* an estimated three million people died). It is an area where the possibility of hostilities reigniting, either by design or by accident, is always present. In those early years especially, it was no place for a soldier's wife.

Harold couldn't see how things could be worse for him, but fate pointed the way. "A few days before I was to leave," he grimaces, "I was helping my mother hook up Christmas lights. I was crawling around on the floor plugging things in, and as I started to get up there was a sound like a skidding tire and I went down like a ton of bricks. I'd torn all the cartilage in my left knee!"

Harold was in agony, but apparently not enough to get a deferment, or even any immediate medical relief. "The doctor at the Duluth air base told me, 'Well, there's not much I can do, and as long as you're on orders, you've got to go. Maybe somewhere along the line they can do something for you.'" Harold glares, "Well, they couldn't—or didn't. Every day my leg swelled up until my pants were tight around the knee, and these were loose-fitting army fatigues!" It was the beginning of another lifelong torment.

He did catch one break when he got to Oakland, California. "I was scheduled to go over on yet another troopship, and one of the sergeants handling the shipments there was giving a briefing. I thought, *Hell, I know him! I taught him to be a railway conductor in Japan!* After the meeting I went up and spoke with him. He asked me, 'Is there anything I can do for you while you're here?' I told him, 'Well, I'm getting damn tired of floating back and forth across this pond. If you can get me on an airplane, I'd be forever grateful!'"

The next day Harold was spread out across three empty seats, flying above the Pacific in a military cargo plane operated by Slick Airways. "When I saw that name on the side of the plane," he snorts, "I thought, *Slick, indeed!*"

As we are looking over his photos of artillery crews training in the fields and mountains adjoining the DMZ, we land on a picture of Harold sprawled out lazily above a broad valley. "This was taken along the Imjin River, and as you can see," he smirks, "I was putting forth a lot of effort."

In truth, he was. Harold was once again with the 1st Cavalry Division, but this time there was no chance of him inadvertently putting together a piece of machinery back to front; as a gun section leader and, eventually, chief of firing battery for the 19th Artillery, the only things he was assembling during this go-around were units of practiced artillerymen.

"I got stuck on umpire teams a lot," he says, explaining that because Korea was no longer a shooting war, training was now the primary focus for units stationed there, and umpires were tasked with observing and rating their performance. "I was an umpire at the battalion, regiment, and division levels," he tells me, "and I was glad to be involved in mock battles, rather than the kind where someone was intent upon killing me."

His knee, meanwhile, had taken up that role.

"They kept putting me into the field," Harold gripes, "even though the pain was becoming more and more unbearable. I insisted that I needed to see a doctor. Instead, my unit sent me to the medics, who gave me water pills and wrapped the knee tightly with an elastic bandage. None of it did me any good, but I soldiered on, doing my job, as ordered—until finally I couldn't do it anymore. My knee was so swollen and painful, I said to the major, 'Either give me transport to the hospital or take me to see the Inspector General and we'll let him sort it out. It's your choice!'" In no time at all, Harold had an ambulance waiting to deliver him to the 121st Evac Hospital.

"I told the orthopedic surgeon there about my problem, and he said, 'Let's have a look; take your trousers off.' I had to practically peel those fatigues past the swollen knee. When the doctor saw that elastic bandage, I thought his head was going to explode! He got on the phone right then and called up the dispensary where I was stationed, and he raised hell with them for applying pressure to the kneecap. It had ground up all the soft tissue underneath."

Harold was admitted to the hospital, where, other than him waking up in the middle of his surgery, things finally started to turn around. Both before and after the operation, he went through days of whirlpool and weight therapy to reduce swelling and strengthen the knee. "They put me into the hands of a gung ho PT nurse named Hamilton, and I just *loved* to watch her go to work on people," he says playfully. "She didn't monkey around! A guy would come in with a bad back, and she would put him face down on the table. Then she'd crawl up, sit on him, and pull his shoulders back until that patient was hollering and screaming!" Harold smirks, "I used to take it all in and agitate things a little. Whenever someone new would show up, I'd tell him, 'Welcome to the torture chamber!' Nurse Hamilton would glare at me, and say, '*Shut up, Stevens!*'"

While Harold was in Korea, Chiyoko had remained in Duluth, living in their apartment and continuing her studies. Throughout the cold winter months she rode the bus into town from West

Duluth, then trudged up the city's steep, San Francisco-like hills to night school.

Living in Duluth also afforded her an opportunity to spend time with her mother-in-law, trying to cement their relationship. Initially, Chiyoko had had a few reservations about Harold's mother. She was not always comfortable with the way his mother treated him when she was displeased—like the time she hit him with a hammer while he was driving! From Chiyoko's perspective, parent-child interactions in the West were no less complicated than in Japan, but things like that were still going to take some getting used to.

Before Harold left for Korea, word had come from Chiyoko's sister that their father had died. When Harold asked her if she wanted to return home to attend the funeral, she had surprised him by opting to remain in Duluth. In spite of how fiercely loyal she had been to her father, Chiyoko seemed outwardly unaffected by his passing. "Not a lot of tears," Harold remembers. "When I consider all the hardships she endured throughout her life, I don't think this was high on the list."

Who could blame her? After selling her into servitude when she was a child, Chiyoko's father had continued to extract money from her well into her adulthood. And yet, she had remained the dutiful daughter to the end, never complaining or permitting others to speak disrespectfully about him. But Harold surmises this may have been the extent of her devotion. "I think her relationship with her dad had more to do with a cultural obligation rather than affection." Harold believes that despite her father's transgressions, Chiyoko felt compelled to honor him while he was living, but that duty had died with him.

There is no doubt, however, that Chiyoko loved and missed the other members of her family, especially her sister, and as that winter drew to an end, she determined to go back to the land of her birth for a lengthy visit. With any luck, Harold might even be due for some R&R there. Plus, it was spring, the time of year when all the blossoms were returning to Japan.

There is no explanation for why some things happen. There is luck, good and bad. Coincidence. Fate. When the Universe decides to connect the dots, nothing stands in the way. Not even two sisters with the navigational skills of headless chickens.

"There was a famous seafood restaurant in Tokyo, and we wanted to go there." Harold is describing to me a night in Japan when the stars inexplicably lined up. But he needed to get somewhere for that to happen, and things were not looking good. "I'd been given one week of R&R in Japan while my wife was there, and we were staying with her sister. The three of us were looking for this restaurant, and the girls were walking me all over town trying to find it. 'It's up this street!' one of them would say. 'No, it's up *this* street!' the other insisted. I kept saying to them, 'I know where the damn restaurant is. I'll take us there,' but they were ignoring me. They were determined to find it themselves," he steams. Harold was beginning to yearn for the days when he and Chiyoko had been forced to take separate routes to avoid being seen together. "They led me around for at least fifteen blocks, and we had backtracked three or four different times until I finally said, '*Halt! Stop, now!* Come with me!' Then I walked us straight to the restaurant." He squints annoyance, "And instead of thanking me, they wouldn't even speak to me, they were so mad." Harold rolls his eyes, but exasperation is quickly supplanted by an expansive smile. "Lucky for me, there was someone else there to talk to. I walked into that restaurant, and I practically ran into Barney!"

I blink. "I thought Barney lived in Chicago…"

Harold nods, "He was visiting family in Tokyo!"

"What were the odds of that?"

He nods more vigorously, "Barney and I were both shocked, and we both said, simultaneously, 'What are *you* doing *here*?!' It just so happened that on that same night, in a city halfway around the world, Barney and Flora and all their relatives were gathered in this restaurant for a big family party!" Harold marvels, "I even got to meet his mother!" The evening, which had begun as a wandering fiasco, had progressed to an improbable reunion with dear friends.

Other than Chiyoko briefly giving Harold the cold shoulder at the restaurant, there was nothing but heat between them during his week in Tokyo. Once again, they laughed, loved, walked in the park, and savored every moment together. Though the couple had been forced apart for extended periods before, Harold's year-long, fourth tour in Korea would be the longest separation of their fifty-seven year marriage. At least, by this time, there was the reassurance that his deployment was drawing to an end, and they would soon be together again in the States. Harold was scheduled to depart shortly via troop transport. Chiyoko sailed for home on a cruise ship. Husband and wife had made plans to reunite in Seattle.

That did not happen.

The night before he was scheduled to leave Korea, Harold tried to jump a strand of barbed wire. On the way over he hooked a boot and tumbled down a ravine. Less than eight months after having his left knee cobbled back together, his fall shattered the tibia plateau on the other leg. He was flown to the evac hospital, strapped to the side of a chopper.

"As my stretcher was being off-loaded," Harold recalls, "I looked up, and there was Nurse Hamilton frowning down at me, shaking her head. She clucked, 'Sergeant Stevens, how could anybody do this *two* times in one tour of duty?'"

There is no explanation for why some things happen. There is luck, good and bad.

# Chapter 29
# SERGEANT

軍曹

HAROLD HAS BEEN battling with the Department of Veterans Affairs over his injuries longer than I have been alive. For more than a half-century he has filed claims, gathered documentation, and cut through enough red tape to wrap the Kremlin. But now he is finally scheduled to make a personal appearance before the VA medical board, and Harold is like a bombardier itching to drop a payload—he is going to give them holy hell.

"Evidently," he scowls, "they cannot understand that my back troubles and the injuries to my legs, knees, and foot, are all tied together. Well, I'm going to lay it out for them!"

"Cascading failure." That is scientific nomenclature for what happens when damage to one or two parts ripples into systemic breakdown. Doctors might refer to it as a degenerative condition. Soldiers have their own word: FUBAR, an acronym for a situation *F\*\*\*ed Up Beyond All Recognition.*

In Harold's case, it began with the crunch of the trail spade that split the bone in his big toe, an injury that has never stopped hurting. Then a torn knee that went untreated long enough to cause permanent weakness. When his other knee was shattered, the subsequent cast and crutches shifted weight onto the compromised leg, wearing that joint again till it was bone-on-bone. "I've walked in

pain for fifty years," he says, and because of the way I've had to move
and bend to compensate for these different injuries, I've developed
the problems with my back. Two doctors who've examined me will
affirm it's all related; the shifting and nerve damage from my injuries
is what keeps popping the discs out of my spine—I've had six back
operations to shave or remove those pieces!"

Now, it is a piece of his mind he wants to give the VA doctors.

"I'm going to show them, in person, what it is I'm talking
about," he smolders, gripping his bum knees. He has even managed
to schedule his appearance in front of the board for the afternoon,
when the swelling typically peaks and his pain is at its worst.

I ask him what it is he's after: an opportunity to affix blame?
Accountability? Money?

It turns out, all of the above. "This goes back to my original
complaint," he notes, "which I filed in the 1950s. I want them to recognize that." He adds pointedly, "*If* they follow the rules, they'll have
to compensate me for all those years. It would be a hell of a payoff!"

"I see…and what would you do with all that money?"

Harold does not miss a beat. "I'm going to buy a Learjet, fill it
with young ladies, and tour the world!"

Japan, Midway, Hawaii, California, Illinois…that was Harold's
globe-trotting itinerary as he journeyed back from Korea—though
all he toured were hospitals and military waypoints, and without
the company of the only young lady that has ever mattered. He had
to rely on the Red Cross to meet Chiyoko in Seattle, to assist her in
getting home.

"I spent quite a while recovering in the naval hospital at Great
Lakes, on the north side of Chicago," Harold recounts. "Eventually,
I asked for leave to go to Duluth. I'd done my full tour in Korea, but
the liaison officer wouldn't bring my request to the CO of the hospital. Instead, he gave me some song and dance about how I'd had to
have been there for so many months before I could qualify for conva-
lescent leave." Harold resorted to what was by then his go-to tactic for
motivating the middle ranks. "I said to him, 'Well then, maybe a little
trip to see the Inspector General…'" Harold smiles, "I got right in to
see the commanding officer, and thirty minutes later I had my leave!"

Harold had a good reason for wanting to get home. Chiyoko was up for her citizenship exam. "She'd been scheduled to report to the federal building," he explains. "She would have to go before a judge, and she was understandably a bit nervous."

Once he was back in Duluth, with his leg still in a cast, Harold lay beside his wife in bed and helped her cram. He relished this opportunity because, when it came to learning, this is the only time he can ever recall Chiyoko asking for his assistance. "She had such an incredible intellect," he puffs. "My wife could overcome any challenge. Anything she set her mind to achieving, she would do it. This was how she'd become a geisha, and now, in the same way, she was determined to become an American citizen."

He illustrates her aptitude with an example: "I recently came across some letters my wife exchanged with my baby sister while I was doing my fourth tour in Korea and Mike was in Japan. I had no idea they'd written to one another...I didn't know Mike could even write in English by that time! She hadn't been in school that long—this wasn't after two or three years of learning," he stresses, "it was only a couple of months! She'd picked up so much in such a short time about American language, culture, and government that I was amazed! Her night school teachers were amazed..."

And the judge was amazed. When the big day came, he took Chiyoko to his private chambers and grilled her on everything from intricacies of the U.S. Constitution to details of American geography and history.

"When she came out again, she was all smiles," Harold says, radiating delight. "It was quite a thing. Her teachers were in the courtroom—they thought enough of her to be there to give her moral support; my sister and my mother were there; and of course, I was the proudest guy in the building..." His voice quavers, "I don't know how I could ever be impressed by any person more than my wife."

Now that she was a citizen, every inch of the United States was Chiyoko's country too. Soon enough, she would discover there was at least one place she might wish to give back.

Lawton, Oklahoma, is a city that would not exist except for the army. Originally the site of a remote cavalry outpost during the

Indian Wars, the subsequent town has relied almost entirely upon the enduring presence of its fort. There is not much else here to draw people. The land is arid prairie, flat as the ocean, and virtually tree-less. Anything taller than grass that manages to take root is levered from the soil by the unimpeded winds that perpetually sweep the plains, and occasionally claw at them—this is, after all, the heart of Tornado Alley. But Lawton's lonely, far-removed location is its greatest asset for hosting a military reservation, particularly one like Fort Sill. It is a hell of a good place to shoot off cannons without bothering anyone.

"*Lovely* Fort Sill," Harold's voice drips sarcasm. "Once my leg was mostly healed, I came out on orders for that glorious place. It's the main artillery training center for the entire United States Army, and so, of course, that's where they sent me."

In Oklahoma, Harold took every assignment the army gave him. His now-familiar, primary role was as gunnery and drill sergeant, tasked with schooling class after class of aspiring artillerymen. Fort Sill was first and foremost a training facility, and in every capacity, Harold strived to turn out top-of-the-line soldiers.

"Whenever I had a platoon," he tells me, "—and I had a platoon of one type or another most of my career—I would brief the new guys by saying, 'There's one thing I want you all to be clear about: *I hate trainees*. Don't get on my bad side, and we'll get along fine.'" It wasn't that Harold was a misanthrope, or even a particular grouch; this was his way of telling recruits that putting forth their utmost was how not to disappoint him, and he would hold them to the highest standards—just as he did himself. "I told those men that I would never have less than the best platoon in the unit," he nods self-assuredly, "and it was very rare that I didn't."

"What about living at Fort Sill," I wonder. "It must have seemed like a pretty forlorn posting—especially after the big cities like Tokyo or Chicago, or a scenically diverse place like Duluth. How did you and Chiyoko cope with suddenly being in the middle of nowhere?"

"Oklahoma has its own beauty," he suggests. "The Wichita Mountains are among the oldest in the country…you can tell that because over time they've been worn down nearly flat."

"Hardly an endorsement for alpine tourism," I laugh.

Harold knuckles under. "Yeah," he concurs, admitting, "being assigned to a place like Fort Sill, it was rare when something exciting happened."

It is such a contrast to the thrill-a-minute black market intrigue of his days at Yokosuka, I tease him, "Couldn't you and Chiyoko have run a gambling operation, or robbed a bank or two—just to spice things up?"

"I became a hell of a good bowler," he offers, "and so did she!"

For Harold and Chiyoko, living in isolated Oklahoma may have felt like Witness Protection, but they could not hide from Harold's family. The couple hadn't been at Fort Sill a year before his mother and younger sister Shirley landed on their doorstep. In terms of rebuilding his relationship with his mother, Harold looks back on this visit as the final course of bricks.

"The grandest time I ever had with my mother was when my sister brought her down to Oklahoma." Harold eyes me sharply, "We even managed to find a few interesting things to show them there: prairie dog villages and buffalo and longhorn cattle. But for me," he recalls happily, "the greatest thing was having my mother all to myself. In Duluth, there was almost always a mob of other family members around, crowding the room and the conversation. Having that privacy with her, day and night, I valued that so much. Mom and I would just sit there and talk…"

When I ask him what these chats entailed, he tells me it didn't matter. "It was questions and answers," he shrugs. "I'd ask her about other members of the family: how many kids does this one or that one have now—and don't they ever do anything but make more kids?!

"'Now son,' she'd scold me with a smile, 'don't get smart.'"

But it wasn't the content of their conversations he treasured as much as the connection they forged by being together, showing one another affection, and enjoying each other's company.

"I think it's the closest that I got to my mother in all the years…" he chokes, his face flooding with emotion, "and I prized that. When I was a kid, I was my mother's orphan. Now, I wanted to be a son to her, and I was getting to the point in my career where I could finally start helping her more in the future."

Over the week that she visited him in Oklahoma, mother and son, once and for all, put to rest any unpleasant vestiges of the past. The struggles that had defined their early relationship, his defiant misconduct, her wearied exasperation, were replaced by deep appreciation on his side, forgiveness and pride on hers, and a genuine and easy affection between the two. All the rest was gone, and just in time, because shortly after this visit, so was Harold's mother.

"I got the phone call from my sister," he recalls, his shoulders slumping heavily, as if the bones and sockets have transformed into lead. "She said, 'Mom's been in an accident. She's alive, but the doctors are saying the family should prepare for the worst.' I got an emergency leave, Mike and I jumped in the car, and we drove nineteen hours straight. I didn't know my mother had died until I got to her apartment in Duluth. Even then," Harold growls, "one of my older sisters, who answered the door, didn't have the decency to tell me straight away. Instead, she eyed me up and down and said, 'Where the *hell* have you been?'" He clenches, "I nearly punched her in the mouth!"

Over the next few days, his siblings did not make things any easier for Harold. "I had all these relatives," he carps, "and guess who had to take care of all the details! I had to deal with the insurance, make funeral arrangements…" he pauses, mellowing. "It was quite a funeral," he breathes. "That church was just packed with people. My mother never met anyone who didn't become her friend. The flowers just kept arriving from all over the country, until finally the florists told us, 'We can't keep sending flowers!' They had to have some for other funerals!"

"How did your mother die?" I ask Harold. "You said she was in an accident…"

"She was on her way to church." He snorts a half-smile, as if to say, *where else?* "She was crossing the street to catch the bus when she was struck by a car. It was tragic, but it was nobody's fault. The young guy who hit her was driving at a reasonable speed, but the road was loose gravel and ice, and he just slid into her. I talked to him some time later, and he was still pretty shaken up. I understood how it could have happened. My older brothers didn't want to talk to him; they wanted to kill him. But that's the way they were."

In his heart, Oklahoma will always be the place where Harold made a meaningful peace with his mother. On the other hand, Fort Sill is where his relationship with the army soured like air burping from a carton of long forgotten milk.

"Being in artillery was a real stumbling block for me," he frowns. "I was stuck in it—stuck with that specialty number. It locked me up so I couldn't get a promotion."

"Why was that?"

"Because there were never any allocations for higher rank in my unit! And I couldn't get a transfer."

"And why—"

He interjects irritably, "A smart commander won't sign off on anything that might risk him losing a good sergeant. I spent five years at Fort Sill, training the apes, and I was damn good at it. *Too* good."

I have to ask him, "Did you even like artillery?"

"Hell no," Harold grumps. "It was too damn hard on my ears!" But then the boy who thrilled at piloting the steam locomotives in Japan emerges. "Of course, I didn't mind going onto the range and firing those big guns..." he concedes.

"Look," he says flatly, "When I was called upon to do something and I was professionally geared for it, I did it. But I'd have liked an opportunity to eventually move on to something else. There was no escape for me from artillery. I was in it for *nine* years! My career had stalled. It was very discouraging."

Harold finally took things into his own hands. "I couldn't get out and I couldn't get a promotion, so I decided, hell, I'll go for warrant officer! I knew I had the prerequisites for that, and more than enough recommendations to get the appointment."

In the U.S. Army, warrant officers straddles the boundary between the enlisted ranks and commissioned officers. They are a corps of specialists, often trainers or advisors, and their strengths typically come from years of experience in their respective fields. Word for word, this was a description of Harold. It was maddening for him then when he was disqualified from applying because of a seemingly counterintuitive technicality—he had accumulated too *many* years of experience.

"They disapproved my application," he fumes, "because I had sixteen years in service, and the cutoff was fifteen years! They didn't want to oversaturate the ranks with experienced men. To me that was the dumbest regulation in the book…" Harold is so angry now he could kick a cobra. "Because when I first went into the army, we looked up to the warrant officers who had the most time. They were the ones who knew the army inside and out—they were the guys who taught the guys coming up! We respected a warrant officer. Hell, he was like a general in a company. But now the army was turning its back on the most experienced candidates, with all their years of service!"

When his application was returned "without action," instead of punching a wall or taking up a bottle, Harold did something out of character but with no less potential for regret after the fact. He took up a pen.

"That's when I sat down and I wrote to U.S. Senator Hubert Humphrey about the things I thought were wrong with the warrant officer program. I'm not a crybaby," he jabs, "but this was something that was affecting many guys, not just me! The army was boxing out a lot of good soldiers. It was almost like punishment, and it was undeserved. So I figured I'd give someone a damn good explanation of what was going on! After I wrote that letter, I took it to the CO of the unit. I said to him, 'Before I hand you this, I want you to know that a copy went in the mail this morning.' I figured he was going to chew me up and down for stepping out of line. He looked it over, and then he looked up at me and said, '*Damn* good, Sergeant Stevens!'"

It was damn good. He'd composed an intelligent, even eloquent, piece of writing that was neither a complaint nor an angry missive, but a thoughtful exposition that laid bare the folly of the warrant officer application regulation. Harold went on to describe, in very personal terms, the hard choice he and other seasoned enlisted men faced when the army limited their opportunities. He wrote plainly, *In simple terms, I have come to the end of the road. I feel that if there is not a higher goal to strive for, men become slow and just go on day after day, doing little or nothing more than what is required of them. This is by no means the type of man who makes a good soldier. I am sure the military does not intend to drive its experienced men from service, nor do I, for one, want to call it quits, but men such as myself, and others in a similar position, have very little choice other than to get out if the door to advancement is closed to us.*

In short order, Senator Humphrey wrote back, *I want you to know that I have your letter and I am going right to work on it.*

Eighteen months later, virtually overnight in terms of government action, the army changed the regulation.

# Chapter 30
# TRANSITION

遷移

THE ARMY MAY have been holding Harold back, but he was still going places. I learn this after telling him I have to take a business trip to England. The announcement of my impending journey has him squirming with excitement, not because he will get a break from his weekly grilling (a chance to catch his breath and restock the candy dish). Rather, he is fired up on my behalf because, in Harold's experience, the British really know how to show someone a good time.

"I went there on an exchange!" he enthuses, excitedly rocking his chair. "That's where I got introduced to Guinness beer…" His eyes bug, "I'll tell you what, after drinking three of those, I could have skipped all the way across London Bridge!"

"An exchange…" I note, "what was that, some kind of troop swap?"

He nods. "The U.S. Army sent an entire artillery unit to Plymouth, England, for a month or so, while the British sent a unit of commandos to *beautiful* Fort Sill." Harold paints with a little scorn over this last bit, making it clear who, in his opinion, got the short end of the stick.

What did his unit do in Jolly Old England, I wonder, other than sample the stout?

"Firepower demonstrations for the Brits," he smiles. "They had to take all their cattle off the fields, and then we went out there and shot up the hills!"

"That must have made the farmers happy."

"I'll tell you what, those people were just great! They couldn't do enough to help us out and make sure we enjoyed our visit!" Harold launches into a case in point. "While we were in Wales, a couple of us stopped in at a pub, where the locals asked us, 'Are you going to the dance?!' Hell, we didn't know anything about a dance. 'Yeah,' they said, 'there's a barn just a few miles down the road, where there's going to be a big dance this evening,' and they practically begged us to come. So we did, and the place was packed. The Beatles were playing, and we danced up a storm…"

When he says, "The Beatles were playing," I assume he means recorded music. Nope.

"Not that I'm a great dancer by any means," he breezes onward, "but the band was really putting on a show, clanging and banging away, and even I managed a few calisthenics out on the floor."

I am nonplussed. "Do you mean to say the Beatles were there performing? You saw them play? In a barn?!"

He nods, "Oh yeah. Of course, at the time I thought, *Who the hell are the Beatles?*"

"*The* Beatles?!"

"Yeah," he frowns, pretty sure he has already answered the question. "They were just getting their start." Harold shrugs dismissively, though he gives the up-and-comers a solid review: "They were loud, but they played some pretty good music!"

Harold had felt vindicated and he was gratified when the army changed its policy and began allowing men with over fifteen years of service to apply as warrant officers, but for him it was too little, too late. In the wake of his own rejection—field trips to Britain notwithstanding—his attitude toward the army was darker than midnight on Pluto.

"Bitter!" he tells me, looking like he has swallowed a worm. "I'd learned to almost hate the army, and I was on the verge of doing something stupid. I was considering getting out. I had sixteen years in by then, and it would have been foolish for me to leave before twenty years when I could retire with a full pension, but after ending up in Fort Sill for so long (I note that instead of 'at Fort Sill' he phrases it like an incarceration) I'd reached a point where I was so damn frustrated…I had to do something different, even if that meant leaving the army!"

Luckily, a cooler head prevailed.

"Whenever I got mad or upset, my wife is the one who would calm me down and clear the air," he says, inhaling a pacifying lungful. "She made me see that for most of my life the army had been good for me. It had taught me a number of important things and had helped me in a lot of ways. And what the army didn't do for me, my wife did," he squares his jaw decisively, "and she was the tougher of the two."

When I ask what he means by this, Harold smiles and reminds me that thanks to Chiyoko's geisha training she was practiced in the manipulation of men, and she never shied from using this knowledge to her advantage throughout their marriage. She instinctively understood the best way to motivate her husband was to play on his insecurities and his hot temper—something he would have found damn infuriating if he had recognized it while it was happening. "My wife was very tricky with me. She didn't hit me over the head by arguing, or yelling, or preaching a sermon; instead, she nudged me with little comments…"

"Such as?"

"Oh, she might quietly express her admiration for somebody who had done what she thought I needed to do. I wouldn't say she shamed me, but these little pokes brought out my competitive side. I wasn't going to have her see the army beat me, and I wasn't going to let anyone shine any brighter in her universe than me. So instead of quitting over this whole warrant officer thing, I picked up the Army Schools catalog and started looking for the toughest damn course I could find!"

In the past, whenever he had applied himself to getting an education, whether it was buckling down to keep the peace with a Wisconsin schoolmarm or studying to pass his GEDs, good things had followed. The confidence he took from bettering his mind had opened new doors of opportunity—such as when he had finagled his way into an advisor position with the National Guard in Cloquet. Harold's fortune had been on the rise when his unanticipated fourth tour in Korea flattened the upward arc, leading him down a progression of blind alleys where he had stagnated professionally. But he was determined to exit the maze, and this time Harold was going over the wall. After scrutinizing the army catalog and with the warrant officer debacle still churning his gut, the man who, as a boy, had quit school after the ninth grade, decided to apply for one of the most academically daunting specialties in the armed forces: Special Weapons.

As in nuclear weapons.

New Mexico was the final pin in the map of a strange and singular journey. Harold had witnessed firsthand the utter annihilation at Hiroshima. On Tinian, he had looked on (albeit unknowingly) as the instrument of that ruin was prepped and loaded into *Enola Gay* for the flight to Japan. Now he was based very near where the bomb had been engineered and assembled, while he studied the weaponry that descended from that Promethean science. Unwittingly, and in random order, Harold had followed the path of the device that ushered in the Atomic Age. And like the scientists who had labored under the same desert sun on the Manhattan Project, he was sweating whether he'd bitten off more than he could chew.

"I was challenging the army when I put in for Special Weapons," Harold acknowledges. "I wanted to prove that I was so much better than what they'd boxed me into." He is quick to admit, however, "I undertook that challenge not knowing if I could pass it. Honestly, I felt like it was probably beyond my capabilities, and that I was going there to fail. Nevertheless, once I set my mind on something," his eyes reflect the resolve of a salmon staring upstream, "that was where I was going to go!"

Where he went was to the tri-service (army, navy, Marine Corps) Special Weapons School in Albuquerque: sixteen intensive weeks of mathematics, physics, and engineering required to understand and maintain the country's nuclear arsenal.

"That was fun," he says acidly.

"Sounds like it wasn't," I reply.

"It wasn't easy, that's for sure!"

Harold had indeed selected "the toughest damn course" in the army catalog. On top of that, he was considerably older and had completed less formal schooling than anyone else attempting the training. But he had two things going for him. First, he would be goddamned if was going back to artillery without a fight. And number two: "My wife was there with me, and she was my biggest booster. Whenever I came out with a negative, she'd challenge me with a positive. When I doubted myself, which I did often, she would coax me over the hump."

"How would she do that?" I ask.

"Same as always," he squints. "She'd say something...but with just the right tone or implied meaning to steer me back on course or get my hackles up, and then I'd attack my studies!"

Of course, it wasn't that simple—or maybe it was. All his life, Harold had considered his headstrong, competitive nature something of a curse. Chiyoko recognized it as a source of strength, if applied productively. Wisely, artfully, cunningly if necessary, she helped him to parlay his instinct for running heedlessly toward a challenge, into realizing his full potential. For this, he is forever in her debt. "Look," he says, eyeing me squarely, "I sold myself short in so many ways, but if I wanted to do something, and pressure was put on me that told me I couldn't do it, or if somebody put a stumbling block in my way, I'd work harder than hell to prove them wrong." Inwardly, however, Harold was plagued with doubt, which he manifested as brooding frustration, even anger. Chiyoko was there to counter these crises, but never in ways he anticipated, or according to his own instincts (like when he and former fiancé Shirley had fastballed shoes at one another). In fact, at first, Chiyoko typically reacted by not reacting. "She would just be moving around, listening, not saying much," Harold explains. "After I'd stewed awhile, she might tell me, 'You can do it,' but in the same matter-of-fact way someone might say, 'you can pick that flower off the vine.' She made it sound *so* easy," he grumps. "Or she'd say, 'Have you really thought about that?' And it would leave me speechless. Because I hadn't. 'I think you ought to give that a little thought,' she'd suggest." He considers, stubbornly, "I knew she was right, and this made me even angrier, but then I would go after the problem with a vengeance! And I'd succeed!" Harold settles back, marveling, "By rallying me in ways that only she could, my wife helped me achieve things that resulted in a better life for us both. This is something I'll never forget. She wasn't just a wonderful wife, she was a damn good teacher. She had to be, to change me."

Chiyoko may have been an expert at raising his confidence and focusing his talents, but in the end, it was Harold who had to attend the classes and tackle the formidable coursework at Special Weapons School; it was Harold who had to pass the exams. Thankfully, he had an aptitude for numbers. Arithmetic had been his favorite subject in grade school and junior high, but it was nearly his undoing in Albuquerque.

"During an important exam, I was stuck on one particular algebraic problem…" he knuckles his skull. "I just couldn't get the formula. I thought if I don't crack this, I probably won't pass the course, because math is a big part of Special Weapons. But, try as I might, I couldn't do it. After the test, I was resolved to the fact that I was probably going to flunk out, when it suddenly dawned on me— the formula, how it worked! I asked the instructor if I could retake the exam, and this time I buzzed right through it. After that, things just started falling into place!" Harold beams and pats his noggin the way one might reward an old dog that has finally gleaned the futility of chasing its tail. "I had more brains than I thought I did!"

Against expectations (or his own, anyway), Harold graduated with high marks from Special Weapons School. The following winter the Beatles came to America and played some of their pretty good music on the Ed Sullivan Show.

Everybody was moving up in the world.

# Chapter 31
# CHECKMATE
# チェックメイト

WORKING WITH NUKES is not always "clean room" surgery, but it is never as depicted in a James Bond movie: a tense and solitary race against time, where cutting the wrong colored wire might trigger Armageddon. There are myriad fail-safe redundancies built into the designs of nuclear weapons that would prevent 007 from inadvertently incinerating a city, and even more rigid security protocols ensuring he would never get a chance to screw up. It takes a long time just to work up to a clearance level where a specialist is allowed to put a hand on a bomb, and even then, that person is never alone. Just to enter the room, he or she has got to be partnered with someone of equal training—the "two-man rule," as Harold calls it. And there are as many different jobs in Special Weapons as there are weapons themselves (munitions ranging from backpack-sized demolition devices that can surgically vaporize a bridge in a mini-mushroom cloud, to megaton-yielding warheads). Harold's first assignment as a nuclear weapons specialist was not working with bombs, and it didn't even get him out of Fort Sill, but it also wasn't training artillerymen, and that's all that mattered to him.

"The army shipped me back to Oklahoma," he tells me, "and cut orders to transfer me to a Special Weapons ordnance unit there. But I couldn't just dive in. Every specialist has to undergo a thorough background investigation. They examine your life from the womb to the tomb," he chuckles, "so it can take months, and while I was waiting for my clearance, I supervised the testing of the testing equipment used for maintenance with Special Weapons." Just these redundant layers of testing have my brain spinning. Harold nods, "That, in itself, was testing *me*—old blockhead, ten years older than anyone else there and picking it up half as fast." He grins, "But it got me the hell out of training recruits!"

Thanks to his new vocation, Harold's attitude had tempered, but the army still rankled. "It was much better for me in Special Weapons, but I was holding on to some pretty bad feelings because of the things I'd gone through," he grumbles. "I still am. Oh, I don't hate the army," he clarifies, "now, or then. I wouldn't have stayed for over twenty years if that was the case. But would you believe, in my last year or so, they stuck it to me again?!"

Harold explains, "I'd gotten to where I only had seven months left before I could retire. I was thinking, boy, this is it…just over half a year and I'm gone! I was excited to get out of the army and work somewhere else—where I could earn real advancement based on my skills and merit." His face clouds, "And then I got a letter from the office of the commanding general in Europe…"

Harold rifles through an album and presents me with the very piece of correspondence. *Dear Sergeant First Class Stevens,* it begins, *You are to be assigned to the U.S. Army Advanced Weapons Support Command in Pirmasens, Germany. I send you my best wishes for a very pleasant journey…*

"After five years at Fort Sill," I remark, "that must have come as a shock!"

He sighs. "I thought, I can put up with anything for seven months. But when I told them I wanted to take my wife, the army said, sure, but if you take your wife you'll have to commit to a full year. That meant extending my service."

According to Harold, this is standard army MO. "They dangle the carrot, but add little conditions and incentives to bend you to their needs." It was the opening gambit in a bureaucratic game designed to get him to delay his retirement, and the chessboard favored the military because Harold was not about to surrender his queen.

"I said, I'm not going anywhere without my wife. I'll do the year—but not a second longer."

From the beginning, Europe was a disappointment. Never mind the fact that when he and Chiyoko arrived it was the middle of the night, and there was no one to meet them (they had to camp with six suitcases in the air base terminal until morning). Or that the following night was another sleepless affair, thanks to the parade of drunks singing their way home from the beer halls. What really popped Harold's cork was the appalling state of the unit he had been sent there to oversee. The smell alone knocked him back on his heels.

"When I first opened the door to the barracks," he gags, "I practically choked on the smell of urine coming down from the toilets on the second floor! I thought, *What the hell?!* Then I walked into the squad room where the guys slept, and every nightstand had an ashtray full of cigarette butts, the bunks were a mess, shoes were in disarray…"

The missiles in Germany weren't the only things armed and ready to blow.

"Well," he observes, seething, "Sergeant Stevens went off the deep end! There were four sections to the barracks and each one had a lead sergeant. I called them all in. I said, 'Gentlemen, you won't be going back to your quarters today. In fact, you won't be going anywhere until this place is spic and span. Do. You. *Understand?!*'" I imagine they could have tethered a wild stallion between Harold's clenched teeth.

"What was going on with that unit?" I ask him. "Why were they such slobs?"

"That's what I wanted to know!" he thunders, tossing his hands with disgust. "I had heard so many great things about the Seventh Army in Europe. I'd seen their drill teams parading on the television, and I thought, this is going to be a crack outfit! Then, to get there and see the run-down conditions…" He shakes his head in disbelief. "Korea was a hellhole, but I'd never seen a barracks there in this poor condition! I mean, in the shower room there was mold growing down the walls, and that smell from the toilets…and these were Special Weapons people!" he stresses, incredulously. "They were educated guys with pretty high IQs—living like animals! I was so disillusioned."

"I'll bet you shaped them up in a hurry."

"Damn *right!* I transformed that barracks. I had those guys scrubbing and painting the walls, shoes were shined and lined up, and you could have bounced a feather off those bunks. I'll tell you what," he mutters, "I was so mad I was practically insubordinate. I told my lieutenant he couldn't set foot in the place until after I was done with it! I don't think they'd ever encountered anybody like me over there!"

Once he had restored personal pride to Europe, Harold could actually start to enjoy the place. From their base in Heilbronn, north of Stuttgart, he and Chiyoko toured as much of the region as time allowed.

"I didn't get a lot of days off," he tells me, "but when I did, Mike and I made the most of it. I had a little Volkswagen, and we traveled all over Germany, up and down the Rhine, and to Holland and Belgium. I would have liked to visit Berlin, but as a nuclear weapons specialist, I wasn't allowed within five kilometers of an Eastern Bloc country."

I ask him why.

"It was to protect us," he says darkly, reminding me that Europe, at that time, was gripped by East-West intrigue that included espionage, defections, and even kidnappings. In terms of Cold War value, the information in Harold's head was worth his weight in gold—or weapons-grade plutonium.

"You were there to support a missile unit," I note, "in case the Russians got out of hand…"

"Yup," he nods.

"When you were working on those nuclear weapons, did you ever consider whether they would actually be used?"

"Let me put it this way," Harold says, "they had to be reliable. You couldn't have any misfires. If it came to that, they had to work. This wasn't a game."

In fact, it was. The tactic was a stratagem game theorists called "mutual assured destruction." A game, by definition, with no winners. Robert Oppenheimer, the architect of the Hiroshima bomb, upon witnessing the first atomic test, recalled a passage from Hindu scripture: *Now I have become Death, the destroyer of worlds.* Oppenheimer's greatest fear was also the check against it ever happening. By the mid-1960s, the world's two opposing ideologies were faced off in Europe along the Iron Curtain, each side armed to the teeth with enough nuclear hellfire to incinerate one another to ashes, which ensured that the ultimate destructive potential of the atom remained speculative. To Harold's mind, deterrence worked like a charm.

"I don't think the Russians ever gave a thought to attempting anything," he maintains, "because if they did, we would counter, and it would be a disaster for everyone. So did I sit and worry about these things? Dwell on them? Never."

In truth, Harold rarely worked hands-on with the weapons in Germany. Even though he was 1st sergeant in charge of the unit, it was six months before he could even enter the maintenance shop. It took that long for his background check to finally clear, and by then, his twenty years in service were nearly up. Of course, it was at that point that the army's pawns began putting the moves on him to re-enlist for another two years.

"I said, hell no!" he frowns. "I'm not re-enlisting, but I would honor the commitment of one year I'd accepted in order to have my wife there with me." When a captain tried to tell him that wasn't how it worked, Harold let him know that was damn well how it was going to work. And for even attempting a bait and switch, Bomb-san called the officer a son of a bitch. How Harold did not end up in irons is a mystery.

"I had made up my mind," he declares. "I'd told them when I went to Europe, 'I want you to understand, I'll do the year, but I'm not extending *one damn day!*' There were several heated phone calls back and forth to army headquarters before they got it through their skulls that I was leaving!"

And that is exactly what he did. When his obligation in Europe was up, Harold retired from the army with full benefits, plus an extra two and a half percent for the additional months and his navy time.

Checkmate.

Decades earlier, on the evening of July 17, 1944, while a sixteen-year-old boy chafed at the months remaining until his mother's signature would secure him enlistment in the navy, much of the town of Port Chicago, California, disappeared off the face of the earth. One moment it was a bustling naval depot where munitions were being loaded into vessels bound for the Pacific theater. Then, in the blink of an eye, it was all gone. For causes that remain a mystery, the equivalent of three-and-a-half-million pounds of TNT suddenly detonated. Entire ships were vaporized or blown asunder in a fireball that by some estimates measured three miles in diameter. The resulting losses in blood (320 people killed, 390 injured) and treasure ($12.5 million in damages) ordained the incident the worst home front disaster of the Second World War.

But even that horrific explosion was the pop of a cap gun compared to the destructive potential of what routinely passed through the site of Port Chicago in the 1960s, when an adult Harold, recently discharged after twenty-plus years of military service, noticed a sign for the Concord Naval Weapons Station and impulsively turned in the gate.

"We had moved to California," Harold explains. "I'd been employed briefly at a Los Angeles electronics firm." When the company reneged on the promised terms of his employment, Harold did what he had always dreamed of doing in the army under similar circumstances—he collected his pay and walked out. "And now I was looking for work in the Bay Area."

San Francisco seemed an ideal place for Harold and Chiyoko to settle. A large population of Japanese immigrants and their descendants lived there, and there were a number of military installations where Harold might find work as a civilian. He runs down a list for me.

"I'd been to the Presidio, Travis Air Force Base, the Mare Island shipyards…I can't remember all the places I'd gone, when I just happened to be driving by Port Chicago, and I saw a little sign that said *Concord Naval Weapons Station.*"

Harold's hands whirl in energetic mimicry of wrestling a steering wheel. Just the word "weapons" was enough for him to pull a tight one-eighty on the highway.

In fact, Concord was the munitions storage depot that supplied warships docking at Port Chicago and the other naval piers in San

Francisco Bay. The magazines at Concord held the navy's principal stockpile of conventional ordnance for Pacific operations. But by the 1960s, the armaments also included a formidable cache of Special Weapons; Concord was where the navy's nuclear arsenal was stored, maintained, and trans-shipped. Aircraft carriers and ammunition ships docked at nearby Alameda, where the nukes were unloaded and convoyed under Marine escort to Concord. There, they were secured, inventoried, and any necessary work was done on them before being redeployed. Although it was a navy installation, the administrators and technicians at Concord were civilian employees of the federal government. It was as if Harold himself had dreamed up the ideal place for him to work.

"I went in there and I told them I had experience with Special Weapons, and I asked to talk to the person in charge. The general foreman himself came down and met with me. I told him about my qualifications and experience, and he said, 'Take an application home, fill it out, and send it back. I'll tell you right now, I'm going to hire you as a weaponsman.' That was the lowest rung on the ladder," Harold explains, "kind of a flunky, who sweeps the floors and cleans parts, but it was a place to start. I couldn't work with nukes right away anyway, not until they finished doing yet another thorough background check on me."

Harold knew from experience that could take a while. He'd had to wait months to be cleared at Fort Sill and in Europe.

"Why a whole new investigation?" I wonder.

"The National Security Agency does government-wide checks on people now, but in those days each branch performed their own," he smiles, "and now it was the navy's turn. But it had to be done. You couldn't get a job in Special Weapons without getting cleared."

"The investigations were pretty rigorous, right?"

"Oh, yes. Very."

"And you weren't worried they'd uncover any of your previous navy shenanigans?"

Harold laughs. "I had a few secrets…" he admits. He tells me that although he was confident they wouldn't get the goods on him, it would be a long wait to find out. "The foreman told me to be patient. He said it might be thirty days or more before I'd have the clearance needed just to be hired—even longer before I could expect to work with Special Weapons. I joked with him as I was going out the door. I said, 'You know…once I'm in, I'll be after your job!'"

All kidding aside, eight years later, Harold would be running the place.

# Chapter 32
# FOREMAN
## ボス

I AM ATTENDING a Labor Day ceremony honoring our Veterans of Foreign Wars, but—to borrow their jargon—something here is FUBAR. The local men and women whose work it has been to protect our freedoms have been led in and seated according to conflict, starting with World War II and progressing right up through the most current actions in the Middle East. Typically, at these events, the flag leads the way, but today the color guard is conspicuous by its omission. Instead, rifle-toting representatives of the various service branches, along with Old Glory, are standing in the back of the auditorium, waiting patiently at attention for marching orders that have somehow fallen through the cracks. When the organizers realize their mistake, the proceedings are brought to an abrupt halt and everyone rises as the Stars and Stripes are finally paraded in. Way down in front, a handful of elderly men plumb their spines to stand at salute, and I know instantly that these are the veterans of the Second World War. I recognize that plaid shirt a mile away.

Afterward, back at Harold's apartment, things are proceeding more according to custom. I'm kicked back on the sofa perusing my notes and his candy dish as Harold neatly folds his decorated veteran's jacket, places it to one side of his chair, and settles in for another interview. I remark that although his dress ribbons peg him as an army veteran, he has actually devoted more years of his life to a different service branch—even if most of these were not in uniform. He nods affirmingly, "I started and ended with the navy."

In fact, Harold's tenure at the Concord Naval Weapons Station lasted nineteen years, and in that period he advanced through every position in the facility, up to and including general foreman. In this sense, he was the equivalent of a CEO who worked his way up from the mail room—although at Concord, any packages they moved gave new meaning to the phrase, *Handle with Care!*

"The first weapon I worked on there was a Mark 31 atomic bomb," Harold tells me, "similar to the one dropped on Nagasaki. It was a big round thing, with an outer shell made up of ninety-six detonators that had to go off simultaneously in order to compress the core and initiate the nuclear reaction. It went together just like a jigsaw puzzle, all the wiring and pieces had to be absolutely precise."

But even after finally receiving his security clearance and being promoted to a full crew member, Harold could not go to work on any old bomb. "A lot of the training I had in the army didn't carry over to the navy," he explains. "There were only a few Special Weapons that the army and navy had in common—mainly smaller demolition bombs—and any dummy can master one of those."

*I certainly hope not!* I'm thinking.

"So I had to go back to school for nearly every weapon," he continues, "and I wasn't alone. Anytime something new came into Concord, the whole crew would head to Albuquerque to attend classes and learn about shelf life and the other aspects of what we were working on. We trained according to the weapons that we received—probably twenty different types in all."

I am curious about what it was they were doing when they serviced a bomb—his mention of shelf life makes me think of weeding through a refrigerator, separating out things with old expiration dates and tossing them. According to Harold, it was exactly like that.

"Oh yeah," he nods, "this was one of our primary purposes. If there were any parts that were on the verge of timing out, we would bring the weapon into the shop and replace those components."

"What parts of a nuclear weapon expire?" I ask, fascinated.

"Retardation parachutes, that was a big one…and pressurized gas canisters in the triggering mechanisms—the pressure only lasted so long before it went below spec. This was tritium gas," he stresses, "really bad stuff, highly radioactive. One whiff of that in your lungs and…" he waves his fingers, "you were a goner."

Contemplating the risks of contamination, I wonder, "What about safety? Were you worried at all? Did you have to wear special suits to ward off radiation?"

"No," he scoffs, "nothing like that. I'll tell you something, I felt safer walking into work than I did into my own house. That's the truth! There were monitors everywhere at the plant constantly checking the air, and, of course, it was very high security—but other than that it was like working in any well-appointed industrial shop."

To make his case, he cracks open an album and shows me a series of photographs of the Concord plant. I see for myself that the weapons maintenance bays could indeed pass as places for assembling industrial wellheads rather than nuclear warheads: high ceilings banked with fluorescent lights, the ubiquitous rolling tool cabinets flanking workbenches, and winches rigged overhead. Of course, the fact that the doors were explosion-proof and the walls between bays were twenty-five-feet-thick concrete—or that a worker could not perform a single task, not even visit the bathroom, without being buddied up per the two-man rule, set this workspace apart. As I tuck a few select photos into my briefcase for future reference, Harold reminds me that Concord was a top secret military installation. "Don't sell those to the enemy!" he winks.

For the second time in his life, Harold was thriving thanks to the navy. But, unlike his black market empire in Japan, at Concord, everything was on the up and up; progress and prosperity came solely as a result of his honest, hard work. "I took every job they gave me and I happily did it," he says. "Even before I'd gotten my clearance, when they had me working with the segregation department loading and unloading ammunition, or in the lumberyard pulling nails out of wooden crates, I didn't gripe. I was getting a good wage, and it all added to my knowledge of how the plant operated." As he climbed the ranks—weaponsman, crew member, electrician, testing-gear specialist, junior foreman—Harold made it a point to thoroughly understand every job and forge relationships with all the division heads of the station, which was key to his moving up and ultimately being appointed the man in charge.

"I'd finally found a career where I could earn advancement by the work I did and the effort I put forth," he says with evident pride, "and it turns out, that was all I needed to succeed."

That, and the wise and supportive woman at his side, I suggest.

Harold nods. "You're never going to get anywhere if you don't try—that was my wife's philosophy." He acknowledges, "It was because of her that I ended up running that plant. In my mind, there's no doubt about that."

With her signature passive, understated brand of encouragement, Chiyoko continued to prop Harold up whenever he flagged or needed a gentle push toward the next stepping-stone. She had nodded her approval when he decided to supplement his education by taking courses at nearby junior colleges. She had nodded her agreement when, after a crisis of confidence brought on by attending meetings surrounded by men with doctoral degrees, a commanding officer told him, "Hal, you've come farther and accomplished more than any of those guys, and you can talk with any damn one of them and know exactly what it's about—so don't ever feel intimidated around these people." And Chiyoko proudly stood beside him, again and again, as Harold was called forward to receive official commendations and awards for the outstanding performance of the Concord Naval Weapons Station under his watch.

Harold deflates slightly. "I think the hardest part of my job," he murmurs, "was that I could never go home and discuss with Mike the specifics about what I was doing. It was very tempting. Most of the things I've been telling you—the layout of the building, the weapons we were working on, the maintenance we performed—all of it was classified at the time. I wasn't allowed to say a word about anything, not even to my wife. It wasn't that I didn't trust her, but those were the rules. Some of the other men's wives and girlfriends resented it—but not her. Over the course of nineteen years, she never once pressured me to share things she knew I wasn't free to talk about."

And yet, I consider, within the intimate confines of a marriage, adhering to such a canon of secrecy must have been dispiriting, maybe even insulting to Chiyoko. "If you trusted her," I press, "couldn't you have bent the rules…just a little?"

Harold lowers his voice as if the room is bugged. "There was always someone listening," he confides. "All I had to do was say something to Mike, and she might repeat it, either forgetting or not knowing it was taboo…" In that case, he tells me, the consequences would have been swift and unforgiving. He saw it happen to others. "We had a warrant officer—he had an important job supervising maintenance on testing and handling equipment—and his girlfriend made a remark at a party, just a casual comment to someone about something going on at the plant. The next morning when he showed up for work, they took his ID card at the gate and told him, 'Sorry, you're done.'"

Still, I think, for Chiyoko, never being able to visit Harold's workplace; never able to discuss with him—other than in the broadest terms—his work day; never privy to the work-related events and concerns that consumed so much of his thoughts and his time… "She must have felt disconnected from you, isolated… lonely," I contemplate. "How did your wife cope during those years in California? What did she do with her time while you were focused on your career?"

"What *didn't* she do!" he laughs, and I suddenly regret that, with all I have come to know about her, I could think for even a moment that Chiyoko might have lacked purpose or struggled to fill her days.

"For one thing," Harold tells me, "we built two beautiful homes in Pittsburg, just over the hill from Concord, and she did all the landscaping for both houses herself. Oh," he shrugs, "I might have helped move a boulder or two, but it was always under her supervision. And let me assure you," Harold emphasizes, "when it came to landscaping, she was as stubborn about her ideas and opinions as I ever was about anything." He cites just one example: "I got the idea that I would build a retaining wall, but when she got wind of what I was planning, she said, 'No, *no*. You can't do that!' I said, 'What do you mean I can't do that? I live here too!'" He chuckles, "Well, I never did make that wall."

Chiyoko's design influences were her Japanese heritage and her own, highly cultivated sense of aesthetic—as a former geisha she sculpted her landscapes with the hand of a practiced artist. In a Japanese garden, everything is representational of the greater world, and she deliberately positioned every plant and stone to achieve an overarching composition of harmonious arrangement and captivating interest. To this end, she was insistent that any stones Harold collected for her gardens were "living rocks," with tiny plants in the cracks, or velveted with lush moss (which Harold cantankerously referred to as 'mold'). But he dutifully hauled and heaved whatever she demanded, and he is the first to admit that every boulder and truckload of gravel was worth the effort.

"The places we lived were a paradise, thanks to her. In fact," he notes proudly, "she ended up working for the contractor that built our second house. He was so impressed by her gardens that he hired her to advise him!"

"Did she ever study landscaping or horticulture?" I ask.

"Not formally. But if she didn't know how to do something, Mike was a person who got books and read until she did. She was also intuitive about design, and she had a natural green thumb with flowers and plants, although I doubt she ever did any gardening until she married me. She certainly never got her hands dirty as a geisha... Yeah," he concludes, "I introduced her to dirt!"

At this, Harold's eyes dart self-consciously around his living room, and he frowns at a few, furry tufts of lint that have collected in the recesses since she has been gone. "She'd kick me right out of this place!" he sighs. "You'd have never found a speck of dust in any of the houses we lived in. She brought that same manicured beauty that characterized her gardens to every room."

Again, in order to achieve her vision for interior design, Chiyoko would not hesitate to put Harold to work. His description of how she motivated him to her purposes seems to me exemplar of their greater marriage dynamic—and how they enriched one another's lives.

"My wife would ask me to do something in the house, lay carpet, or finish a fireplace...things that were never a part of my schooling or my military training, and I would tell her, 'Mike, I don't think I can do that. I just don't have the skills!' She'd give me that little smile of hers that said to me, *I think you can or I wouldn't have asked.* So then I'd think about it, and decide I can't let her down. I've got to try. I'd start working it out, drawing up plans, educating myself— and then I'd do it! Afterward, I thought, that wasn't so hard! But the huge smile on her face when it was done, that was my real reward. Whenever I achieved something that was difficult, it would please her, and that meant everything in the world to me. In so many ways," he concludes, "she was my inspiration. My hero."

There are heroes who inspire with examples of wisdom, talent, or generosity, and there are heroes who earn admiration by coming to the rescue of others despite great personal risk. Harold had become the latter when he'd smuggled a boxcar full of electric motors out of Yokosuka to gain his future wife's freedom. He never imagined that, years later, in California, he would be called upon to rescue her again. By then, Harold had achieved more happiness than he ever dreamed possible. In one terrifying instant, he watched it all vanish.

"We had been to dinner with a bunch of people over in Concord," he recounts. "That was just over the mountain pass from where we lived in Pittsburg. Mike had come there to meet me. I was driving my pickup, and she had her car. On our way home, she was following me, and just as I crested the pass an object suddenly appeared from out of nowhere in front of me. I managed to swerve, and I just missed hitting a big concrete divider that had somehow ended up right in the middle of the road. In my rearview mirror I saw Mike's car swing to one side, and then it plunged out of sight over the ninety-foot embankment...

"I pulled over, jumped from my truck, and raced back to where she'd gone down." Though it only took minutes, to Harold, it felt as though the river of time itself had thickened into a viscous liquid, and he was swimming upstream. "As I went sliding over that steep edge I was calling, '*Mike! Mike!!*' Her car had rolled, over and over, all the way to the bottom of the gorge, where it finally came to a stop, upside down with its roof flattened. She was still inside."

When he reached the wreck, Harold was confronted with a gut-wrenching scene: all the windows of the little car were smashed or broken out, there was glass everywhere, and the air was scented with the ominous perfume of gasoline pouring from the ruptured fuel tank. Chiyoko was alive, conscious, speaking, but making little sense. *"I'm captured! I'm captured!!"* she kept repeating, deliriously.

"I was trying to reassure her," Harold recounts. "'Mike!' I said, 'I'm here, I'll get you out!' I tried to open the car door and it wouldn't budge."

Harold could not imagine how things could get worse, but he soon found out. Another motorist had stopped to help, and Harold was alarmed to see the man scrambling down towards him, illuminated in the sputtering halo of a road flare.

He shakes his head with incredulity, "There's gasoline all over the place, and this guy's climbing down with a burning flare! I shouted at him, 'Put that *goddamn* thing out!' He said, 'I'm bringing you some light!' I told him there was gas everywhere, and to get rid of the flare or I'd—" Harold bites his tongue, then spits hotly, "I wanted to *kill* that idiot!" This anger may have provided the extra squirt of adrenaline he needed to summon the strength of Hercules. "I went back to that door and I didn't have anything to pry it with, so it had to be sheer strength. I put my foot on the frame and I got hold of where the door had opened a small crack, and I gave a jerk—and the whole damn thing came flying off!"

In the meantime, Mister Lady Liberty had arrived (sans torch, thank heavens), announcing, "I've been trained as an EMT, and you're not supposed to move her!"

Harold glared at him, "I don't care how much emergency training you've had! That's my wife in there, and I'm getting her out— can't you smell the gas?!"

There wasn't a second to waste. "I put my jacket down to cover the broken glass and I reached into the car and got hold of Mike. I tried to move her, but she kept saying, *I'm captured! My foot! My foot!'* What had happened was the heel of her shoe had somehow jammed beneath the seat, trapping her leg. I managed to work it free and I inched her sideways—I had to be so careful with her because of all the glass—but I got her out! Then I tore the back seat out of the car," he says, with astonishing nonchalance, "and I laid her down on it. Soon after that the firemen showed up, and when we finally got Mike up to the ambulance, the highway patrol was there interrogating a woman who had been driving up the road, fumbling with a cigarette and a damn beer, when she'd hit this concrete divider, knocking it across our lane. *She'd* caused the accident!"

I reflect that it is a good thing the cops had found this woman before Harold did. "Your wife..." I ask him, tentatively, unsure I want to hear the answer, "how badly was she hurt?"

"She was pretty banged up and bruised, but in terms of more serious injuries, she only had three cracked ribs and a broken collarbone." He marvels, "It's amazing to me that she lived through that crash—the roof of the car had caved in right down to the seats...the rings on her fingers were so crushed we had to use pliers to round them out in order to remove them."

"You saved her," I smile. "For the second time, you saved her."

Harold waves his hand, rejecting any notion that his actions were extraordinary, or heroic, or more than a husband's most fundamental instinct. Plus, by his accounting, the ledger still placed him heavily in his wife's debt.

"She saved me," he whispers. "She saved me, just by marrying me."

# Chapter 33
# STRANGER

失名氏

EVEN A MAN strong enough to rip the door off a crumpled car (or a woman capable of riding out such a wreck) cannot hope to wrestle old age and win. Harold knows the score, and rarely complains, but when he does, it is not just gripes about his aches and pains or being the last survivor in his family that rise to the surface. Occasionally, he bemoans how growing older has wreaked havoc with his ability to throw a punch.

Since childhood, being a fighter has been a defining part of Harold's identity—a competency integral to his machismo and his self-assurance. When he grouses about his frustration at his physical decline and how it has stripped him of his ability to defend himself, it is chillingly clear what a formidable combatant he must have been. "I know that today," he laments, "if I punched someone's rib in order to drive it into his heart, I'd probably break my hand."

The fact is, Harold tells me, he has lost fights to just two people in his adult life. The first was an insolent young recruit at Inchon, Korea, who lipped off once—and that was one time too many—so Sergeant Stevens took him to the woodshed to knock a little sense into him. Unfortunately, as they wrestled, Harold landed badly, with a shard of rock knifing into his spine. "That was one I lost," he admits, quickly clarifying, "but just the first round. Later, I turned that guy's bunk upside down on top of him. He never ran his mouth again, after that."

Shockingly, the only other person to get the better of Harold in a physical altercation is the one who was most precious to him in the world. Of course, he could have fought back, but even then, at an age when he was still able to defend himself, there was a line he would not cross. As he considers this, Harold's face dims with dismay, not because it was a woman who took him to the mat and inflicted real injury, but at the circumstances that caused his wife to attack him in the first place. "It was so easy for her to go from love to hate..." he says, shaking his head miserably, "but I couldn't blame her, not for any of it."

At this moment, however, that is all he will say.

With any luck, a married couple's golden years are just that—precious time. Ideally, the stresses of having to earn a living and the tedium of the daily grind are replaced by opportunities to kick back and enjoy life, and one another's company. For Harold and Chiyoko, it certainly started out that way.

"After forty-plus years in government work, I was ready to focus my energies exclusively on Mike and her happiness," he says, evoking shades of Yokosuka, long ago.

When Harold announced his retirement as general foreman of the Concord Naval Weapons Station, he had more feathers in his cap than a Polish chicken. He'd overseen the station for eleven years, and during that time, in addition to his team's primary functions, they had successfully cleaned up a major contamination on Guam, completed a covert inventory of Special Weapons in Spain, and he had personally overseen the construction and transfer of operations to a brand new maintenance facility at Concord. Along the way, Harold had collected enough certificates of merit and letters of accolades to fill an entire mailbag—or an album.

With his two pensions to draw upon, money was not a concern for the Stevens (how Harold wishes his mother could have lived to hear those words). Neither was filling time. Harold had a honey-do list a mile long under the tireless supervision of his head gardener, but he also managed to sneak away now and then to dive for abalone on the coast with friends. Together, he and Chiyoko enjoyed visiting with family at home and abroad, including in Japan. They both loved to travel and experience new places (after his five-year non-disclosure agreement expired, Harold walked his wife through the National Atomic Museum in New Mexico, to give her a thorough report of what he had been up to, all those years).

Eventually the couple decided to trade the hustle and bustle of California for the secluded beauty of the Rocky Mountains. They relocated to Lewiston, Idaho, where they downsized to a condominium, but with ample room to put up guests, and, crucially, space in the yard for a Japanese garden.

"Did you ever think about moving back to Japan?" I wonder.

"No," Harold states categorically. "Mike wouldn't consider it."

"*Mike* wouldn't?"

Harold nods. "One of my sisters actually asked her that very question. Mike said, 'I could never live there now.' Let me put it this way," he says, in response to my dubious furrows, "my wife loved the country of her birth. She was very proud of her Japanese heritage. But she loved her adopted country too. There were so many things about living here that she enjoyed, and she'd grown accustomed to the lifestyle in the United States. She always looked forward to visiting family in Japan," he adds, "and they came to see us in Lewiston—both her brother and her sister. But America had become her home."

Another regular visitor to Idaho was Harold's brother Lorin. Against all odds, the sibling Harold once regarded as a bigoted pressure cooker, ever at risk of venting racially offensive comments and opinions, had become Chiyoko's favorite in-law, and Lorin made at least three trips to Lewiston that Harold suspects had less to do with seeing him, and more to do with how much Lorin enjoyed Harold's wife. By now, the brothers had moved beyond their contentious childhood relationship, burying their hatchets rather than swinging them at one another (although during one visit, after the pair had become hopelessly mired in snow while trying to drive over a remote mountain pass, Lorin had speculated there was a high probability the Forest Service would find two skeletons in the spring, with their hands around each other's throats).

But Harold and Chiyoko did not just sit around the house waiting for family to darken their doorstep. At least once a year they also hit the road, doorstep and all. "I bought a gorgeous twenty-six-and-a-half-foot motor home," Harold says, waxing nostalgic at the utilitarian luxury of their house on wheels. "It had a spacious bedroom," he gushes, "a big shower with a separate bathroom, and an all-natural hardwood interior." Best of all, however, the RV had a windshield the size of a movie screen. "I enjoy driving," he declares, "especially if I'm going through country that is scenic. I love the wide-open spaces. In the evening, when all the stars come out and you can see the horizon in a complete circle all the way around you, it's just pure beauty." As they road-tripped, Harold would often pull over in the middle of nowhere, step outside under the wheeling heavens, and say, "Mike, come out here. You've got to see this!"

It was a year or two after they moved to Lewiston that Harold first began to notice her strange behaviors. He did not know it at the time, but these were the first sand grains washing to the sea in an erosion of his happiness that continues to this day.

"There was a discount store across the street from our condo," he frowns, "and Mike started coming home with shopping carts full of odd stuff. Not things we needed. This was very out of character for her."

Unbeknownst to him, she was also hoarding cash. "I'm still finding money," Harold frowns, "tucked in books and drawers. She was able to draw from our accounts anytime she wanted," he says confoundedly, "so I don't understand why she felt compelled to hide money!" A little here, a little there, but it added up. Much later, Harold was stunned to discover that his wife had amassed over seventeen thousand dollars in a secret bank account. He suspects she was sending money to her family in Japan, which was probably true, but it was another example of unusual shifts in her personality. Whether these were symptoms of aging, disease, or long dormant manifestations of an undiagnosed brain injury from her traumatic car accident, it marked the onset of a perplexing mental illness.

"Whatever this was—and I still don't know for sure what it was," he mutters grimly, "it came upon her gradually. She slowly grew into it…so slowly I hardly noticed as it was happening. But it got to the point where she starting seeing a psychiatrist, who put her on medication—and that's when things really started to unravel."

Unravel is exactly right. It was as if Chiyoko's personality was fraying and splitting apart into a snarl of unrecognizable strands. Eventually, the kindest, calmest, most even-tempered woman Harold had ever known, was transformed into a quarrelsome and combative stranger. "And of course, I didn't know what was going on," he sighs wretchedly. "I had no idea. She was so irritable, and she didn't want to discuss it with me. She would complain about everything, and she'd raise her voice because she thought I wasn't listening, even though I was. And this just started boiling over…" Harold pauses, swallowing hard, "into violence."

I blink. "Violence? Violent how?"

"She didn't think anything about hitting me, and she would scratch me and kick at me… If she caught me off guard, she could knock me to the floor!"

I hardly know what to say. "I'm so sorry, Harold. What was going on with her? What did the doctors think was wrong?"

"It was that medicine," he states flatly. "The psychiatrist had prescribed a very strong medication for her, and I knew that was what was causing these rages. Mike had *never* been this way before that. The *doctors*…" he snorts, "they weren't so sure. They wanted to observe her. Plus, they said this medication wasn't something you could just stop taking."

At his wits' end, Harold made an appointment for Chiyoko to be admitted to the hospital for observation. When they arrived to check her in, however, it was a disaster—and no fault of hers, Harold asserts. "The staff there were cold and indifferent," he grumbles. "They completely ignored us for over an hour! And when they did finally admit her, they tried to put her in a *brown* room—it was the most depressing color I could imagine…any idiot knows you don't put somebody suffering from mental troubles in a room that feels like the inside of a cardboard box!" But when they tried to confiscate her personal items, her toothbrush and other toiletries, that's when Harold said, *"Enough! She's not staying!"* This was no way to treat a person, especially his wife. "There was no attempt at compassion!" he thunders. "I made the decision then and there, those doctors and that hospital weren't qualified to evaluate anybody!"

Chiyoko's moods went up and down, and while he tried to figure out how best to help her, Harold had little choice other than to ride out the low points. Together, they managed one tolerable cross-country expedition to Maine, with a stop in Illinois to visit Barney and his family, but a year later, shortly after setting off on a swing across the southern states, Harold's patience crumbled.

"Sure enough, not long after we'd started this trip she was cranky as hell and complaining about everything, so I pulled over and I said, 'Mike, I can't go on like this. You have to make a choice: either you're going to calm down and quit picking at me, or we're going back home and I'm going to sell this damn motor home and get a camper so I can travel, and you can stay at home if that's what you want!'

She said, 'I want to go home!'"

True to his word, Harold traded in the RV for a pickup camper. "And the next time I was ready to go on a trip," he sighs, rubbing his brow, "guess who hopped in the cab? *Now* she wanted to go on trips with me!"

Of course, one of their travels was to Minnesota. In retrospect, Harold should have known better. Here, surrounded by family, Chiyoko's anger and paranoia thrust their personal struggles into the open, which only added to her husband's misery. Plus, the delusions struck a particularly sensitive nerve.

"That drug would make her think up all kinds of bad things about me. When we were with my family, if I left the room, she would tell them a bunch of fictitious stuff. She said she had found letters from various women in the trunk of my car that proved I was having affairs. I didn't have any letters in the trunk of my car, and I wasn't having affairs!" Even so, the specter of Chicago and the guilt that still haunted him from that misguided fling only compounded Harold's heartache.

Everything came to a head on the morning they were leaving Duluth to return to Idaho. Harold made a stop at a niece's house to say their good-byes, but Chiyoko would not get out of the truck. She wouldn't even speak; in fact, she seemed to have retreated into her own mind.

"She just sat there," Harold recalls. "She wasn't angry or anything, but she wouldn't talk and she wouldn't move…nothing. I couldn't reach her. So I did the only thing I could think to do. I drove her to the hospital emergency room. I told them, 'This is my wife, and I can't handle whatever it is she's going through. Right now she's not violent, but I can't get any response from her at all.' They kept her there for five or six days in a special ward, and I visited her every day, until finally she looked at me and said, 'I want to go home.' I told her, 'Okay, Mike. Okay. Let's go home.'"

I ask him if the Duluth hospital offered them a diagnosis or any more information about what was afflicting her.

He nods. "They confirmed it was the medication. They said I needed to get her off that damn dope."

Weaning someone off a psychiatric medication is a tricky business. Withdrawal may exacerbate existing symptoms or result in new and dangerously adverse side effects that can persist for months, even years. It is definitely not something to be attempted cold turkey, without medical supervision. For Harold, finding a way to safely free his wife from the drug and the raging episodes that now governed her personality was his only priority—for her sake, and his own. He wanted his wife back, and he was damn tired of getting beaten up.

"In her sickness," he tells me, "there were times when the abuse got pretty serious."

I ask him if there was anything in particular that caused things to escalate.

He shakes his head. "It would happen like lightning. It might be something that I said—but it could be anything—and it would just set her off. She would get angry. She would come out of her chair. Then she'd stand there, hollering at me. In the worst cases, she would literally assault me. She didn't think anything about punching me, or scratching me, or biting. To defend myself, I would have to grab her wrists and hold her down, and I always felt so bad when I restrained her. I *hated* that…" he says, achingly. "I always tried to ease off just enough to prevent her from getting her claws in me, because hurting her was the last thing I wanted to do."

I wonder, "Did she ever injure *you?*"

His face snaps toward me, "I've got scars! Oh yeah!" His hand moves instinctively to his flannel sleeve. "There are places on my arms where you can see how she dug her sharp fingernails into me. But the day she bit me on the chest, that was the worst! I had pinned her so she couldn't bite my hands or my arms, and she went for my chest… I'll tell you what, she left an impression of her teeth there that a dentist could work from!"

Most times, however, Harold managed to hold his wife at bay. But then the words would come, he tells me, and that was almost worse.

"What would she say?"

"That she hated me. That I wasn't a good husband…anything she could think of to get at me. She searched for the words that would hurt me most—and she found them."

"God, that must have been hard on you, Harold."

"It wasn't *her*," he stresses emphatically. "This wasn't my wife. It was the rage and the pills talking." He exhales dismally, "But I pity any husband, or wife, who ever has to hear things like that from a spouse."

I ask him how these episodes would end. What would it take to calm her down?

"Just me talking to her. I would have her pinned on the couch or the bed, and I'd tell her, 'Mike, this isn't you.' I'd say, 'You don't know what you're doing. You say these things, and you make me feel real bad, but it's the medicine talking.' Then I'd tell her how much I loved her, and she would start to ease off. Eventually I could let go, and we could have a conversation, and we'd talk her away from it."

"What would she say to you afterward?" I ask him. "Was she embarrassed…or sorry? Would she apologize?"

He is not minimizing his wife's suffering, and I cannot fault Harold for his opinion that, in this one respect, her illness was harder on him than it was for her. "She would forget everything," he sighs. "For her, it was as though none of it ever happened."

# Chapter 34
# HEARTBREAK
## 傷心

HAROLD IS AT the end of his rope with the medical profession. Never mind the fact that his appearance before the VA medical board resulted in yet another bureaucratic stalemate, just the sight of a white coat and stethoscope raises his ire. The Hippocratic Oath? More like *hypocritical*, if you ask him. Time and again, over the years, he has been attended to with bedside manners ranging from withering indifference to dismissive condescension. As a result, he's like the turf at a private country club: there is no counting how many times he has been teed off by doctors.

But there is at least one physician who has earned Harold's respect. During Chiyoko's illness, this doctor had listened as Harold described the waking nightmare of his wife's capricious rages and the suspected cause—then he passed her off to someone of real competence, someone without even an M.D. Refreshingly void of medical ego, the doctor had said, "If it's her medication that's the problem, I want you to talk to my nurse. She knows more about meds than I ever will."

Real help, real hope, at last. But Harold should not have had to move halfway across the country to find it.

The results of Chiyoko's observation during her hospital stay in Duluth had been inconclusive in terms of diagnosing an underlying psychological condition. Nevertheless, Harold had been impressed with the compassionate care she had received, and by the respect they'd both been shown while she was there. It had seemed to him the polar opposite of everything they'd experienced in Idaho.

"I thought, *no more of this*," he shakes his head decisively. "We needed to get the hell out of Lewiston! I had a nice condo there where we'd been very happy before my wife's medical condition, but I sold that place on a dime and moved us to Duluth."

"Why here?" I ask him. "Why Minnesota?"

"I felt like Duluth had excellent hospitals, and the Mayo Clinic was also nearby…and it turned out to be the right choice!"

Indeed, no sooner had they settled into a house in Duluth than Harold secured Chiyoko an appointment with the disarmingly helpful doctor, who quickly referred them to his nurse, the acknowledged expert about psychoactive drugs. "She was excellent!" Harold nods definitively. "She explained to us that we had to be very careful in terms of getting Mike off this particular medication, but we could do it safely, and she would help us every step of the way. Under her supervision, I started reducing the dosage, just a little at a time, and monitoring her progress, and I could see we were gaining ground!"

I ask him whether that means she had stopped attacking him.

"There were still times when I was fighting her off," he replies, "but less and less often. I cut back her medication slowly, twenty-five milligrams at a time. I had to be mindful in my eagerness that I didn't jump the gun, because I had to wait quite a while between adjustments. It took over four years…"

"Four *years?!*"

"*Over* four years," he confirms, "and when I gave her that last twenty-five milligrams, I was the happiest guy on earth! We got her completely off that damn drug, and once she was free of it…" Harold brightens, his mouth slowly curving into a weary grin, "she was back to her old self! Cured!"

I assume he means no more rages.

"No more *anything!*" he stresses. "She was just like before— before she ever started having problems with her mind in the first place!"

In keeping with the nature of miracles, this was beyond all hope or reason; Harold's lost wife, returned to him. He had been granted more time with the gentle, sunny, familiar woman he'd loved for over six decades.

Which made what happened next all the more cruel.

Just the word inspires terror. Six letters in Latin, for a scourge older than antiquity—older than humanity (it has been found in the fossil bones of dinosaurs). Greek and Roman physicians were the first to observe how it invaded the body, sending aggressive appendages outward, crab-like, and named it thus. Even transposed upon the night sky, it seems a sickness—among the ancient constellations of the zodiac it is a collection of anemic stars, dark and eyeless, lurking between the dazzling suns of the Lion and the Twins. Cancer.

While working the coal piles at Yokosuka, Harold had breathed in toxic lungfuls of black dust and ashy diesel exhaust. During the Korean War and throughout his years as an army sergeant he had smoked umpteen thousand unfiltered cigarettes. He had spent the second half of his career working in close proximity with deadly radioactive isotopes. But a malignancy does not always ripen according to reason or fairness; it was Chiyoko who developed lung cancer.

"We had about two years of very pleasant life together after we got her off that medicine," Harold sighs. "By that time my knee had screwed up my back so badly that we'd moved into *this* place," he says, a grouchy reference to his pricey retirement complex. "But for several years we were happy here. We would walk down the hall to the lunchroom, hand in hand, like a couple of kids, and she would tell me, 'I'm so happy!' When I asked her, 'Mike, why are you so happy?' she'd turn to me and say, 'Because I have you.'" Harold's eyes fill. "You can't imagine how much those four words meant to me: *because I have you.*" He quivers a long breath, "That was about the time they discovered the cancer."

It still weighs on Harold—whether it might have been prevented. "She used to have an X-ray as part of her annual physical exam," he breathes shakily," and for one reason or another, we skipped a year. The next time she went in, they found a spot on her lung. I don't know whether that one missed X-ray would have made any difference…maybe, maybe not." But, by that time, conjecture was meaningless. The reality was that Chiyoko had terminal cancer.

The doctor advised them that she could try chemotherapy. It might slow things down, but at the age of eighty-seven, it could also make the time she had left abject misery.

Harold had spent a lifetime trying to shield his wife from pain. Now he was faced with an impossible decision—though it was not his to make. "I said to her, 'Mike, the choice has to be yours. We can ask the doctors to do everything possible to help you, or…'" he swallows hard, perhaps wondering now why he offered her any alternative other than to grasp at salvation, "'or,' I said, 'you don't have to take these medicines that will make you sick.'"

He could not imagine his life without Chiyoko, but the doctor had also told them the cancer was almost certainly slow-growing, and this offered hope for Harold that they might still have many months together—maybe even years. The bottom line for him was that chemotherapy would put his wife through a living hell, and after everything she had endured with her drug-induced rages, he could not bear the thought of her ever suffering again. "I told her, 'I love you, Mike. I don't want to lose you, but it's your decision. The one thing I can promise you is that if you don't have the chemotherapy, I'll make sure you are never in pain.'"

Chiyoko was not hurting; she had no symptoms other than perhaps some shortness of breath. She decided to forgo treatment, and to get on with living out her life, however long that might be.

"Were there a lot of tears over her diagnosis—or her decision?" I ask quietly.

"There were with me," he chokes. "It was very, very difficult for me…it still is."

"What about for her?"

He contemplates his doomed, brave wife. "I think that if the whole world was falling down around us, she could still smile."

And, of course, it was.

Chiyoko's cancer was not slow-growing. In fact, within just a few months, her health began to nosedive. "She was getting weaker," Harold says dispiritedly, "and going downhill fast. Soon, she wasn't able to do much other than lie on the couch or in bed. One day I was helping to support her, and I saw her flinch…" Harold's eyes had widened, and he asked her, "Mike, are you in pain?!" When she admitted she was, he immediately phoned the clinic and got a prescription for morphine, to be administered by him, two times per day. Significantly, the doctor also told him that if she was still hurting, he should not hesitate to give her more.

As his wife's illness progressed, Harold never left her side. They would sit together, he tells me, just as he and I are sitting now, reminiscing about people and places from their storied life together. Now, when they went to lunch, he pushed her in a wheelchair, and despite everything, she still insisted, "I'm so happy…because I have you."

"Then, one morning," Harold's face clouds, "she couldn't make it from the bathroom back to her bed. With my bad back, it took everything I could muster just to get her there. I had to drag her gently across the floor. I sat down behind her facing away from the bed and I hugged her under the arms, pulled her up on top of me, and rolled her over into bed." Clearly, Harold needed help. He arranged for a nurse to come regularly to help Chiyoko bathe and use the bathroom.

The morphine kept his wife comfortable, but the day came when he finally had to begin administering extra doses to manage her pain. The additional narcotic put her into a state of nearly perpetual sleep. Now Harold was mostly alone, a distressing portent of an impending future.

In his despair, he did something unusual—although Harold had done it once before when a flood of frustration and helplessness threatened to overwhelm him. He took up a pen and he wrote a letter. But this time it was not an appeal to a senator or any other Supreme Being. In fact, he wrote it without any expectation of a response or comfort…well, perhaps that's not quite true.

He hands me those same sheets. The words scrawled like a title across the top of the first page say it all: *A Last Good-bye, Until We Meet Again, For the One True Love of My Life.* I wonder aloud what it was that moved him to write this.

"Sitting here," he tells me, "I could see her sleeping in that bed-room," he points. "I knew she was dying…and I knew it wouldn't be long now before she would leave me forever. I felt a sudden urgency to share my feelings. I wanted her to know how much I loved her… how much I would miss her." He shrugs bleakly, "So I decided to write it all in a letter."

I ask him whether he actually intended to give the letter to Chiyoko, or was it more of an exercise for focusing his thoughts as he prepared himself for their final good-bye. Or was it simply an out-let for emotions bottled up behind the dutifully selfless facade of a caregiver. His answer, of course, is that it was all of these things.

"I was writing it to her, but I was composing my feelings. I would have read it to her if she'd been conscious, but by that time, I had in-creased her morphine, and she was sleeping almost around the clock."

For that reason, Chiyoko never would hear what Harold wrote, but as I read it, I have no doubt she would have relished every word—it being as fine a love letter and as heartfelt a good-bye as I can ever imagine. He begins:

*As I sit here just a few steps from where you are resting, I know that it will not be long now and I will be left alone without you. I don't know what time I have left in this world, but however much there is, I know there will always be an empty place in my heart that you have filled for more than sixty years…I have loved you from the first time I met you.*

As he progresses, Harold outlines the same history he has shared with me over the past months—the joys and the trials that have defined their relationship.

*The first nine years of separations and reunions were a test of our devotions for each other. Whenever we were separated, there was always something missing in my life, and I just had to get back to you. And when we were married, my life turned around and I knew that I had to make a better life for both of us. You were my inspiration for this.*

He acknowledges that it was not always an easy life, particularly for her.

*As my military service demanded so many moves and changes in our lives and friendships, you were the one who made the most sacrifices. You always accepted these changes without complaint.*

He extols her beauty. Her patience. Her intellect. He provides a long list of her varied skills and talents, including her innate ability to buoy any floundering soul she encountered, and one in particular.

*Somehow, whenever I was depressed, you had the power to encourage me to look on the bright side of life. I want you to know, like me, all our friends and family always looked up to you and admired you. Your smile seemed to lift people's troubles and send them away...you lifted us all!*

He even manages to inject some of his signature, crotchety humor amidst his reflective grief.

*I loved you so very much all the time you bossed me—and even though I lost out in all the final decisions.*

In the end, however, Harold's letter is a testimony to Chiyoko's greatest gift to him; proof, poured out in ink and tears, that the boy who once professed, "I didn't know anything about love," was now a man of intimate familiarity with limitless affection. At an age when time had reduced them both to withered and infirm shadows of their former selves, as he looked upon her, just a few feet from him, but slipping further with every labored breath, Harold still saw the geisha.

*My darling, Mike. My promise to you is that I will never forget the treasure I discovered so many years ago in Omori. I shall carry you in my mind and heart, as I have since the first day we met, for as long as I live. To be so well loved through all our years together is something that can never be lost, and it will somehow keep me going. The pain I have suffered in my body I would gladly feel all over again, if only I could have you with me. But that is not to be...*
*Good-bye, my love. I already miss you so very much.*
*I will always be yours,*
*Harold*

The morning after Harold wrote the letter, Chiyoko's crisis peaked.

"I'd doubled up on her morphine, and she'd been going in and out of consciousness and couldn't leave bed. I telephoned the hospice and told them I needed help. They sent a nurse over right away. When she arrived, I explained to her that when I felt I could no longer care for my wife at home, my plan was to move her to the hospital. The nurse went in and checked Mike's vitals, and when she returned, she asked me if I had a sense of when I thought it might be time to take her there.

"I said, 'Right now.'"

Sitting beside Chiyoko's hospice bed, Harold gently gripped and stroked his wife's hand, comforting her until late in the evening. Early the next morning he returned with a dozen red roses, and held her hand again all day long. Family—his sister and several of their nieces—visited in the afternoon. Through it all, Chiyoko barely stirred from the warmth and floating bliss of her drug-induced slumber. She experienced no pain, or Harold might have also died that night.

"At around eleven-thirty, I had to visit the bathroom, and I called for a nurse to sit with her while I was gone. When I came back, the head nurse was there, and she said to me, 'Harold your wife will be taking her last breaths in just a few minutes...' So I sat there, mumbling my love to her and gripping her hand. It was a peaceful thing," he chokes. "Her eyes fluttered—I think she was trying to see me, and I hope she did. It seemed to me that she smiled slightly...she always smiled. Then she took three more breaths, each one farther apart... and she was gone."

Harold is weeping freely now. "And ever since," he sobs, "my heart has been in pieces."

# Chapter 35
# RECKONING
# 決算

THE MAN IS an oak. A gnarled trunk, bent with time. Each twist is a record of adversity that would have broken lesser timber. Moreover, like an enduring tree, Harold is the lone survivor. Not long after Chiyoko died, he lost his last surviving siblings, two sisters, just four months apart. Barney is gone, and Harold recently received word that Flora Nozaki, too, has passed. In a thinning forest, as age and disease exact their toll, the venerable oak persists until it is the last living wood standing—unless an acorn has sprouted among its stony roots.

For a full year after his wife died, Harold sat in his recliner, paging through his albums, grieving, remembering…wondering. Then he decided to call Margaret.

It was not that easy, of course. He had no idea where Margaret was, or—presuming she had married—what her last name might be, or even if she was still among the living. But tracking her down, he reflected, could not be harder than making the decision to try. He had given his word more than half a century earlier not to intrude upon her life, and other than his marriage vows, Harold had never made a more determined promise. Nevertheless, he made up his mind to find her. Because of the boy.

"I'd thought about him for fifty-six years," Harold confesses, as we sit for one last interview. He's dressed in black and white plaid, like the checkered flag at the finish line of our conversations.

Harold has answered the question before, but I cannot help asking again whether he was ever tempted to find his son while Chiyoko was still living.

"Never," he says, definitively. "I would never have risked the hurt it might have caused my wife. But the boy was often in my thoughts, and after Mike died I wondered about him every day for over a year…" Finally, Harold asked a friend who is savvy with computers to see what he could find out about Margaret. Savvy is an understatement.

"I knew she'd had the baby in the hospital in Sheboygan, and that's all the information I had about her. About a week later my friend stuck a folded piece of paper in my shirt pocket. He said, 'I don't know what you want to do with that, but it's there if you want it.' On the paper, he'd written her current name, address and phone number."

Harold draws a deep breath, "The next morning I sat here with that telephone number debating, should I, or shouldn't I? At last, I called. A man answered the phone. I asked him if Margaret lived at that number. He said, 'Yes, *she's my mother…*'"

Looking at Harold, I am reminded he is a man who is no stranger to life-changing moments: the magnetic flash in the okiya when Chiyoko first entered the room; making the final payment on her debt and watching that realization spread across her face; the skipped heartbeat on the night when she first allowed his hand to wander beyond her wrists; the heartbeat that never came on the night she died. And there was the time he had looked into the eyes of an infant and known in an instant Margaret had given birth to his child. Many people believe destiny is in the hands of a Higher Power. Others insist it is cause and effect—an accumulation of our deeds or misdeeds that determines our salvation. The smart ones pray that the Fates will be kind, and cover their bets by living charitably. But there are no guarantees. For every set of lottery numbers that add up, a wrecking ball swings; either way, nothing is ever the same again.

Harold considers his to have been a good and productive life. Despite the way he started out, he never did spend more than a few nights in jail. On the contrary, by the time he retired from his second consecutive twenty-year career, Harold was privy to closely guarded secrets of national security. In between, he had fought doggedly for his country, had proven himself a worthy son, and against seemingly insurmountable odds, managed to literally free his soul mate. He's been blessed to know the joy of a true and abiding love, even if it has meant seesawing between that bliss and crushing loneliness, here at the end. Harold has regrets, certainly, but, after so many years together, perhaps his wife's cultural inclination to submit without complaint to events that were beyond her control has rubbed off on him. Things that might uproot or topple a lesser man, he takes in stride.

Like an oak.

The man on the phone was not Harold's son.

Margaret had had several sons, she explained, when Harold finally spoke with her. And she had also lost one.

"She told me our son had died…" he trembles, mustering heart-breaking self-control. "She told me he was being treated for sleep apnea, and he'd been given a new medicine. He took it, went to bed, and never woke up. He was fifty-one years old when he died. I saw him once as a baby, when I lifted him up out of his crib for those few minutes, and then I never saw him again. Except there…"

He is pointing to a photograph propped on a nearby shelf. Up until now, I've always assumed this is a picture of Harold himself. It is a portrait of a handsome, twenty-something man with a strikingly similar profile. The fact that he is wearing a military dress uniform makes the resemblance all the stronger.

"I thought it was damn nice of Margaret to send me that photo." He stares hard at his son's face, a face frozen in the only expression Harold will ever know. "My heart sank when she told me he was gone. Otherwise, if she had allowed it, I would very much liked to have met him."

I am surprised to learn that in the two years since he first con-tacted Margaret, Harold has visited her twice in Sheboygan and he checks in with her by phone periodically, yet he still knows almost nothing about his son's life. He is blindfolded by guilt. Harold firmly believes that because of the debt he owes Margaret, her life is inviolable. To his way of thinking, she sacrificed mightily so Harold could have his happiness, his life—his wife. For that reason, he adamantly refuses to impose upon her any questions on the subject, even though he yearns for answers. "I don't have that right," he insists. "I think she's told me everything she wants me to know. If she doesn't volunteer things, that's her decision."

Whether it is his tragically haunted conscience or a sense of gratitude long overdue that prevents him from pressing for details, the fact remains, he will not delve further into Margaret's family history or try to contact other members of her family. By inference and through tidbits Margaret has offered up voluntarily, Harold has learned that his son had five children of his own. He served in the military. He died relatively young. And that's about it.

I ask him if Margaret has even told him his son's name.

He nods. "Randy," he breathes. "His name was Randy."

Surely, Randy must have wondered about his father…

"I've never asked Margaret about that," he reiterates. "She has a right to her privacy, and so whatever the boy asked or didn't ask, whatever she told him or didn't tell him, I need to let it lie."

The same applies to his grandchildren.

"Because if it's peaceful right now for that family," Harold acquiesces, "I don't want to stir anything up… But I did try to open one conversation with Margaret," he admits. "I was interested in knowing one thing—was he a good man? I'd settle for just knowing that."

"What did she say?"

It's nearly imperceptible, but the smile is there. "She said when he was young, things were hard with him. He just had to try things, and then he joined the army…"

It is high time we pay Chiyoko a visit.

Throughout Harold's narrative, he has done his best to convey his wife's side of things, however, it has been clear from the beginning this story would be told exclusively from his point of view. Chiyoko's perspective has vanished with her. But even though I will never have an opportunity to interview his wife, Harold still goes to speak with her regularly, and this communion colors his every word. Now, at the end of our visits, he has been kind enough to let me accompany him.

"She wasn't supposed to be here," he tells me, braced firmly upon his cane before the polished stone. "She always said she wanted her ashes in some beautiful place, with mountains or hills, and I wanted to do that for her…but I got greedy," he sniffs, with a trace of his trademark irascibility. "She's been at my side nearly my entire life, and that's where I decided she was going to stay. Besides," he reflects, "at this time of year, there are few places on earth more beautiful than this."

He is right about that. The leafy canopy throughout the cemetery is aglow with autumn's luminous, ocher hues. There is arguably no finer pageantry in a forest than this breathtaking metamorphosis of birch trees and sugar maples—except, perhaps, the spectacle of a blooming cherry. It seems fitting that she be planted here, among kindred glory.

Harold tells me it was a beautiful funeral. Quite a turnout. More well attended, he estimates, than any of the multitude of other burials he has attended in recent years. But not because of him.

"She was just so loved and admired by everyone," Harold boasts. "Nobody wanted to let her go. I didn't think they were ever going to lower her into the ground. I finally had to tell the people to go home! I said, 'It's time now to let her rest.'"

He looks from side to side, as if measuring the throng that assembled here to pay his wife their respects.

"They all loved her, and they knew how much I loved her, but I don't think any of them truly understood what she had done for my life…"

"What about what you did for her life?" I counter. "You paid her debt."

"My family knew about that in bits and pieces." He shrugs, indicating they remained generally unimpressed. In their minds, all he had done was steal to get money for something he wanted, and that, they figured, was just ingrained in his DNA. On the other hand, what Chiyoko had wrought was nothing less than Harold's transformation from teenage smuggler to the chief administrator of one of the nation's key nuclear weapons depots. "Make no mistake about it," he emphasizes, *"She saved me."*

Harold presses his hand to his breast, as if he can feel the emotional heat kindling behind his ribs, and his gaze lowers to the footstone that proclaims, *Beloved Wife.* "From the moment I met her, I worshiped this girl. She was in a different category than me: smart and sophisticated, with so many capabilities, and filled with..." He nods, considering the brilliant leaves, "She was filled with such *light.* She inspired me, but she didn't pressure me to raise myself up—getting more education, advancing myself, I did that because I wanted to be a better man than when I married her."

Harold shifts uneasily on his cane, not because he is weary of standing; rather, it's a response to where his thoughts have led him. "I wasn't a perfect husband," he acknowledges. "I made that one, big mistake." He droops, voice cracking, "I did that," he repeats, "but it wasn't because I didn't love my wife. She was my life!" He stiffens, "I was weak," he concedes, "and I'll carry the weight of that until the day I come here for good."

Of course, at this, Harold's perennial survivor guilt flares. "I think about how much time I've got left," he ponders. "I think about that quite often. It's *hell* to be alone... I wonder, why am I the last of fifteen siblings? Why am I the one still living at nearly ninety years old? What have I been spared to accomplish?"

His answer is still the same.

"It must be this book," he concludes. "I've been hanging on so I can help you finish the book." But then Harold adds something he has never said before. "I told her I was going to write a book. Before she died, I told Mike I was going to write it all down. In my mind, I was determined to create a monument to her..." He glances down again. "I wanted something even more permanent than this stone. I said to her that I thought we'd had an interesting and unique life together, but more than that, I wanted people to remember the kind of woman she was, and the kind of wife she'd been. This book—all these things I've told you over the last year—it's an expression of my love for her. My only ambition left in life is to tell the story of the wonderful wife I had, and how she made me a better man. If I've done that, maybe now I can finally go, too."

I tell Harold this does not give me much incentive to finish the job. Perhaps we should keep talking…

He laughs, but mindful of where we are standing, I could not be more serious.

The Stevens' plot is a double. Harold's marker is here too, engraved and waiting, just a single date on it yet to be filled in. It must be strange, I think, to contemplate one's own grave.

As if reading my mind, he nods, but his voice registers more anticipation than melancholy when he says, "I just look at this, and I think, soon enough, it's going to be home."

If home is where his heart is, there is no doubt this is it. In fact, below the name *Stevens* on the imposing headstone, the only adornments are a chiseled heart encircling two grasped hands, and the date of Harold and Chiyoko's wedding day. I cannot imagine a more fitting memorial to this couple, one that hearkens back to Harold's declaration during our very first meeting: *From start to finish, this is a story about love.*

"God, I miss this girl," Harold breathes.

They were married for fifty-seven years, but he still refers to Chiyoko as his girl, because he has never stopped seeing her as he first did, and he has never stopped feeling what that first glimpse stirred in him, a love worthy of grand larceny. Harold has preserved those feelings in granite, and now in print.

I imagine he's telling her that right now.

I have stepped away to allow him a few private moments with his wife. From a distance, it is a singular and poignant tableau, particularly for this time and place—a cherished geisha, resting now, as she will forever, beneath the splendid maples, and beside a solitary oaken man.

# ALBUM, PART TWO

Living fast & dangerously!

ARMY:

Soldier

Diesel-Electric
Locomotive Mechanic

KOREA (FIRST TOUR):

SEOUL KOREA

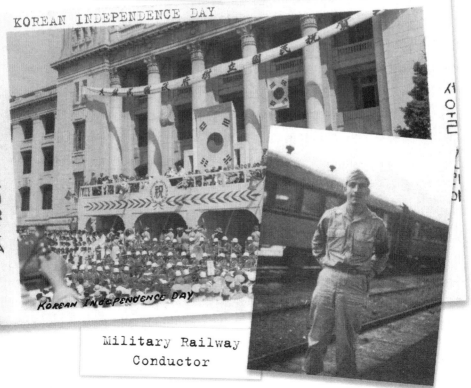

KOREAN INDEPENDENCE DAY

KOREAN INDEPENDENCE DAY

Military Railway
Conductor

Reunited

Conductor

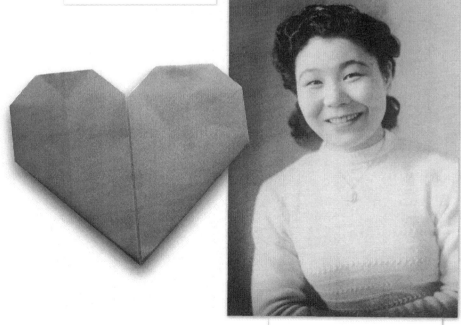

Geisha (off-duty)

Christmas, 1947

In the hills

Flora, Barney & Chiyoko

Taura

Holiday party

KOREA (SECOND TOUR):

War!!

Driver for War Correspondents

Artilleryman

Gun Sergeant

Wedding Day

Coca-Cola models

Chiyoko & Buffy

Manager, Exchange garage

Beautiful Hokkaido

Hokkaido hot springs

# HOMECOMING:

Passport photo

Aboard troopship

Arrival in U.S.

Meeting Mom

Welcoming
the Newlyweds
home

CHICAGO:

120mm anti-aircraft battery

DULUTH/CLOQUET:

Family reunion
at the Zoo!

KOREA (FOURTH TOUR):

R&R, Tokyo

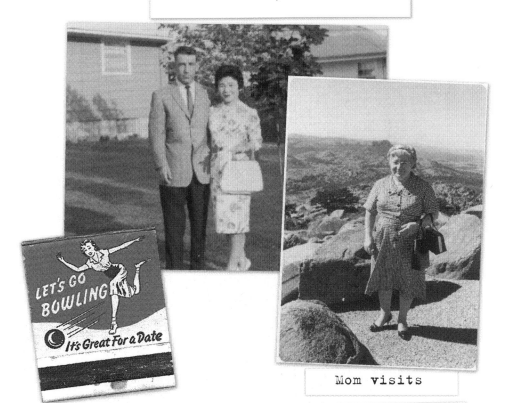

LET'S GO BOWLING
It's Great For a Date

Mom visits

Troop exchange to England

ALBUQUERQUE:

ALBUQUERQUE:

Special Weapons school: studying hard!

GERMANY:

Heilbronn,
West Germany

Landscaping by Mike

Concord Naval Weapons Station

General
Foreman
receiving
another
award

Mike's car, after the wreck

Brother
Lorin
visits
Lewiston,
Idaho

Near the
Imperial
Palace,
Japan

Cherry
Blossoms

50th Wedding Anniversary

"I'm so happy, because I have you."

# AFTERWORD

HAROLD MADE IT.
On the day I handed him a proof copy of this book, a smile pinched his cheeks as joy bloomed like bursting cherry buds. He was over the moon. My primary emotion, I will admit, was relief, at having been spared the "journeying solo" provision in our agreement. Although this pact had given Harold necessary and practical reassurance regarding the outcome, for me, the plausible prospect of suddenly losing him midway through our collaboration was a source of constant dread.

But he made it—despite the fact that Harold's enthusiasm to share his story unwittingly prolonged the goal. Throughout the lengthy process of creating the book, his determination to get it all down on paper was front and center in his thoughts, and this gave rise to a mixed blessing for me, his memoirist: a mountain of information that grew larger with every conversation.

As a born raconteur, Harold reveled in the interviewing phase of our project. The man lived to bend my ear. I informed him from the start that once our dialogues were complete, I would disappear from his radar to focus on the actual writing. That plan turned out to be unworkable. If he didn't hear from me during a particular week, Harold phoned me, or showed up at my house, insistent that we schedule yet another interview. In the end, I probably sat with him at least a dozen times more than planned. Inevitably, we covered the same ground more than once, but new stories and specifics would spontaneously emerge, like when he attended the Beatles concert in a Welsh barn—details that have added to the richness of this memoir and ensured every conversation between us was time well spent. Not to mention a delightful exercise in listening. I have never met anyone who could spin a tale like Harold Stevens.

Despite the lofty alp of seemingly limitless material (don't get me started on his photo albums), I managed to shape the clay. As the writing progressed, I brought Harold each newly completed chapter and read it to him for his consideration and approval. He never changed a single word. Instead, he would nod, laugh, or weep along with the narrative, and then, afterward, he would tell me the whole story again, as if it had yet to be written. As I have said, there was no shortage of source material, nor lack of urgency on his part to communicate it—while he still could.

Harold made it…but barely. Mere days after I gave him the proof copy—days he spent excitedly roaming the halls of his retirement complex, showing the book to everyone he met—the old tree finally crashed to earth. Harold suffered a devastating stroke. At this writing, he is still, as he would say, "above ground," but our conversations appear to be finally, definitively…mournfully, at an end. His neurons, so recently like the steel strings of a bass fiddle, straight and strong and capable of communicating such clear and reverberating emotion, are now in tangles.

Of course, some stroke victims are able to recover their former mental acuities. Health-wise, Harold has been battling upstream for so long and he was already weary of fighting the current; whether he has the strength or even the will to keep rowing in the face of this latest deluge remains to be seen. I do know he was very much looking forward to hawking this book.

On the other hand, Harold delighted in the observation that his life reads like a movie script, and there is astonishing cinematic poignancy in how these final events have unspooled. Just in time—just as he always believed he would—Harold gifted his dream to the world. Then, as he also predicted, once he saw that his Forever Girl was secure, his age and his body's many torturous afflictions, so long held at bay, climactically overwhelmed him.

His audience, his readers, particularly those of us who knew him whole, are left to ponder Harold's story and marvel at his extraordinary devotion to Chiyoko, and how he used nearly every last second of precious clarity to ensure her memory was preserved for all time, even as we ourselves endure what was ever his most acute distress, the hollow anguish of irretrievable loss.

*Shikata ga nai.*

David Pagel
*Duluth, 2017*

67529941R00194

Made in the USA
Lexington, KY
14 September 2017